WICKED PROBLEMS MANAGE DESIGN STYLE AGILITY

Design Thinking

Integrating Innovation, Customer Experience and Brand Value

Edited by
Thomas Lockwood

ALLWORTH PRESS
NEW YORK

dmi
Design Management Institute

14 13 12 11 10 7 6 5 4 3

Published by Allworth Press
An imprint of Allworth Communications, Inc.
10 East 23rd Street, New York, NY 10010

Cover design by Jon Craine and Alan Lee
Interior design by Alan Lee
Page composition/typography by SR Desktop Services, Ridge, NY

ISBN-13: 978-1-58115-668-3

Library of Congress Cataloging-in-Publication Data
Design thinking : integrating innovation, customer experience, and brand value / edited by Thomas Lockwood.
p. cm.
ISBN 978-1-58115-668-3
1. Industrial design. 2. Product design. I. Lockwood, Thomas.
TS171.4.D4865 2009
658.5'752—dc22

2009026966

Printed in the United States of America

Dedication

This book is dedicated to the creative class. To all the right-brainers out there—and the left-brainers with a creative spark—our opportunity to make a difference is now! There has been no greater time of need for social, economic, and environmental improvement than today, and no better people to make a difference than "design thinkers": those who venture outside the box, who are open-minded, who enjoy collaborative ideation, who have an eye on design and an eye on the future, who have a passion for change, who tell visual stories, and who do all of these things with a spirit of goodness. We can make the world a much better place, by design, in every moment.

Contents

SECTION 4: MEANING: CREATING CUSTOMER EXPERIENCES THAT MATTER

Acknowledgments

I would like to express my gratitude to all of the contributing authors whose work is included in this book. Their professional insight and research is greatly appreciated and have made working on this manuscript a true pleasure. I would also like to thank all of the other contributing authors who have written articles for DMI's *Design Management Journal* and *Design Management Review* over the years. Equally, I would like to acknowledge the work of the former president of DMI, Mr. Earl Powell, who founded the DMI publications and served as their publisher until 2005, and Dr. Thomas Walton for his outstanding work as the editor of the *Design Management Review* since its inception. Collectively, all of these efforts have significantly increased our understanding of design management, thinking, strategy, and leadership, and advanced our knowledge about the important role of design in business.

Foreword

THE IMPORTANCE OF INTEGRATED THINKING

When our publisher suggested that I put together a book about design thinking, I wondered aloud: Hasn't someone already done this? Well, evidently no one has, at least not in the sense of the current meaning. The publisher asked when I first encountered the idea of design thinking. He was surprised when I answered that it was about thirty years ago, when I was a young designer at CAMP7, one of the leading manufacturers of down sleeping bags and mountaineering gear at that time.

Years ago, state-of-the-art clothing for skiers and mountain climbers consisted of cotton long johns, wool sweaters, puffy down jackets, and a cotton/poly 60/40 outer layer that shed wind but not water. I was the head of design and development at CAMP7, and one day an engineer from 3M contacted me to discuss a new microfiber he was working with. We got to talking about clothing for outdoor sports, and he asked me if I knew why down keeps people warm. I realized that I did not. I thought it was something about those little puffy down "pods," the more loft in them the better, but I finally had to admit that down equaled warmth to us in the industry, and in a way we basically thought of it as some kind of magic. But the 3M engineer knew much more than I did, and he explained that the "magic" was due to the combination of teeny-tiny nodes, which protrude from teensy-tiny barbules, which stem from the little tiny branches, which protrude from a single pod of down, which creates a tremendous amount of surface area, yet is invisible to the human eye. He even showed me microscopic photography of this. That day, the realm of scientific research arrived on the doorstep of the design of ski-wear and mountaineering gear.

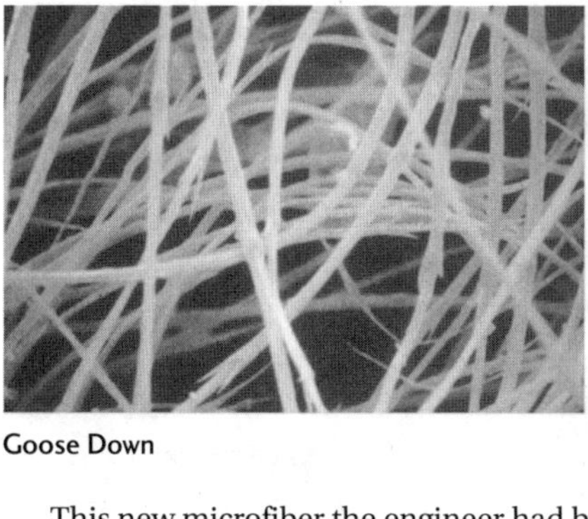

Goose Down

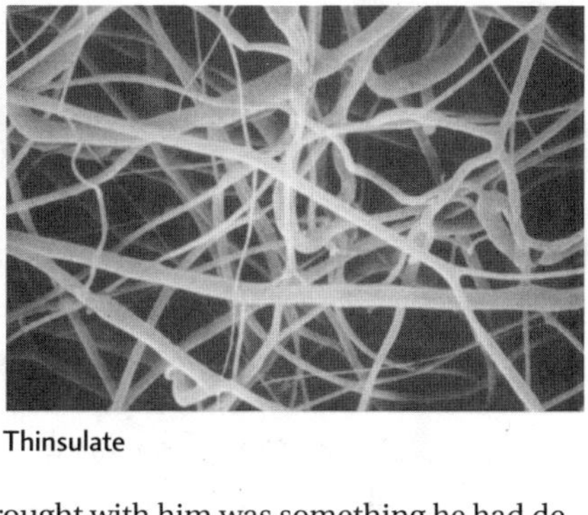

Thinsulate

This new microfiber the engineer had brought with him was something he had developed while working on a project to invent better brushes for commercial floor scrubbers: a synthetic material with maximum surface area for more scrubbing friction. He gave me a few sample yards of material and asked if I could make some outdoor gear out of it. So we made clothing and sleeping bags, used them in the Colorado mountains, and found they kept us warm, even in wet snowy conditions. It turns out that the greater surface area stops air movement due to friction, and thus helps prevent heat loss. The engineer invited me to 3M headquarters, where they photographed our current products and our new prototypes using a form of photography they had just developed called thermography. With thermography, it was possible to see exactly where heat was being lost. We all got very excited about this.

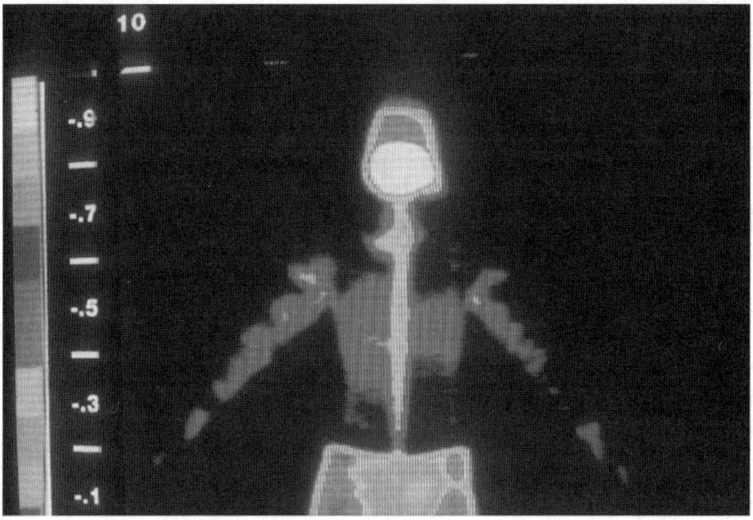

Not long afterwards, I started a research collaboration with the University of Colorado's physiology department to study heat loss in cold-weather conditions. I discovered that there was very little existing research about how and why people lose heat when exercising in severely cold weather. We recruited students to exercise in a very large walk-in meat freezer on campus by working out on stationary bikes and treadmills in front of large fans simulating wind chill—really difficult conditions. We tested new prototype synthetic materials and variations of product designs against the traditional wool, cotton, and down. The results amazed us. For the first time, we were able to provide scientific evidence of how certain synthetic materials, such as polypropylene and polyolefin, when developed as a microfiber, wick moisture away from the body and in doing so keep people warmer as they exercise in freezing temperatures than traditional natural materials do. The 3M prototype material, a microfiber polypropylene, was later named Thinsulate.

We also tested another prototype material, which had a waterproof and breathable synthetic membrane, but allowed more moisture transfer and actually kept our test students warmer in action. This material was later named Gore-Tex.

In the coming year, CAMP7 was the first company in the world to make skiwear from Thinsulate and combine Thinsulate with Gore-Tex, and to be able to prove that these worked better than the century-old "status quo" materials. One reason we were relatively fast to market was because our CFO was also an avid skier and wanted to be involved with the testing. So, while we evaluated various designs, he considered potential business opportunity scenarios with us. Although our rough prototype clothing was rather "patchwork," it worked very well. Soon we added western-style GoreTex shoulder yokes over the prototype Thinsulate ski jackets, and these worked well even in wet, snowy conditions. We gave prototype samples to our friends. They used them on climbing expeditions. This soon got the attention of the U.S. Nordic ski team, which trained in the area. The team members tested our prototypes, helped refine the components into a layered system, and then used our radical new clothing in the Winter Olympics.

The point of the story is that our innovation was successful, better products came to market, and people were more satisfied because a few open-minded designers teamed with some thoughtful engineers and with users who liked to experiment, developed and tested very rough prototypes, discovered flaws and reworked quickly, and included business analysis during the development process. I call this design thinking, and it was very successful. This was my first job, and it taught me quite early in my career some principles that have stayed with me to this day.

THINKING FROM BOTH SIDES

I suspect that the reason I dealt with the challenge of new synthetic materials—an example of what we now call "disruptive technology"—so positively was because I studied design as well as business in undergraduate school. I found it very natural and interesting to apply my right-brain strengths and my left-brain strengths equally. I must admit, many of my design school peers had no idea what I found interesting about business, and my business school peers thought I had a rather strange creative side they did not understand. But this is exactly the point of design thinking. Businesses need to be ambidextrous, so to speak, and to think from both sides. All too often, it seems, businesses either excel at the creative side, in which case innovations usually fail, or they excel at the analysis side, which generally leads to only incremental innovation or, more likely, stagnation. The challenges of today's economy require much more.

Books like Richard Florida's *The Rise of the Creative Class* (2002) and Daniel Pink's *A Whole New Mind* (2005) have really cemented the foundational requirements of design thinking. Coupled with the insights Tom Kelley first presented in *The Art of Innovation* (2001), these books present a very clear shift towards a more creative and more collaborative way of working—one in which intuition counts heavily, experimentation happens fast, failures along the way are embraced as learning, business strategy is integrated, and more relevant solutions are produced.

After a career progression from designer to creative director to owning my own design consultancy and working in corporate design and brand management, I still find a compelling and natural integration between my creative passions and my business acumen, which I have found to be my "sweet spot" in design management. By mid-career, not content with my experience as a practitioner, I decided I wanted to go to graduate school. Knowing that, traditionally, schools in England have been at the forefront of design management education, I jumped at the opportunity to earn an executive MBA in design management from the University of Westminster in London via a cohort in Boston. I enjoyed the experience so much that the day I graduated I re-enrolled with Westminster into their PhD program.

The focus of my research became design integration, and my thesis set out to establish new models for how large organizations can coordinate all the design disciplines in order to enable design innovation for the business, design coherency for the brand, and design relevancy for the user. I found no existing research on that topic whatsoever, which meant it fit doctoral criteria. I interviewed fifty-two design managers and executives responsible for all of the major design functions at Caterpillar, Kodak, Levi Strauss, Microsoft, Nike, Starbucks, and Sun Microsystems. Of course, I learned a great deal from these organizations, but particularly interesting was the need for design managers to work in cross-functional teams, develop deep user insights, collaborate, visualize ideas, and actually solve customers' problems rather than just apply branding or fancy design styling. It took about four years to develop a model, which I called "integrated design management." This research was directly related to design thinking—which I think, by the way, is a perfect term to define a perfect way of working.

So, back to the question posed by my publisher, who wanted a book about design thinking. "Yes," I said, "I've thought of this before." But design thinking is not exactly science, and there is no one "correct" take on the subject, so I've designed this book as collection of opinions. Fundamental methods in design thinking are collaboration, embedding diverse points of view, and integrative thinking, and so it is in this book.

COLLABORATION OF THOUGHT LEADERS

This book includes work by thirty-four authors, representing ten countries. And it includes case studies about companies such as Streetcar, Dyson, Linux, Samsung, Whole Foods, Ritz-Carlton, Volkswagen, Nike, Procter & Gamble, Apple, Banana Republic, Coca-Cola, Océ, State Farm, and IBM, as well as many of the world's leading design and innovation consultancies. This is the heart of design thinking, and integrative thinking, in action. What's more, as a sampling of opinions this method offers not only a more comprehensive point of view but also a faster path to market so the information is more timely.

In my role as president at DMI, I have a "macro" view of the international design and design leadership community, and a "micro" view of the individual players. It allows me to be incredibly integrated within the global community. And because the institute is dedicated to advancing the role of design in business for the triple bottom line (i.e., the social and environmental as well as the economic aspects) and focuses on the "how" of design, we have access to best-of-class thinking about design methods, processes, strategy, research, and operations, including the emerging notion of design thinking. The following is a synthesis of my point of view of design thinking. Synthesis: to combine two or more elements to create something new. Yes, this is what design thinking is about.

OVERVIEW OF DESIGN THINKING

Design thinking is essentially a human-centered innovation process that emphasizes observation, collaboration, fast learning, visualization of ideas, rapid concept prototyping, and concurrent business analysis, which ultimately influences innovation and business strategy. The objective is to involve consumers, designers, and businesspeople in an integrative process, which can be applied to product, service, or even business design. It is a tool to imagine future states and to bring products, services, and experiences to market. The term *design thinking* is generally referred to as applying a designer's sensibility and methods to problem solving, no matter what the problem is. It is not a substitute for professional design or the art and craft of designing, but rather a methodology for innovation and enablement.

There are several key tenets of design thinking that seem to be common. The first is to develop a deep understanding of the consumer based on fieldwork research. Using an empathic approach can be both a source of inspiration and an aid to reaching consumer insights and discovering unarticulated user needs. The best way to do so is by getting out in the real world with consumers, with open-minded collaboration, even with codesign concepts. Often, this involves observational research and ethnographic methods, by watching, listening, discussing, and seeking to understand. The key is to start from a seeking to understand point of view—not in seeking persuasion, as has been the practice in many traditional push-product development methods. Sometimes, this approach is aided by sociologists or anthropologists, but most often it's just designers and researchers getting out and working with the target audience and being empowered to be open-minded.

Having the users involved early on also makes it possible to get user evaluations of a concept. Therefore, a second important aspect of design thinking is collaboration, both with the users and through forming multidisciplinary teams. This helps to move a company toward radical innovation, rather than incremental improvement, and of course seeks added value.

The third part is to accelerate learning through visualization, hands-on experimentalism, and creating quick prototypes, which are made as simple as possible in order to get usable feedback. Since design thinking is focused more on radical than on incremental innovation, the more experimentation the better, and quick, simple prototypes also help grasp a potential implementation well before many resources are spent in development. Ideas are often mocked-up as very rough articulations of a concept, product, or service. Often the goal is to fail quickly and frequently so that learning can occur.

In fact, failing quickly is a stated objective at award-winning Pixar Animation Studios because it leads to better work done more quickly.

Prototypes can be concept sketches, rough physical mock-ups, or stories—or role-playing or story boards, for a service design—and always include a form of visualization of concepts, which is the fourth criterion. The objective is to make the intangible become tangible, and visualization is the best way to do that. The power of visual communications is undeniable. They say a picture is worth a thousand words, which makes me realize why some large, well-known, traditional management consultancies are known to write so many words—perhaps that's necessary when there's no visual information to aid in communication. Using visual explanations also provides context, which is greatly helpful when the consumer is a partner in your concept development.

The fifth and last aspect, which may not be on everyone's list but which I endorse, is the importance of concurrent business analysis integrated during the process rather than added on later or used to limit creative ideations. This can be a tricky balance, but the key is to enable integrative thinking by combining the creative ideas with more traditional strategic aspects in order to learn from a more complete and diverse point of view. In collaboration, constraints can be removed and great ideas can emerge. This is also helpful in anticipating what new business activities may be required by a conceptual new product, service, or experience offering, as well as the resources it may require and the competitive landscape in which it will appear.

DESIGN THINKING/DESIGN MANAGEMENT/DESIGN LEADERSHIP/ DESIGN STRATEGY

There are so many seemingly similar terms. I am often asked to simply clarify the difference between design thinking and design management. My point of view is that design thinking is primarily an innovation process. It is a way to help discover unmet needs and opportunities and to create new solutions. It is part of the "fuzzy front end" and is also being adopted to help reinvent businesses, as in solving "wicked" problems and business transformation. Design management is primarily the ongoing management and leadership of design organizations, processes, and designed outputs—products, services, communications, environments, and interactions. Design leadership and design strategy may be viewed as outputs of effective design thinking and design management.

Generally, design management and leadership lie in the area of integrating design into business and in continuous development and improvement, whereas design thinking is more interested in front-end innovation and radical improvements. I suspect that making this distinction may clarify things for some, yet the differences tend to blur as we proceed. For example, this book is organized into four sections, as an overview and cases of various aspects of design thinking. But some of the methods presented could very easily be classified as design management. Many people use the two terms interchangeably or, as Bruce Nussbaum is fond of saying, "just call it a banana."

DESIGN THINKING AS INNOVATION AND BUSINESS TRANSFORMATION

Years ago it felt as though business was easier, or at least less complex. Today, it seems that everything is being challenged. The old status quo is no longer relevant, disruption abounds, and there is no better time than now for out-of-the-box thinking and new methods of problem solving. We need new, transformative corporate strategies that are based on human needs, not just financial analysis. We also know that innovation drives business differentiation, and that design drives innovation. As Marty Neumeier so simply observes in *The Designful Company* (2009), "Creativity in its various forms has become the number-one engine of economic growth."

But our problems go far beyond just business problems. I've recently had the opportunity to collaborate and critique work at MIT and Harvard on problem-solving at the systems level: big issues such as our food supply system, child obesity, and emergency healthcare. As a designer and design thinker, it is very exciting to have these opportunities to help me explore solutions to problems I never thought I could influence. And I was surprised to find that these are problems that don't necessarily need big solutions; what they need is a complete reframing. Here is where we see the leading edge of design thinking. Similarly, there are discussions emerging about using design as a method for business transformation, as well as using design thinking methods to create corporate strategy. Beyond traditional analytics, design thinking connects people and business by using design as a medium, which makes perfect sense.

As the following chapters suggest, big issues are indeed possible to solve by using the methodologies of design thinking. You'll hear new terms such as *abductive thinking* and *open collaboration*; ideas that challenge norms, such as seeking to fail quickly and being roughly ready rather than seeking design perfection; and concepts such as deep understanding, unpacking complexity, and challenging constraints towards breakthrough solutions—all great stuff. Big issues need new ways of thinking, which is exactly the point of design thinking.

So, we begin with a simple discussion of terms by comparing and contrasting the two most important areas: design thinking and design management. To aid in that consideration, Craig Vogel looks back at the development and history of both. Then, we look into tools to achieve business strategy and tools to transform businesses. We also look at the idea of design-driven innovation. We explore the value of developing creativity and consider ways to "think like a designer."

For a simple analogy about design thinking, consider the process of digital photography. In the first step, we look for the big picture as well as the details. Our thinking and observing is in zoom mode, using both macro and telephoto views. By thinking like designers—being able to see the details as well as zoom out to the big picture—we can really add value by challenging the status quo. We collaborate with the subjects and hunt for the best angles to represent the picture of our ideas and observations. In the second step, we process information. We visualize; we go for quick previews; we sort, trash, rezoom, rethink, and immediately share the findings and observations with others. Just as in taking a digital picture, design thinking moves through process, preview, and share modes. And in the third step, we demonstrate our results by producing final, visualized concepts. We apply business methodology to best prepare the idea, just as we might use image-enhancing software. The final image—the result—is a plan for a product, service, experience, or business strategy.

I include a chapter on the seminal research by Brigitte Borja de Mozota. She originally summarized the four powers of design (DMI *Academic Review*, 2002) and now further defines design as differentiator, as integrator, as transformer, and as good business. I find her thought leadership about design for business transformation especially valuable, as I always find it interesting to see educators leading practitioners into the future. The section concludes with my perspective on making the transition to becoming a design thinking organization. This chapter is research-based, yet from the experience of a practitioner, an effective combination, in my opinion.

DESIGN THINKING IN THE AREAS OF BRAND VALUE

It's just a pleasure to see businesses prosper in the innovation arena with design thinking, and so too to see businesses increase their brand value. The question is: What is the best way to use design thinking toward better brand value? Some very interesting points arise from the chapters that follow—for example:

- The importance of embedding a brand ethos into the business
- All touchpoints matter. As Paul Rand said, "From little buck slips to big buildings, the design challenges of a large organization are never-ending."
- The need to apply integrated design processes
- A focus on customer first, but based on meanings
- Developing customers' emotional connections

The brand value section begins with Jerry Kathman's take on the importance of articulating the brand strategy and leveraging the design franchise—that is, the equity of the brand, which is based on design assets. Those assets are what is used in creating compelling brand expressions and experiences that best showcase the brand identity at all touchpoints. In essence, Kathman says, design thinking can enable brand improvements and improve branded innovations, but only after you find the core design franchise to build upon.

It is also critical for users to connect to the brand on an emotional level, so it's important that they have their input during the creation phases. As Marc Gobé suggests in his essay, the role of postmodern brands is not to dominate but to stimulate, and therefore we need to draw on emotional insights when creating new projects. After all, the product is really the starting point of a customer's journey and experience. This is supported by Tony Kim, who notes that brands must connect to consumers' lifestyles and values. He invokes a handy acronym—PESTE—to describe trends formed by changes in political, environmental, social, technological, and economic factors.

Ultimately, a brand is about fulfilling a promise, and this includes creating value for the customer. Often, innovation is the way to create value, and design is the key to bringing innovation to life, especially with design thinking methods. Phil Best relates design thinking to a five-step innovation process that includes immersion and understanding, discovery of opportunities, creating a vision, validation with key stakeholders, and finally, integration and activation. The section also looks into the importance of private-label branding and the sociocultural roles of brand in business value creation.

DESIGN THINKING FOR SERVICE DESIGN

It is often said, based on the U.S. gross national product, that we live in a service economy. Service design is relevant in the public as well as the private sector, and I find it to be a very interesting and meaningful arena, so I include a series of chapters on it.

Like many design disciplines, design thinking in services involves multidisciplinary teamwork, prototyping as a means for dialogue, open design architectures, and integration between functional and emotional connections. Yet designing for services does require a somewhat different mindset than for the more static product design. In essence, although people are at the center of each, product design is generally about the object, whereas service design is about the journey. That's a challenge for some designers, because industrial designers are traditionally taught to create the ultimate form, and graphic designers to create persuasion, whereas designing experiences that constantly change through multiple touchpoints is an entirely different idea that requires different interests and skill sets. Service design frequently involves much complexity, even entire systems, and touchpoints that are out of scope for traditional product, graphic, or brand design roles. In service design, it could be argued, alignment is more important than ideas. It may require new touchpoints, new technologies, new relationships with customers, and new revenue models. Although design thinking readily applies, service design often requires new methods of design management.

Service design begins with discovering what processes need improvement and how to best serve people's needs. But the value of design thinking in service design lies beyond that. It includes the methods of design thinking I've outlined, but it also requires making new service concepts come to life with methods such as storytelling, storyboarding, acting, and role-playing. In the book section that follows, chapters begin with appraising and measuring service design, followed by a five-stage framework for service innovation and several chapters that demonstrate cases of service design in retail environments and in virtual environments.

DESIGN THINKING FOR CUSTOMER EXPERIENCES

Here is a catchy phrase from Marty Neumeier: "Seek customer experiences that rivet the mind and run away with the heart." Similarly, as frog design's Hartmut Esslinger is wont to say, "Form follows emotion." In this section we find many of the key principles of design thinking in creating customer experiences. Four points stand out:

- Experience is constantly in motion.
- Experience is a result of the customer's perception.
- All touchpoints have influence, but budgets do not always reflect this.
- From a brand view, it is necessary to achieve internal alignment before customer experience can be properly designed.

This section begins by looking at the mathematics of brand satisfaction and the interplay between expectations and experiences. Each interaction moves our "satisfaction dial"—our accumulation of experiences with a brand. In other words, the customer's journey is one of experience building, and it can be a brand-building experience as well, if properly managed. Dave Norton provides a very thorough overview of this journey, noting a shift in experience strategy from making things convenient to making experiences that customers care about—in essence, a shift from using design to make things simple and easy to design being about making people care. With strong links to Mark Gobé's discussion of the importance of emotional design, this idea fits very well with the methodologies of design thinking and design management. Several chapters in this section explore the value of internal culture and brand management via design and demonstrate with cases how brands must align with meaning. Here, we look into branding from the inside out and explore the importance of transparency: creating authentic interactions so that brands and people's lives actually may fit together. The section concludes with chapters about customer loyalty and the elements of user experience in building enduring relationships on the Web, segments on shaping brands for customer experience and living the brand, and several case studies in design thinking.

A GREAT PLACE TO BE

Welcome to the fascinating world of design thinking—it's deep and wide! Let's face it: we live in the age of innovation, and innovation is the route to growth, better customer experiences, and a better world for all. The innovation imperative celebrates nonlinear behavior and presents many challenges—not just for product and services development, but also to inspire ideas for new initiatives. Design thinking challenges traditional management processes and styles and requires adaptive, dynamic systems. One of the key objectives of nearly every organization today is to innovate and to create meaningful value for its stakeholders and its customers. To that end, the successful, innovative organizations of the future will be those that make the best use of the principles and methods of design thinking.

Many of these chapters were originally prepared as articles in the *Design Management Review*, while others were created specifically for this book. Therefore, this represents the latest of DMI work regarding design thinking, so to speak. However, there have been some previous books on the topic that are worth noting. For example, early works such as *How Designers Think* (Lawson, 1980) and *Design Thinking* (Rowe, 1991) sound similar but represent something that is very different from a content point of view. We will surely see much more literature about this powerful way of working in the future, not just in the design press, but in the business press as well. For example, Thomas Walton and I have published two related books, *Building Design Strategy* and *Corporate Creativity*. In addition, Roberto Verganti's interesting article in the December 2006 *Harvard Business Review* titled "Innovating Through Design" raises many insightful new points, and in the June 2008 *Harvard Business Review*, Tim Brown added to the conversation with his "Design Thinking" article. Brown, the chief executive of IDEO, offers this definition: "Design thinking can be described as a discipline that uses the designer's sensibility and methods to match people's needs with what is technologically feasible and what a viable business strategy can convert into customer value and market opportunity."

Although this presents the business and economic point of view, design thinking can be just as beneficial on a social and environmental level. Design thinking can be applied as a method to transform business and develop new processes and systems, and a consideration of the bigger picture of our societies at large shows us there is much room for improvement in our world today. Design thinking and using the sensibilities of designers is a methodology and a process that can help us take on the larger and more complex challenges we face, and envision and realize solutions for a better future for all. Let's design our way forward. There's no better place to start than with this introduction to design thinking.

Thomas Lockwood, PhD
President, DMI

SECTION 1

DESIGN THINKING METHODS

CREATE

METHODS

CHANGE

TRANSFORM

SYSTEMS

MANAGE

RESEARCH

CULTURE

Chapter 1

Notes on the Evolution of Design Thinking: A Work in Progress

by Craig M. Vogel, Director of Center for Design Research and Innovation, College of Design Architecture, Art and Planning, University of Cincinnati

From the late nineteenth century onward, the nexus between design and business is a story of new challenges met with vision, creativity, and innovation. Craig Vogel summarizes the progression of design thinking and explains how this is bringing new opportunities for the design community to engage.

FIVE YEARS AGO, I left Carnegie Mellon University to come to the College of Design, Architecture, Art, and Planning (DAAP) at the University of Cincinnati (UC). As director of the newly formed Center for Design Research and Innovation (CDRI), I was expected to develop a strategy for increasing the size of the graduate program in DAAP's School of Design, to establish a more consistent way to conduct research, and to work more effectively with corporations. Working with the support and guidance of UC President Nancy Zimpher and Dean Robert Probst, and with Procter & Gamble's chief technology officer, Gil Cloyd, and vice president of innovation, Larry Huston, I was able to conceive and develop the Live Well Collaborative (LWC), a nonprofit company. This initiative focuses on consumers over the age of fifty. It is design driven and multidisciplinary in its approach to running project studios for its member companies. To date, there are four corporate partners, and the LWC has completed a dozen projects.

The LWC is an example of what I believe companies and universities must do to leverage the capability of both undergraduate and graduate education—working with practitioners to effectively and comprehensively design for the future. The concept of the LWC has helped Dean Probst to move design thinking to the center of the university and has created a new model for innovation among universities and companies focusing on a compelling and unmet global human need. Along the same lines, business schools and engineering colleges in universities are also seeking to work with design schools to forge new interdisciplinary programs.

For various reasons, the way designers are educated to think is now perceived as particularly relevant to companies that seek to change their long- and short-term strategies for developing new products and services. These design insights are required to effectively respond to constantly changing social, economic, and technical forces (also known as SET factors). The interaction of these three forces results in the emergence of new, "preferred" states for customers and consumers.

The consistent theme throughout the twentieth century is that design has flourished in companies in which a design leader has been able to represent a full range of value to corporate management, from design strategy and brand equity to design implementation. Design leadership must have corporate champions at the CEO and CTO level who see the value of design and allow it to play a central role in the planning and execution of corporate strategy. This was as true in 1907, when AEG hired Peter Behrens, as it is today at HP, where Sam Lucente is director of design.

However, during most of the twentieth century, corporations and cultural institutions asked designers to play a focused and limited role in product and service development. Today, that role is expanding and the core of the field, design thinking, must expand with it. Design thinking has a rich history, and it is important to trace how it evolved to help understand why design is now so valued.

Indeed, the LWC represents a synthesis of a number of design influences that have developed during the last century. This article provides an overview of those influences.

CASE STUDIES FROM THE TWENTIETH CENTURY

During the late nineteenth century, with the rise of the Industrial Revolution, a schism occurred in the attitude toward the production of new products and buildings. On one side were John Ruskin and William Morris, who shared the belief that the Industrial Revolution was rapidly growing out of control, particularly in the second half of the century. They reacted against the dehumanization of labor and the lack of craft sensibilities in mass-manufactured goods and services (the other side). Morris's designs for products, graphics, and architecture expressed Ruskin's argument and influenced others to become part of a major craft revival. The Arts and Crafts movement was a reaction to the emerging dominance of standardization requiring quantitatively driven management and cost approaches used by industrialists. The quantitative approach was viewed as a necessary approach in managing the dramatic increase of raw materials and finished goods in the service of emerging mass markets. The Arts and Crafts movement was a reaction against the process of industrial production, emphasizing the quality of the product and experience created for consumers.

By the end of the nineteenth century, the two clear sides of the argument about how best to manage change were fully developed. On one side were the industrialists, represented by Carnegie, Rockefeller, J.P. Morgan, and Ford. Supported by Fredrick Taylor's theories of scientific production, they promoted the rapid growth of the modern corporation. The opposing position was held by Arts and Crafts advocates, represented at that time by Charles Rennie Mackintosh, the Viennese Secessionists, Frank Lloyd Wright, and Gustav Stickley, who extolled human-scale production and consumption. Many of their designs combined historical reference with a modern interpretation. Wright's Prairie Style architecture integrated ideas from Japan, as well as from Native Americans, and emphasized the horizontal nature of the prairie with modern concepts of reinforced concrete and open-space planning. Wright stated that his buildings all contained "subliminal mathematics," an underlying logical order of visual elements that resulted in an elegant integrated whole, or Gestalt. In contrast, because of the necessities of using the assembly line and other cost controls, the design elements of Ford's Model T were merely a compilation of parts. The current theory of human-centered design includes the esthetics of the Arts and Crafts movement while also incorporating the scale of mass production.

The schism lasted throughout the twentieth century and persists into the present. For most of the previous century, the dominant argument driving change was in the area of mass manufacture and distribution as directed by captains of industry using statistical methods of management and the emerging scientific method employed by corporate research and development. Two types of CEOs emerged after the turn of the century. One focused primarily on cost control and on engineering and manufacture. The other was open to integrating design and saw the value of brand identity in response to foreign competition and the emergence of consumer segmentation in America. The opportunity for practitioners in fields of design in the early twentieth century was to fill the gap between insensitive, cost-driven mass production and the craft refinement of human-scale production and local distribution of goods and services.

PETER BEHRENS: CORPORATE IDENTITY AND BRAND DIFFERENTIATION

Architect Peter Behrens was one of the first designers who tried to synthesize the two polar positions of technology and craft. In 1907, Behrens was hired by Emil Rathenau, the founder and president of the German electric company AEG. The company needed a new approach to make electricity more acceptable to consumers; Rathenau hoped they would learn to use the technology more broadly during the course of the day, and more evenly in every season. Behrens's work is particularly notable in that he designed not only AEG's buildings and products but also the company's corporate identity and print advertising. Behrens has been called the first industrial designer, but he also paved the way for corporate design strategy and clearly understood the challenge of brand differentiation. Behrens sought to marry the sophistication and human scale of craft heritage in European products with the emerging massive systems of electrical power generation and distribution. Indeed, he succeeded in finding a way to connect the system of electrification, as a new and underutilized source of power, to the quality and tradition of products in the home that could use electricity. Behrens's logo design is still in use (although the brand name is now owned by Electrolux), and his design standards and guidelines for elements in graphic communication predate the grids developed by Dutch and Swiss graphic designers later in the century.

THE BAUHAUS: A NEW DESIGN STRATEGY FOR EDUCATION

Behrens's work ended as a result of the outbreak of World War I, but his influence remained. His apprentices before the war were architects Walter Gropius and Ludwig Mies van der Rohe. The Bauhaus, founded in 1919 by Gropius, was the first school in the twentieth century to take Behrens's ideas and translate them into a curriculum for higher education. Mies served as its last director, for in the early '30s, pressure from the Nazi government forced him to close the school. Both he and Gropius were among many Bauhaus designers who moved to the United States. After World War II, the Bauhaus philosophy of finding a balance among art, science, and mass production received significant support from leading art and design critics in the U.S. The Bauhaus immigrants formed several branches and influenced design across the American landscape, and indeed their school became one of the most influential design movements in the world.

Walter Gropius taught architecture and planning at Harvard, and Mies van der Rohe went to the architecture school at the Illinois Institute of Technology (IIT) in Chicago, while other disciples, including Lazlo Moholy Nagy and Josef Albers, founded new programs. Josef and Anni Albers eventually went to Yale, and Moholy Nagy founded the New Bauhaus in Chicago, eventually merging with IIT's architecture program to form the Institute of Design. Herbert Bayer became head of design for Container Corporation. Each Bauhaus disciple brought from Germany a variation of Behren's core argument that he or she further developed in the U.S., continuing the struggle to balance art, science, and mass production in their work and teaching. Attempts to achieve this balance are exemplified by Mies van der Rohe's glass and steel architecture and furniture designs.

For example, in Chicago's Lake Shore Drive Apartments, Mies expresses his curtain wall exterior with an elegantly proportioned glass and steel façade. The structural support and mechanical core are the consequence of the new systematic and efficient approach to the construction of modern skyscrapers. Mies's theories and students influenced the design and construction of skyscrapers around the world for several decades.

CORPORATE AND CONSULTING DESIGN IN THE UNITED STATES

In contrast to the design thinking that started with Behrens and the Bauhaus, there is an equally influential argument represented by the founders of American industrial and graphic design who worked in corporate and consulting firms during the 1920s and '30s. These designers include Harley Earl, Henry Dreyfuss, Walter Dorwin Teague, and Donald Desky (all born in the United States), and Raymond Loewy (a French immigrant who came to the U.S. in 1919). Their contribution lay in developing methods by which design thinking began to serve the needs of emerging U.S. corporations. Where the influence of the Bauhaus in America originated primarily in education and then moved into practice, the success of these designers influenced the content of the curriculum of American design programs, which began to graduate practitioners who could fill the demand for corporate and consulting designers. Pratt Institute, Art Center College of Design, the Center for Creative Studies, the Cleveland Institute of Art, the Rhode Island School of Design, Carnegie Tech (now Carnegie Mellon), and the University of Cincinnati all developed distinct variations on the approach to graphic and industrial education.

Harley Earl and General Motors: Market Segmentation in the Auto Industry

Harley Earl, GM's head of color and trim from 1927 to 1959, was the first designer in the United States to apply market segmentation in a strategic way to the design of cars.

By the mid 1920s, the Ford Model T had dominated the automobile market for nearly two decades. (The Model T famously came in only one color: black.) Earl's cars were designed to meet the diverse needs of the U.S. market segments that were emerging and growing during the Roaring '20s. Earl, working with the support of GM President Alfred E. Sloan, designed five distinct brands, ranging from the low-end Chevrolet to the high-end Cadillac. The strategy worked immediately; in 1927, Ford was forced to close

its River Rouge plant and retool for the Model A. Harley Earl, one of the most influential designers of the twentieth century, capped his career during the 1950s with designs for Chevy and Cadillac that became icons of American culture for that period. He introduced and perfected clay modeling and the idea of concept cars. GM maintained its market segment approach until the reduction of car sales in recent years forced the closing of the Oldsmobile brand. (By then, consumers had realized that GM was using common platforms across all brands, thus reducing the perceived value of the high-end variants.)

Ford has, in contrast, always used styling on a limited range of vehicles under the Ford, Mercury (always a distant second), and Lincoln brands. In essence, Sloan at GM empowered Harley Earl in the same way Emil Rathenau empowered Peter Behrens at AEG. Consider that, in 1927, GM used the same strategy to compete with Ford that Target uses today to compete with Wal-Mart: Only one company in a market can be the cheapest; the rest need design.

Raymond Loewy, Design Consultant: Updating Existing Technology

Raymond Loewy's 1934 refrigerator redesign for Sears and Roebuck is another story that should be mandatory for design, as well as business, students. Loewy merged aesthetics, materials, and manufacturing to transform the loud and ugly electric refrigerator of the 1920s into a modern kitchen appliance. The consumer response was immediate. In one year, sales of Sears's Cold Spot increased from 65,000 to 250,000 units—without any significant change in core technology.

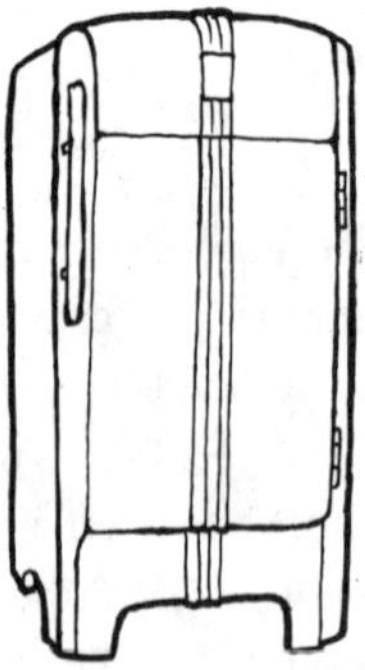

The Cold Spot is an indicator of how design thinking at the product level can transform a product category. Loewy integrated contemporary aesthetics and human factors into a product that incorporated sheet metal stamping technology from the auto industry with an ergonomic door handle, and a systematic organization of interior storage that used no-rust aluminum shelves. Loewy became the design consultant recognized as having the most skill at marrying business strategy with design. He is the only industrial designer to ever grace the cover of *Time* magazine (October 31, 1949). He also developed and managed one of the largest design consultancies in the world for more than three decades.

Henry Dreyfuss: Integrating Human Factors as a Core Component of Product Design

The work and thinking of Henry Dreyfuss overlaps with that of Loewy but needs to be differentiated in a significant respect. Dreyfuss developed a more scientific approach to human factors and integrated that perspective with product aesthetics. The Dreyfuss phone for AT&T was the first attempt to integrate human factors into the integrated speaker and receiver. The resulting design, combining ergonomics with streamlining, fit the hand as well as the ear and mouth of the average (fiftieth percentile) head.

Dreyfuss made a significant contribution to the modern field of anthropometrics when he applied statistical data of human dimensions to the development of products and to considerations of human/machine interaction. His approach was distinct from a parallel field, human factors engineering, because he always integrated human factors with appropriate aesthetics rather than depend solely on statistical analysis. The publication, in 1960, of *The Measure of Man* (now *The Measure of Man and Woman*) and its revised versions have been used by industrial designers as the definitive reference and baseline for human factors in product and machine interface design ever since. His work formed a unique argument within the emerging field of human factors and ergonomics by always emphasizing the need for logical approaches that produced elegant solutions.

Dreyfuss, whose aesthetic philosophy was influenced by product design pioneer and set designer Norman Bel Geddes, received his moral education at the progressive School for Ethical Culture in New York. The motto of the school's founder, Felix Adler, was ". . . to develop individuals who will be competent to change their environment to greater conformity with moral ideals." This became the basis for Dreyfuss's human-centered approach. He expressed those ideas in his 1955 book, *Designing for People.*

Dreyfuss was a more articulate practitioner of human-centered design than was Loewy. His ideas and research were expressed in his writing and in the publications for which his firm is most noted. Although Loewy was a dynamic salesman and understood the business of design, his writing and personal philosophy was less focused on human factors research.

Paul Rand and Elliot Noyes: Corporate Identity and the International Movement

In the years after World War II, Elliot Noyes became one of the most influential designer/architects in the United States. However, his work with large corporations often involved collaboration with the more famous corporate identity designer, Paul Rand. Their comprehensive redesign of IBM and Westinghouse directly descends from the approach Peter Behrens took with AEG—not surprising, given that Noyes was educated as an architect at Harvard and studied under Gropius and Bauhaus furniture designer Marcel Breuer. Rand, for his part, was heavily influenced by what had come to be called the Swiss Style of graphic design and helped to build a relationship between Switzerland's Basel School of Design and Yale University. The strategic redesigns carried out by Rand and Noyes for IBM and Westinghouse became a blueprint for modern global corporate identity systems and spearheaded what came to be known as International Style.

One of the first strategic design decisions Rand and Noyes conceived for International Business Machines was to reduce its long and awkward name to IBM. Modern identities, they believed, needed to be easy to read and pronounce in all applications and all languages. The new logo and identity system was integrated with an approach to curtain wall architecture that was applied to the new buildings at IBM, as well as to the outer panel construction design of mainframe computer systems.

Both IBM and Westinghouse developed large design centers for product, identity, and graphic design while also maintaining a relationship with international design consultants. As for Rand's and Noyes's work, it persists to this day. (For example, IBM's nickname, Big Blue, derives from the color Rand used for the original logo.) Their work continued the design principles defined by Behrens and taught by the Bauhaus, and introduced the principles of the Basel School of Design to corporate America.

George Nelson and Charles and Ray Eames: Systems Design for Home and Work

When George Nelson was appointed design director for Herman Miller in 1945, he brought a new level of design thinking to the concept of furniture design for the home and office. Working with a number of designers, he redirected the strategy of Herman Miller and made it the leader in systems design for the modern office. Modern office buildings were being designed using a systematic approach, and Nelson saw the interior office landscape similarly—as a potential opportunity for the application of modular design systems. Each individual piece of furniture would act as one in a series of flexible parts with multiple configurations that would fit the modern open office that had come into being in the 1950s and '60s.

The design thinking expressed in Nelson's own designs and strategic plans epitomized the perceived function of the modern design manager. As well, Nelson was able to take the goals of the company and inspire a team of designers to creatively interpret them.

The husband-and-wife team of Charles and Ray Eames contributed some of their most important designs under this new strategy. Both of them studied at Michigan's Cranbrook Academy of Art, and both were influenced by Finnish architect Eliel Saarinen, who had designed buildings for the Cranbrook Educational Community and who also became the president of and a professor at the Cranbrook Academy. The Eames lounge chair and airport seating solution, for Herman Miller, are two of the most influential design projects of the twentieth century. The lounge chair was designed for the home and is the classic modern lounge chair; however, the systematic design approach taken by the Eameses contained all the elements that also made it a prototypical example of the modern office chair. The design integrated three structural shell components with soft leather pillow interface modules, a star-shaped base with a structural pivot center post, and knock-down capability, which reduced shipping volume and allowed for easy assembly upon delivery. The airport seating design is a case study in maximizing use of materials while meeting all customer, end user, and stakeholder needs. Originally designed for Dulles Airport, it is still in use in airports around the world and has stood the test of time as the best all-around solution for modern public interior seating.

The ideas and work of Charles and Ray Eames represent a unique and vital branch of design thinking. Their work is as powerful and influential as that of Frank Lloyd Wright; yet they are virtually unknown outside of the fields of design and architecture.

FROM PRODUCT TO ENVIRONMENT AND SOCIAL CHANGE

In 1975 Bill Hannon founded the Design Management Institute (DMI) in Boston, Massachusetts. This was the first professional organization in the world dedicated to improving the role of design in business, and helped to define design management as a new practice. Along with colleague Peter Gorb of the London Business School, DMI helped to add management discipline and process improvement to the design creativity process and helped set the foundations for design thinking. In 1976, Victor Papanek published his *Design for the Real World,* asking designers to see the potential of design thinking for social and environmental responsibility. He accused designers of catering

to the small percentage of consumers who have everything, while ignoring those in lower income levels and emerging economies, as well as people with disabilities. Papanek was an early proponent, along with Buckminster Fuller, of the belief that design could be an effective tool to use for environmental and social improvement. In 1982, Ralph Caplan wrote in *By Design* that Mahatma Gandhi's concept of nonviolent protest was one of the most effective design solutions in history. The philosophies of Papanek, Fuller, and Caplan introduced social change to design thinking.

At first, Papanek's criticism, which challenged the status quo, was rejected by most industrial design practitioners in the United States. His thinking received greater acceptance by European and American design educators. Papanek was an early proponent of what is now referred to as universal, or inclusive, design, and his ideas undoubtedly led to one of the mainstream success stories in universal design—the first set of products for OXO International, developed during a collaboration between Sam Farber and Smart Design in 1990. Using the concept of universal design, OXO has now developed more than 500 low-tech, high-touch product solutions that improve the way we hold everyday objects. The only real technological breakthrough the company realized was the use of neoprene; the rest came about from the thoughtful integration of ergonomics and aesthetics to create assistive devices that empower rather than stigmatize the person using them.

The concept of design for social responsibility is now a growing argument in all fields of design. Corporations are trying to build a kinder, more humane brand message that connects to the social value systems of their customers, by integrating universal design, multicultural design for emerging economies, and environmental responsibility into their products. Bruce Mau, one of the leaders in this movement, echoed a contemporary version of Papanek's ideas in his manifesto, Massive Change, and Papanek would surely have recognized an extension of his ideas in C.K. Prahalad's 2005 book *The Fortune at the Bottom of the Pyramid.* Emily Pilloton's nonprofit firm, Project H Design, is an example of how an empowered individual can address global problems with a humanitarian design strategy.

William McDonough and Michael Braungart have argued for a more proactive approach to design in their book *Cradle to Cradle.* McDonough believes it is possible to have a responsible consumer society if we stop thinking in terms of cradle to grave. He believes the concept of throwing things away is over and that everything must be continuously reused or recycled; thus, cradle to cradle. McDonough and Braungart have created a method for analyzing materials and processes and have developed new methods and materials for minimizing environmental impact. Herman Miller's Mirra Chair, designed by Studio 7.6, was built using the cradle to cradle approach.

The Nobel laureate Herb Simon stated that there are really two types of science. One concerns the world humans are responsible for producing (the science of the artificial), and the other concerns the world in which humans evolved (the science of the natural). The science of the artificial is still relatively young and ineffective, especially in its attempts during the last two centuries to change existing situations into preferred ones on a large scale. The fields of industrial, interior, graphic, and interface design, as well as architecture, have emerged as one branch of the science of the artificial. Although interest in the practice of design grows, research, graduate, and doctoral programs in design fields must grow with it to pull even with the more established branches of engineering, applied science, and business.

The global economy we face today is as strange to us as the one confronted by designers in the early twentieth century. Environmental responsibility and universal design were once an option; now they are becoming a virtual mandate. Experience design, interaction design, and service design are new domains for designers. We live in an era in which the world is "flat" and countries in every continent are contributing ideas to emerging trends, creating new global hybrids at an unprecedented rate. P&G and Apple are today's AEG, and we need a new educational model in the spirit of the Bauhaus, a model that emphasizes equally both education and research.

Design thinking is always most effective when it successfully connects strategic planning with execution of products, services, and communication. Behrens was able to work with AEG to find a way to make consumers understand how to integrate electrical power into their lives. Currently, A.G. Lafley, the CEO of Procter & Gamble, is one of the biggest proponents of design thinking and implementation throughout a corporation. His ability to strategically redirect P&G into almost a decade of meeting expectations of shareholder value makes him an excellent example of Herb Simon's definition of design as "changing existing situations into preferred ones." In his book *Game Changer*, Lafley describes the various experiments in innovation P&G has used to maintain its competitive advantage. He has championed design thinking by growing internal design capability, but he has also connected with design and business innovators and with outside consulting firms.

Lafley transformed P&G from a chemical company into an "experience" company, and design played a significant role in that transition. P&G thinks globally and in terms of billions. The company has successfully found a way to make products in several categories that consumers can personalize into their own patterns of use. This is a unique twist on the concept of mass customization.

Science, engineering, and technology factor shifts have occurred in each decade in the last century, opening new opportunities for designers. The key ingredient for business success is the presence of both an innovative CEO who sees design as an investment, not a cost, and a strategic design director or consultant who can place the value of the design at the center of the company. If either one leaves, the value of design is jeopardized. The rise and fall of the role of design in corporate America is directly related to a change in this relationship more than any other factor in the economy.

Suggested Reading

Dreyfuss, Henry. *Designing for People* (New York, N.Y.: Simon & Schuster, 1955).

Kagan, Jonathan, and Craig M. Vogel. *Creating Breakthrough Products: Innovation from Product Planning to Program Approval* (Upper Saddle River, N.J.: Prentice Hall, 2001).

Lafley, A.G., and Ram Charan. *The Game-Changer: How You Can Drive Revenue and Profit Growth with Innovation* (New York, N.Y.: Crown Business, 2008).

Meggs, Philip, and Alston W. Purvis. *Meggs' History of Graphic Design* (Hoboken, N.J.: John Wiley, 1998).

Neuhart, John, Marilyn Neuhart, and Ray Eames. *Eames Design: The Work of the Office of Charles and Ray Eames* (Germany: Ernst, Wilhelm, & Sohn, 1989).

Pulos, Arthur. *The American Design Ethic: A History of Industrial Design to 1940* (Boston, Mass.: MIT Press, 1983).

Simon, Herbert. *The Sciences of the Artificial*, 3rd. ed. (Boston, Mass.: MIT Press, 1996).

Chapter 2

The Designful Company

by Marty Neumeier, President, Neutron

In a challenging business environment, there is no substitute for having an innovative and distinctive brand expressed in "experiences that rivet minds and run away with hearts." Marty Neumeier identifies how design drives this reality, embracing not only products and services but also processes, systems, and organizations. To succeed, companies must be agile, nurture inventiveness, and have an enterprise-wide appetite for radical ideas.

INDUSTRIAL AGE THINKING has delivered some dazzling capabilities, including the power to churn out high-quality products at affordable prices. Yet it has also trapped us in a tangle labeled by Berkeley professor Horst Rittel as "wicked problems"—problems so persistent, pervasive, and slippery that they seem insoluble. Unlike the relatively tame problems found in mathematics, chess, and cost accounting, wicked problems tend to shift disconcertingly with every attempt to solve them. Moreover, the solutions are never right or wrong, just better or worse.

The world's wicked problems crowd us like piranha. You know the list: pollution, overpopulation, dwindling natural resources, global warming, technological warfare, and a lopsided distribution of power that has failed to address massive ignorance and Third-World hunger. In the world of business, managers face a subset of these problems: breakneck change, ultra-savvy customers, balkanized markets, rapacious shareholders, traitorous employees, regulatory headlocks, and price pressure from desperate global competitors with little to lose and everything to gain.

In a 2008 survey sponsored by my consulting firm, Neutron, and Stanford University, 1,500 top American executives were asked to identify the wickedest problems plaguing their companies today. While the top 10 included the usual suspects of profits and growth, they also revealed concerns that hadn't shown up on corporate radar screens until now: aligning strategy and customer experience, addressing eco-sustainability, collaborating across silos, and embracing social responsibility. The number-one wicked problem cited by corporate leaders was the conflict between long-term goals and short-term demands.

Clearly, these were not the concerns of twentieth-century managers. The last management obsession of that century was Six Sigma, the total-quality movement inspired by Dr. W. Edwards Deming and his postwar work with the Japanese. Six Sigma has been so successful that quality has virtually become a commodity. Customers now expect every product and service to be reliable, affording no single company a competitive advantage.

Unfortunately, the more progressive elements of Deming's philosophy were all but ignored by a business mindset that preferred the measurable over the meaningful.

When we look around and see today's companies and brands beset by distrustful customers, disengaged employees, and suspicious communities, we can link these problems to a legacy management style that lacks any real human dimension. The model for twentieth-century management was not the warm humanism of the Renaissance, but the cold mechanics of the assembly line, the laser-like focus of Newtonian science applied to the manufacture of wealth. The assembly line was intentionally blind to mo-

2008 SURVEY OF WICKED PROBLEMS*
(Sponsored by Neutron and Stanford University)

1. Balancing long-term goals with short-term demands
2. Predicting returns on innovative concepts
3. Innovating at the increasing speed of change
4. Winning the war for world-class talent
5. Combining profitability with social responsibility
6. Protecting margins in a commoditizing industry
7. Multiplying success by collaborating across silos
8. Finding unclaimed yet profitable market space
9. Addressing the challenge of eco-sustainability
10. Aligning strategy with customer experience

*A wicked problem is a puzzle so persistent, pervasive, and slippery that it can seem insoluble.

rality, emotions, and human aspiration—all the better to make your competitors and customers lose, so you can win.

Business at bottom is not mechanical but human. Today, we find that innovation without emotion is uninteresting. Products without aesthetics are not compelling, brands without meaning are undesirable, and business without ethics is unsustainable. The management model that got us here is underpowered to move us forward. To succeed, the new model must replace the win-lose nature of the assembly line with the win-win nature of the network.

In 2006, when Ford Motor Co. announced plans to close fourteen factories and cut thirty-four thousand jobs, Bill Ford made a revealing statement: "We can no longer play the game the old way," he said. "From now on, our vehicles will be designed to satisfy the customer, not just fill a factory." Too little, too late, Bill. While Ford was figuring this out, Toyota had already been satisfying customers for years.

We've spent the last century filling factories and making minor tweaks to the same basic idea of efficiency. The high-water mark in the quest for continuous improvement was Six Sigma—yet the *Wall Street Journal* cited a 2006 Qualpro study showing that of fifty-eight large companies that announced Six Sigma programs, 91 percent trailed the S&P 500.[1] We've been getting better and better at a management model that's getting wronger and wronger.

In an era of Six Sigma parity, it's no longer enough to get better. We have to get different. Not just different, but really different. In my book, *Zag*, I proposed a seventeen-step process to create the radical differentiation necessary for companies, products, and brands to stand out from a marketplace of increasing clutter. Thanks to unprecedented market clutter, differentiation is becoming the most powerful strategy in business and the primary beneficiary of innovation.

So, if innovation drives differentiation, what drives innovation? The answer, hidden in plain sight, is design. Design contains the skills to identify possible futures, invent exciting products, build bridges to customers, crack wicked problems, and more. The fact is, if you wanna innovate, you gotta design.

Imagine a crazy wonderland where most of what you learned in business school is either upside-down or backward—where customers control the company, jobs are avenues of self-expression, the barriers to competition are out of your control, strangers design your products, fewer features are better, advertising drives customers away, demographics are beside the point, whatever you sell you take back, and best practices are obsolete at birth; where meaning talks, money walks, and stability is fantasy; where talent trumps obedience, imagination beats knowledge, and empathy trounces logic.

If you've been paying close enough attention, you don't have to imagine this *Alice in Wonderland*-style scenario. You see it forming all around you. The only question is whether you can change your business, your brand, and your thinking fast enough to take full advantage of it.

The management innovation destined to kick Six Sigma off its throne is design thinking. It will take over your marketing department, move into your research and development labs, transform your processes, and ignite your culture. It will create a whip action that will bring finance into alignment with creativity, and eventually reach deep into Wall Street to change the rules of investing.

DESIGNING THE WAY FORWARD

The discipline of design has been waiting patiently in the wings for nearly a century, having been relegated to supporting roles and stand-in parts. Until now, companies have used design as a beauty station for identities and communications or as the last stop in a product launch. Never has it been used for its potential to create rule-bending innovation across the board. Meanwhile, the public is developing a healthy appetite for all things design.

One survey by Kelton Research for Autodesk found that when seven in ten Americans recalled the last time they saw a product they just had to have, it was because of design.[2] They found that with younger people (eighteen to twenty-nine), the influence of design was even more pronounced. More than one out of four Americans was disappointed in the level of design in America, saying, for example, that cars were better designed twenty-five years ago.

In Great Britain, a recent survey by the Design Council found that 16 percent of British businesses say that design tops their list of key success factors. Among "rapidly growing" businesses, a whopping 47 percent rank it first.[3]

The ballooning demand for design is shaped by a profound shift in how the First World makes its living. Creativity in its various forms has become the number-one engine of economic growth. The creative class, in the words of Toronto University professor Richard Florida, now comprises thirty-eight million members, or more than 30 percent of the American workforce. McKinsey authors Lowell Bryan and Claudia Joyce put the figure only slightly below, at 25 percent. They cite creative professionals in financial services, healthcare, high-tech, pharmaceuticals, and media and entertainment who act as agents of change, producers of intangible assets, and creators of new value for their companies.

When you hear the phrase innovative design, what picture comes to mind? An iPhone? A Nintendo Wii? A Prius? Most people visualize some kind of technology product. Yet products—technological or otherwise—are not the only possibilities for design. Design is rapidly moving from posters and toasters to include processes, systems, and organizations.

Dr. Deming, the mid-century business guru who inspired Six Sigma, had some far-reaching ideas beyond quality control. You'd expect his thinking to be stuck in the rusty past, but it remains remarkably progressive by modern standards. His trademark 1982 System of Profound Knowledge was an attempt to get managers to think outside the system they work in. It featured a list of "deadly diseases," including a lack of purpose, the mobility of executives, and emphasis on short-term profits (sound familiar?). Among the diseases was an over-reliance on technology to solve problems.

The sure cure for Deming's diseases, as well as for the top ten wicked problems, is design. It's the accelerator for the company car, the powertrain for sustainable profits. Design drives innovation, innovation powers brand, brand builds loyalty, and loyalty sustains profits. If you want long-term profits, don't start with technology—start with design.

BRAND AND DELIVER

There are really only two main components for business success: brands and their delivery. All other activities—operations, finance, manufacturing, marketing, sales, communications, human relations, investor relations—are subcomponents.

In my earlier book, *The Brand Gap*, I defined a brand as a person's gut feeling about a product, service, or company. I showed how brands derive their financial value, drawing a distinction between me-too brands and charismatic brands. Charismatic brands support higher profit margins because their customers believe there's no substitute for them; they form unbreachable barriers to competition in an era of cut-throat pricing.

A former editor of *Windows* magazine, Mike Elgan, illustrated the difference between ordinary brands and charismatic brands in two succinct sentences: "Microsoft CEO Steve Ballmer is famous for a crazy video in which he yells, 'I. LOVE. THIS. COMPANY.' With Apple, it's the customers who shout that." This may explain why *BusinessWeek*'s top 100 survey placed Microsoft's brand value at only 17 percent of its market cap, and Apple's at an impressive 66 percent.

The well-documented connection between customer loyalty and profit margins has encouraged many companies to launch so-called loyalty programs by using incentives or contracts to lock in customers. The trouble is, customers don't like to be locked in. It makes them disloyal. Not only that, loyalty programs are expensive to manage and easy to copy. They're nothing more than Band-Aids on a much deeper problem—offerings so uncompelling that customers prefer to keep their options open.

In the previous century, a little brand loyalty went a long way. Often, what passed for loyalty was merely ignorance. If customers didn't know what their options were, they would simply stick with the devil they knew. Today's Microsoft, with its low brand score, may be one of the last major companies to profit this way. In the new century, customer ignorance won't be enough to keep competitors at bay.

To build a brand that fosters voluntary loyalty, it's better to do what Google does—to use design to create differentiated products and services that delight customers. If you can deliver customer delight, you can dispense with the high cost and relationship-straining effects of loyalty programs. Organic loyalty beats artificial loyalty every time.

The central problem of brand-building is getting a complex organization to execute a bold idea. It's as simple and as vexing as that. First, you have to identify and articulate the right idea. Next, you have to get hundreds or even thousands of people to act on it—in unison. Then you have to update, augment, or replace the idea as the market dictates.

Stacked against this challenge are two prevailing headwinds: the extreme clutter of the marketplace and the relentless speed of change. The antidote to clutter is a radically differentiated brand. The antidote to change is organizational agility. Although agility was not a burning issue when business moved at a more leisurely pace, in 2008 it showed up as wicked problem number three. Companies now need to be as fast and adaptable as they are innovative.

AGILITY BEATS OWNERSHIP

Today, there's no safe ground in business. The old barriers to competition—ownership of factories, access to capital, technology patents, regulatory protection, distribution chokeholds, customer ignorance—are rapidly collapsing. In our Darwinian era of perpetual innovation, we're either commoditizing or revolutionizing.

A visible victim of change was Kodak at the turn of the new century, when its ownership of the patents, distribution channels, and dominant market share protecting its film and camera businesses became irrelevant against the steady advance of digital photography. Though Kodak could see the revolution coming a mile off, it couldn't extricate itself from its own culture—a culture based on squeezing profits from a commoditizing film business. By 2004, its share of the camera market was down to 17 percent, despite the company's having been the first on the scene with a digital camera fifteen years earlier.

Why does change always have to be crisis-driven? Is it possible to change ahead of the curve? What keeps companies from the continuous transformation needed to keep up with the speed of the market?

A company can't will itself to be agile. Agility is an emergent property that appears when an organization has the right mindset, the right skills, and the ability to multiply those skills through collaboration. To count agility as a core competence, you have to embed it into the culture. You have to encourage an enterprise-wide appetite for radical ideas. You have to keep the company in a constant state of inventiveness. It's one thing to inject a company with inventiveness. It's another thing to build a company on inventiveness.

To organize for agility, your company needs to develop a "designful mind." A designful mind confers the ability to invent the widest range of solutions for the wicked problems now facing your company, your industry, your world.

"He that will not apply new remedies must expect new evils," warned Sir Francis Bacon 500 years ago, "for time is the greatest innovator."

NEXT, ECO-EVERYTHING

Necessity may well be the mother of invention. But if we continue to manufacture mountains of toxic stuff, invention may soon become the mother of necessity. Our natural resources will disappear and our planet made uninhabitable. On the top ten list of wicked problems, eco-sustainability is number nine with a bullet. My hunch is that it will move up rapidly until it settles in at the top three.

The problem with consumerism isn't that it creates desire, but that it fails to fully satisfy it. Desire is a basic human drive. But part of what we desire is to feel good about the things we buy. We yearn for guilt-free affluence, to use the words of Worldchanging's Alex Steffen.

As a thought experiment, imagine a future in which all companies were compelled to take back every product they made. How would that change their behavior? For starters, they would make their products with parts they could salvage and reuse at the end of their life cycles. This, in turn, would spawn whole industries dedicated to the design of reusable materials. As companies struggled to afford the full cost of manufacturing, the prices of products and services would rise. To keep prices under control, companies would localize their operations to save on transportation costs. Localizing businesses would change the nature of communities, creating a network of quasi-independent economies more akin to the Agricultural Age than to the Industrial Age.

As you can see, the domino effect caused by a focus on waste reduction would alter our commercial landscape beyond recognition, creating more wicked problems, but also more opportunities for innovation.

In France, where the Agricultural Age is still in evidence, the large-scale Boisset Winery is currently rediscovering the value of the old ways. It's replacing heavy, diesel-burning tractors with horse-drawn plows and grass-munching sheep to restore the compacted, depleted topsoil. It's also discovering value in new technologies, bucking the French tradition of corks and glass bottles by shipping its wine in recyclable Tetra Pak containers that reduce oxidation and cut transportation costs.

In Germany, Volkswagen is demonstrating that corporate responsibility doesn't end at the loading dock. The company is already selling cars that are 85 percent recyclable and 95 percent reusable, and it's building a zero-emissions car that operates on a fuel cell, twelve batteries, and a solar panel instead of fossil fuels.

The European Union has announced a "20/20 vision." It wants to get 20 percent of its energy from renewable sources by the year 2020. If this were to come from sun power, it would require twenty-five times the current annual production of solar panels to meet the need. In Silicon Valley, Applied Materials has a complementary vision: to have its equipment used for making three-quarters of the world's solar panels by the year 2011.

American furniture manufacturer Steelcase is currently attacking the waste stream with its Think chair, which is nearly 100 percent fixable and recyclable. The company has also set up three factories around the world to lower transportation costs and support local economies.

Industrial giant General Electric once found itself in the penalty box for dumping toxic chemicals into the Hudson River. Today it spends nearly $1 billion a year on research into eco-friendly technologies to improve energy efficiency, desalinate water sources, and reduce dependence on fossil fuels. The motive? Profit. As CEO Jeffrey Immelt says, "Green is green."

While eco-sustainability isn't yet top-of-mind for most CEOs, when the tide finally turns, it'll turn fast. There's already a significant migration of talented executives from traditional technology to green technology. As venture capitalist Adam Grosser put it, "They have had their consciousness energized, and they believe there is a lot of money to be made."

BUSINESS IS DESIGN BLIND

Until a decade or so ago, the public's taste for design had been stunted by the limitations of mass production. Now people have more buying choices, so they're choosing in favor of beauty, simplicity, and the "tribal identity" of their favorite brands.

Yet if design is such a powerful tool, why aren't there more practitioners working in corporations? If economic value increasingly derives from intangibles like knowledge, inspiration, and creativity, why don't we hear the language of design echoing down the corridors?

Unfortunately, most business managers are deaf, dumb, and blind when it comes to the creative process. They learned their chops by rote, through a bounded tradition of spreadsheet-based theory. As one MBA joked, in his world, the language of design is a sound only dogs can hear.

This is illustrated by a story about railroad baron Collis P. Huntington, who visited the Eiffel Tower just after its completion. When an interviewer for a Paris newspaper asked him for a critique, he said: "Your Eiffel Tower is all very well, but where's the money in it?"

It's not that spreadsheet thinking is wrong. It's just that it's inadequate. A designer might have offered a completely different critique of the tower: "What a stirring symbol of progress! From now on, people will never forget their visit to Paris." According to one estimate, more than $120 billion worth of Eiffel Tower souvenirs has been sold since 1897. The trinket business alone has been worth the investment.

The lesson of Paris has not been lost on cities like London, with its majestic London Eye, or Bilbao, with its shimmering Guggenheim Museum. Frank Gehry's design has not only captivated the world's imagination, it has catalyzed an economic turnaround for the whole region.

For businesses to bottle the kind of experiences that rivet minds and run away with hearts, not just one time but over and over, they'll need to do more than hire designers. They'll need to be designers. They'll need to think like designers, feel like designers, work like designers. The narrow-gauge mindset of the past is insufficient for today's wicked problems. We can no longer play the music as written. Instead, we have to invent a whole new scale.

Endnotes

1. K. Richardson, "The Six Sigma Factor for Home Depot," *Wall Street Journal* (January 4, 2007).

2. 2007 Autodesk "Design for Living" survey, conducted by Kelton Research between March 23 and March 28, 2007.

3. The Design Council, "The Value of Design Factfinder Report," *Design in Britain* (2007).

Chapter 3

Creating the Right Environment for Design

by Julian Jenkins, Senior Consultant, 2nd Road, Australia

Without changes in a company's attitudes and processes, the investment in design may never pay off. Julian Jenkins identifies nine "cults" that thwart the commitment to this resource. He also outlines the qualities of a design-friendly culture and proposes seven ways design managers can help ensure that their contributions yield the most creative and beneficial outcomes.

THE CITY OF Sydney has been weighed in the balance and found wanting. According to a recent study by Danish architect and urban planning guru Jan Gehl, Sydney has squandered the extraordinary natural advantages provided by its stunning harbor. Instead of encouraging a vibrant, people-friendly city, its leaders have allowed a soulless urban environment to emerge, one clogged by traffic and cut off from the water by major freeways and rail infrastructure. Sure, Sydney may have its Opera House—one glorious expression of design that can inspire the human spirit. However, taken as a whole, Gehl argues, the center of Sydney is not a healthy, life-enhancing ecosystem, but a monument to the culture of progress and development at the cost of human values and relationships.[1]

If the way we have built our modern cities often gets in the way of meaningful human interaction, then it is no great stretch to suggest that we have an even bigger problem with our modern business corporations. At least cities make a conscious effort to consider design, and devote substantial resources to urban planning and beautification. The same cannot be said of most organizations. The more enlightened of them may pay attention to the physical environment, creating workplaces that are intended to stimulate creativity and encourage collaboration. However, a human ecosystem consists of more than the physical environment—it also includes all the social, cultural, and behavioral elements of human interaction, the way people work together and get things done.

One organization I have worked with recently had just moved its entire staff to a shiny new campus that has won a number of design awards for its vibrant use of color, its community feel, and its resort-like facilities. Judging by the external environment, one would assume that the organization is a paragon of creative, up-front, human-centered thinking. Yet when I started to interview staff about its invisible infrastructure—the management systems and processes that enable it to operate—I discovered it was seriously dilapidated and in need of urgent renovation. Not only were there gaping holes that needed filling, and dirty windows that didn't allow for any sort of clear visibility or communication, but some of the core systems were so onerous that people had left the organization rather than continuing to live in that mess any longer.

The great challenge that will confront those who wish to champion design in business will be to grapple with organizational ecosystems that are both dysfunctional and inherently obstructive to the spirit and processes of design. To be successful, a design leader will have to do a lot more than introduce design thinking and practices to the corporate world. Erecting a shiny new building called "design" in the midst of the corporate "city" will not be sufficient if all the infrastructure and processes in the surrounding organizational environment are fundamentally misaligned. The designers in the organization may well be cut off from their natural habitat just as effectively as the office workers of Sydney are separated from their natural harbor surroundings.

HOW THE ORGANIZATIONAL ECOSYSTEM IS OFTEN ANTAGONISTIC TO DESIGN

Having worked as a consultant to organizations that endeavor to introduce design as a new capability, it seems clear to me that the real challenge for design leaders is to reshape the modern organization to create an ecosystem that is conducive, not antagonistic, to design. The major obstacles typically encountered in the process of installing a design capability arise out of existing attitudes and behaviors within the organization that will squeeze the life out of design if they are allowed to continue unchecked. Design leaders and their organizational sponsors need to be aware that their task is not just to create a new functional area or new approaches to innovation across the organization—they actually need to undertake an entire cultural transformation.

While due attention has been paid to the differences between the left-brain, analytical thinking that dominates the corporate world and the right-brain, creative thinking used by designers,[2] there is still limited awareness of the fundamental difference in values between these two worlds, and the practical impacts of these values in shaping the organizational ecosystem. This divergence in values—and the cultural forms that emerge from them—go a lot further than the rather obvious surface differences between a design firm and traditional corporate culture (e.g., dress code, work hours, physical surroundings).

To highlight the differences, I have identified nine cultural mindsets that are endemic within the modern organization and that are enemies of design. I have called them cults, because they are based on values that have some inherent validity but have become hardened into unhelpful dogmas and dysfunctional behaviors. These nine cults stand in stark contrast to the sorts of cultural values that are necessary for design to flourish:

The negative behaviors and work practices emerging from these cults are myriad,

Dysfunctional organizational cults	Design-friendly cultural environments
Cult of control and hierarchy	Culture of empowerment and authorization
Cult of performance and short-term success	Culture of learning from failure and looking for long-term outcomes
Cult of efficiency and cost-cutting	Culture of effectiveness and value creation
Cult of productivity and busyness	Culture of reflection and focused action
Cult of competition and empire-building	Culture of collaboration and shared purpose
Cult of compliance and assurance	Culture of judgment and trust
Cult of risk avoidance	Culture of possibility and experimentation
Cult of blame-shifting and arse-covering	Culture of truth-telling, of honest critique
Cult of rigorous process as salvation	Culture of heuristics and agility

and are so deeply embedded with the typical organizational ecosystem as to be almost invisible. For instance, the cult of productivity and busyness creates organizational environments in which calendars are full and it is almost impossible to get the necessary group of stakeholders in a room at the same time to establish intent around a design project or to make important design decisions. The cult of risk avoidance ties new ideas up in interminable business case processes rather than letting them flourish, proliferate, and emerge into new forms. The cult of rigorous process as salvation insists that an activity will produce a good outcome if only the people concerned follow a rigorous procedure (which all too often means applying a set of preordained steps without having to think too hard). Designers, however, prefer to proceed with a flexible toolbox of heuristics and an agile, curious mind. They don't know yet what the outcome will be of their creative explorations, and therefore cannot define what specific steps may be required to get there.

While many values that underpin the modern corporation are expressed in subtle and informal ways within the organizational culture, in many cases these same values permeate some large formal systems and processes, compounding each other in the process. Throw together the cult of performance and short-term success with the cult of productivity and busyness and what do you get? A performance management system that rewards those staff who are seen to work long hours, achieve quick wins, and fix short-term problems, rather than recognizing the value of staff who take the time to think and play with ideas; who take on large, complex challenges with no easy solutions; and who apply a long-term, strategic view. Or allow the cult of efficiency and cost-cutting to flourish alongside the cult of competition and empire-building and you create a budgeting process where business units ruthlessly compete for scarce resources and refuse to cooperate for the wider good. Creating a design-friendly organizational ecosystem may often mean completely reshaping many of the core processes that underpin the way the organization currently goes about its business.

BEING A DESIGN LEADER MEANS RESHAPING THE ORGANIZATIONAL ECOSYSTEM

If introducing design thinking and practices to an organization is actually an exercise in cultural transformation, then it is surely the role of a design leader to be the catalyst for transformation. In effect, the design leader must be willing to take on the organization itself as the object of design, not just a particular product or process. This means both actively working to reshape the underlying cultural values on which the organization is based and being willing to challenge and rebuild some of the major organizational systems and corporate processes.

For many of us who aspire to be design leaders, moving beyond what Richard Buchanan[3] calls first- and second-order design (design of language and symbols, and design of tangible objects) into third- and fourth-order design (design of systems and cultural environments) may seem like a scary proposition, especially given the size and complexity of the modern corporation. It is tempting to stay on the sidelines, to eke out a place for design on the edge of the organization and hope that somehow the design virus will flourish. However, such an approach is likely to condemn design to ongoing frustration or marginalization as it tries to justify its existence and propagate its processes in a culturally antagonistic and impenetrable environment.

The design leader who does want to have a transformative influence on the wider organization needs to have courage and commitment, as well as a clear strategic view of cultural transformation as the ultimate goal. While the task may be a challenging one, it is by no means insurmountable. There are a number of important steps a design leader should take to maximize his or her chances of success.

1) **Be selective in choosing which organizations to work with.**

   When an organization approaches you with a hopeful gleam in its eye and an interest in "doing something" about innovation through design, don't be too flattered or idealistic about the opportunity and rush in where angels fear to tread. Take some time to get to know who or what you will be working with, what level of openness there is to new ideas, and who wields the real power in the organization. Find out how much the organization is willing to invest in design—not just in terms of dollars, but also in terms of time and resources, particularly at the executive level. Assess whether there is any existing recognition that the organization's current core systems and work practices may well be broken and need fixing, and how widespread the appetite for change is across the organization. Declare boldly that successfully introducing design involves a significant cultural transformation and see what response you get.

2) **Work with senior leaders to build strong intent and an embedded culture of design.**

Cultural transformation cannot occur unless it is sanctioned and modeled from the top down. To be effective, a design leader needs the strong support of a key leader or group within the organization. Ideally, the CEO and/or board should be strong advocates for design and should be willing to embrace the cultural changes necessary for design to thrive. Where this is not possible, a business unit leader may be able to act as a voice of intent, though clearly the scope of his or her authority to implement change will be more limited. Trying to champion a design-oriented cultural paradigm shift without strong intent from within the organization is an exercise in futility; the design leader must place himself or herself strategically near the center of power and clearly articulate the vision, opportunities, and transformations required to embed a new design culture within the organization.

Of course, to be powerful, a declared intent should be matched by a strong commitment to lead by example. For design to be fully authorized as a legitimate and valued activity and as part of a company's cultural DNA, the leaders of the organization need to show the way by incorporating design thinking

LEADING CHANGE WITH AN INTENT WORKSHOP

Having a key leader to supply a strong voice of intent within an organization is vital, but ideally you also need to secure a wider, collective intent around any specific new initiatives or around the overall cultural change program. One effective way to achieve this is to start any new design activity or change program with an intent workshop. This involves inviting all the key stakeholders to attend a facilitated conversation, an open, yet carefully structured discussion that is intended to achieve two important goals: to create a shared view of the problem or opportunity that has paved the way for a design initiative; and to agree on the desired outcomes or vision of what an ideal future would look like. Not only does the intent workshop establish important parameters in terms of scope and specific issues that need to be addressed in the design, but it also creates a strong sense of engagement and common ownership of the problem among those with a direct interest in influencing the outcome.

into their own work. For example, they should be able to demonstrate a strong awareness of where and how to use design, use a shared language about design processes, and ask good questions that reflect their familiarity with design thinking. To support this, the design leader needs to devote considerable attention in the early stages to building awareness and capability within the leadership team and encouraging team members to apply design thinking to specific organizational problems or opportunities. At the same time, the leadership should also champion design by embedding it into key organizational processes, such as capital investment, resource planning, recruitment, training, performance and recognition, and reporting, and by finding opportunities to showcase the fruits of design thinking as signposts to a new cultural environment.

3) **Be a systems thinker.**

Traditionally, the sciences have applied a reductionist approach, breaking everything down into component parts, whether atoms (physics), molecules (chemistry), or cells (biology). It is only relatively recently that scientists have recognized that the physical world cannot be explained purely in terms of its parts—you must look at major systems (such as climate), recognize what drives them, and understand how complex systems interact with each other to create a whole. At one level, this involves relinquishing the illusion of control, but the payoff is in finding opportunities for insight and leverage on a larger scale.

The same shift in thinking is required in relation to the organizational ecosystem. You need to understand the systems and processes that drive the organization and suck up all its energy—and then find ways to intervene and redesign them. Recently, I was building up momentum around a new design project when it was unceremoniously stopped in mid-flight because key stakeholders were consumed in the annual budgeting/planning process. All too often, organizations expend all their creative energy on perpetuating the current system, rather than on renewing it and allowing room for innovation. Ask an average middle manager which organizational processes take up most time and feel most onerous, and you will probably get a quick insight into which systems need an overhaul. Being able to think about an organization as a series of interrelated systems, and being able to identify where to intervene to achieve a major cultural impact, is an important skill for a design leader. This may well mean pushing upstream from second-order design projects focused around a specific artifact (for instance, a project report) to third- and fourth-order projects involving reviewing and redesigning the wider system (for instance, the whole web of conversations and documents that make up the project reporting system).

4) **Focus on human interactions and social processes.**

   One of Jan Gehl's seminal books is *Life Between Buildings: Using Public Space.* Challenging the architect's overarching focus on the physical infrastructure, he asserts that an important part of the urban environment is the open spaces and the opportunities for human interaction that emerge. It is tempting to jump quickly in to characterize the organizational environment as "life between meetings," but this would be to misdirect the analogy. In organizational culture, meetings are the equivalent of public space and an important opportunity for human interaction, although unfortunately they are typically devoid of any good design and therefore end up being as soulless and meaningless as many urban spaces. A more apt analogy would be to think about "life between budgets, business plans, and PowerPoint presentations." Too often, organizations put enormous energy into implementing formal planning cycles and writing long documents that gobble up a huge amount of resources and pay no attention to the social processes and the quality of human interactions that surround them. Knowledge, insight, and new ideas tend to come from humans interacting in both formal and informal settings. The formal processes and documents should play a subservient, supporting role, not dominate. Creating an organizational environment conducive to design means maximizing the opportunities for human interactions, communication, and connection, and breaking down the formal structures and silos that keep people apart.

5) **Exercise well-directed discipline when implementing new processes.**

   Discipline may not be a word that readily resonates with many designers, but it is an important part of any cultural change process. A well-directed discipline is required to prevent the habits of thinking and behavior characteristic of the old ecosystem from reemerging and smothering the new attitudes and practices of design. The law of entropy is alive and well in organizational culture change—new ideas and processes atrophy very quickly unless a concerted effort is made to ensure their longevity. The design leader, working closely with the client sponsoring the change process, needs to hold firm on key design elements during the implementation phase or all the hard work to create a new way of doing things will be quickly undone. Wherever possible, incentives should be built into the system itself or into the accountabilities of the relevant managers to provide some extrinsic motivation for adopting the new ideas. An engagement strategy should also be developed to ensure that the rationale and benefits of the new system or process is understood by those expected to use it.

6) **Kill some sacred cows.**

   Nothing accelerates change like killing a few sacred cows. One of Jan Gehl's recommendations for Sydney is to dismantle the Cahill Expressway, an

THE IMPORTANCE OF HOLDING ONTO KEY DESIGN PRINCIPLES

I learned the value of firm discipline to achieving cultural transformation early in my career, when designing a new reporting system in a major government agency. We asked the senior managers in one major business unit to present their annual strategic reports to an executive committee using a new streamlined format, which was designed specifically to limit the amount of detail they could supply and focus instead on answering a set of key strategic questions. Uncomfortable with the relative brevity of the report and the demand for answers to specific questions, the senior managers tried various stratagems to maintain their existing habits and behaviors—such as insisting that certain questions did not apply to them, or tabling additional supporting documents to supplement the main report. But the executive committee remained firm in its commitment to the design principles underlying the new reporting format and insisted that the most important element in the exercise was having a meaningful conversation about the key strategic issues raised in the report, rather than getting lost in a sea of detail. As a result of maintaining good discipline, within a few years this process had become the main strategic planning and decision-making activity for the organization.[4]

elevated road and rail connection that has played a major role as a piece of transportation infrastructure for half a century, albeit at the cost of cutting the city off from its foreshore (see photos on next page). For New York, Gehl has proposed removing cars from Times Square. Taking a dramatic step to change the existing environment is often important to show that you mean business and that the status quo is not the only possible reality. Whether it is firing a manager who does not want to embrace the new cultural environment, scrapping the current business case process and insisting that the argument for a new idea should be communicated in no more than a page, or generously rewarding an employee who comes up with a good idea, sacrificing a sacred cow can open up new and unsuspected opportunities and undermine the cynicism of those who have given up aspiring for something better.

Judiciously choosing which sacred cows to sacrifice is important—drive-by shootings or wholesale massacres are unlikely to produce a positive result! Having the support of a strong voice of intent is clearly important here, as the design leader is unlikely to be able to enforce these decisions alone. However, the design leader should be pointing the way and working with the organizational sponsor to ensure that the right moves are made.

Sydney Harbour Bridge from Circular Quay. The Opera House is on a parallel peninsula less than 100 meters to the right.

Same view toward Sydney Harbour Bridge from forty meters further back (Cahill Expressway in foreground).

7) **Help the organization to learn more about itself from experience.**

One organization we worked with on introducing design was confident that it had an open and collaborative culture that would be receptive to design, and in many ways it was right—it had a better culture to work with than many other organizations we have encountered. So we proceeded to undertake a major design project and achieved some real success and momentum along the way. However, we also encountered some unexpected pockets of resistance at management level, frontline staff who were reluctant to get involved in prototyping a new process, and lengthy delays in moving from ideas to implementation. Even in the best of environments, then, there are cultural obstacles and existing processes that get in the way of effective outcomes from a design process. Sometimes, the only way to recognize that things need to change is to enable the organization to experience design, and see what unexpected obstacles emerge. The key for the design leader here is to take the time to step back from the process, to identify with the organizational sponsor which factors presented difficulties, and to work together on changing these parts of the ecosystem for the future. The design leader must ensure that the design process itself does not get blamed for less-than-satisfactory outcomes that arise from unhelpful organizational behaviors or processes. Setting realistic expectations for the time frames required for successfully introducing design to an organization and achieving the necessary cultural alignment is also a vital part of this process.

CONCLUSION: IT CAN BE DONE

The typical response that Jan Gehl receives when he suggests a more human-centered approach to urban design for cities like Sydney, New York, and Copenhagen are initial protestations that "it can't be done here." The existing structures and transport systems seem too firmly entrenched, too monolithic. But those cities that have had the courage to believe in his ideas, and to institute change, even if incrementally, have reaped the benefits in making their city centers more accessible and attractive to people. For all its civic pride, Sydney looks enviously at Melbourne's vibrant bar and café culture, which has emerged in the wake of Jan Gehl's 1994 recommendations for that city. Transforming the organizational ecosystem may seem like an almighty challenge, and is likely to provoke similar protestations that "it can't be done here." But with some courage and a lot of faith in the power of design to create better, more human-friendly organizational ecosystems, the design leader can be a significant agent of cultural change.

Endnotes

1. Jacqueline Maley, "Man with Sydney in his Sights," *Sydney Morning Herald,* Weekend Edition (December 1, 2007): 33.

2. See Daniel H. Pink, *A Whole New Mind: Moving from the Information Age to the Conceptual Age* (New York, N.Y.: Riverhead, 2005).

3. Richard Buchanan, "Wicked Problems in Design Thinking," *Design Issues* 7:2 (Spring 1992).

4. For a complete account of this design process, see my article, "Information Design for Strategic Thinking: Health of the System Reports," *Design Issues* 24:1 (Winter 2008): 68–77.

Chapter 4

Designing Business: New Models for Success

by Heather M.A. Fraser, Director of Business Design Initiative,
Rotman School of Management, University of Toronto

To maximize the impact on corporate outcomes, design should be the path to understanding stakeholder priorities, the tool for visualizing and prototyping concepts, and the process for translating cutting-edge ideas into effective strategies. This involves the methods of design thinking and Heather Fraser presents her point of view on the process steps.

GREAT DESIGN HAS long been recognized as an important strategy for enterprise success. It is also broadly understood that the same methods and mindsets that create new "objects of desire" are instrumental in enhancing services and user experiences in meaningful ways. But the greatest payout of design thinking is in the design of business itself: the design of strategies and business models for enterprise success. Through expanding design thinking across the organization and throughout the business development process, an enterprise can open up new opportunities, set more dramatic growth strategies, and evolve its business model to better seize market opportunities.

ENTERPRISE NEED: THE ABILITY TO NAVIGATE THROUGH CHANGE

The world today is dynamic and ever-changing.

- Economic instability around the world calls for new ways to address big challenges. There is no question that our global economy contains some flawed economic and social models.

- Social values are shifting and causing higher expectations for corporate social and environmental responsibilities. Commercial ambitions, political agendas, and social needs are inextricably linked and must be considered as a broader ecosystem.
- Global access to world markets opens up new opportunities for commerce and expanded access to talent and business resources. This creates new opportunities for some and poses threats to others.
- Technology has profoundly changed the ways in which people connect and the ways business gets done, both locally and globally.
- Marketplace expectations are higher than ever. Consumers have come to expect better, more sophisticated offerings and greater customization within the plethora of goods and services. The expectation now is that all people in all markets should have access to life-enhancing solutions.

Many companies are finding models and infrastructures that were successful in the past are now too rigid to rise to new challenges and opportunities. They are searching for better, faster, and more efficient ways of tuning up their organizations, mobilizing their human capital, and evolving their business models to get ahead of the curve. An emerging group of business leaders believes that design thinking plays a valuable role in unlocking new opportunities.

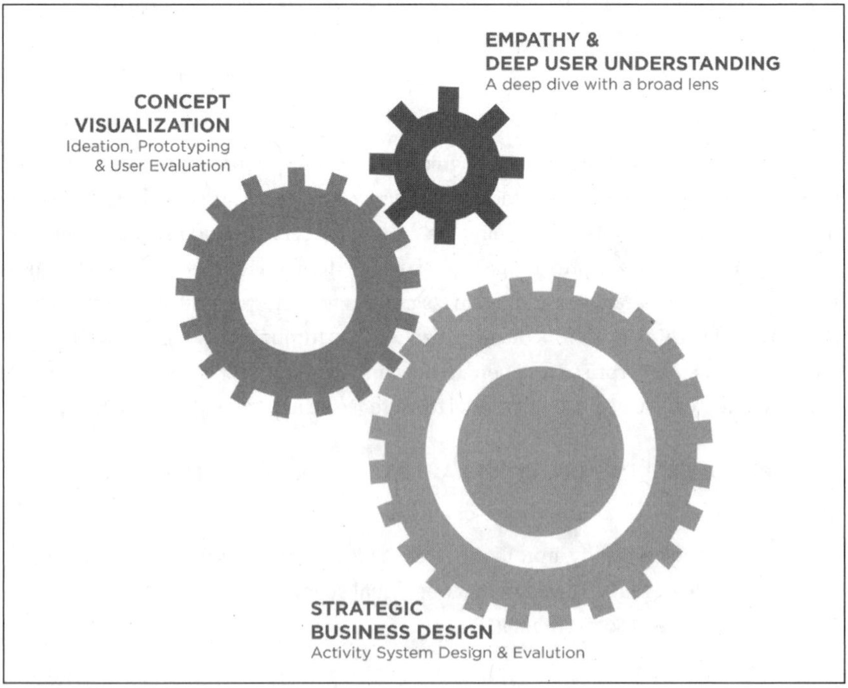

Figure 1

THE ROLE OF BUSINESS DESIGN

There is compelling evidence that the methods and mindsets behind great design in fields such as engineering, industrial design, and architecture are equally powerful in designing an enterprise model. Business design is about creating a model for symbiotically delivering market value and enterprise value. It embraces important design factors such as fostering multidisciplinary collaboration, considering altogether new possibilities rather than aiming for incremental improvements, sourcing creativity from constraints, prototyping early and iterating quickly (both in the lab and in the market), and creating new and better models through systems thinking. Like all great design, business design requires skill and discipline, along with a healthy dose of courage, open-mindedness, imagination, and perseverance.

THE METHOD: THE THREE GEARS OF BUSINESS DESIGN

Drawing from and integrating the many tools and techniques used in both the design world and the business world, the methodology we call the Three Gears of Business Design (figure 1) incorporates empathy and deep user understanding, concept visualization and prototyping, and strategic business design. It is not a linear process, but rather a framework for iteration that knits together user needs, powerful ideas, and enterprise success. By cycling through these three gears, work teams can get to bigger breakthroughs faster—using insights and unmet needs to inspire high-value conceptual solutions and extracting strategic intent from the concepts to recast strategic business models.

Gear One: Deep user understanding. The first step is to understand your customer (and other critical stakeholders) more broadly and deeply. This helps reframe the business challenge wholly through the eyes of the ultimate end user and establish a human context for innovation and value creation. Companies are often quite well versed in measurement of the human factor in their business (in terms of demographics, habits, and segmentation), but are often lacking in broad and deep understanding of the customer. It is this deeper understanding of needs that reveals important opportunities.

To broaden the lens of opportunity, it is important to look beyond the direct use of a company's product or service to the context in which it is used. For example, a food company will discover more game-changing opportunities by exploring the broader theme of healthy eating and lifestyles than by investigating the more narrow idea of consumption of products such as frozen dinners. By exploring a broader set of activities, one gains deeper insight and a broader behavioral and psychographic perspective on the user's life. It also allows one to understand consumers in the context of a given activity—what they do, how they feel, and how their needs link to other parts of their life.

As an example: Nike's deep understanding of the runner goes way beyond the utility of the running shoe. Runners are deeply motivated by the standards set by winning athletes, their own drive for personal best, their achievement of personal goals, and the motivation they get from sharing their passion with others. In keeping with its mission to innovate and inspire the athlete in everyone, Nike tapped into this mindset with the

Nike+: a chip inserted into a uniquely designed running shoe that communicates to your iPod while you run, measures and motivates personal performance, and connects you to an online community of runners. Before this initiative was launched in 2006, Nike accounted for 48 percent of all running-shoe sales in the U.S.[1] By late 2008, Nike had sold over 1.3 million of these sports kits to passionate runners who had logged more than 100 million kilometers online. Today, Nike's share of the running-shoe market is 61 percent, with a significant amount of its growth attributed to Nike+. In this case, everyone wins. The avid runner has a new means of pushing personal performance and connecting to a broader community, and Nike is rewarded with stronger sales and loyalty through a deeper and more engaging relationship with its consumers. Partners (Apple, in this case) win by being part of a broader ecosystem of consumer value. And all of this was inspired by a deep understanding of the user.

Deep user understanding is also highly relevant in an institutional context. For example, the healing process in a hospital is enhanced by a multitude of factors beyond the essential medical expertise and patient flow (the logistics of moving a patient through the treatment process). Cues to reduce patients' anxiety are rooted in many dimensions: their connection to the outside world (physical cues to nature and spirituality); the physical design of the hospital (the width of the halls, the artwork on the walls, the flicker rates of the fluorescent lighting); a sense of control or empowerment (the information they receive in communications before, during, and after their hospital visits); and the practices and manner of the people on staff. All these cues—people, objects, environment, messages, and services—can enhance the healing process or hinder it if they are not heeded.

An example of how this approach has helped one hospital re-image the patient experience is a project currently under way at Princess Margaret Hospital, a leading cancer hospital in Toronto. Design-style patient research was conducted to define the underlying needs of patients going through chemotherapy treatment as a brief for the redesign of a new systemic treatment center. Research revealed a number of foundational needs, including the need for an environment that creates a sense of calm and wellbeing, a communication system to help patients manage their time and diseases better, and a program to engage them during the process and turn lost time into found time. All of this pointed to an opportunity to completely redesign the patient experience as a means to promote healthy healing, and to redefine capital priorities to focus investment on the things that really matter in the delivery of better patient experiences and outcomes. The result was a focus on three development priorities: a complete overhaul of the space, a new kind of treatment chair, and an IT system that would enable both patients and staff to better manage time and relationships as well as the ongoing treatment. This foundation was also applied broadly to hospital practices at Princess Margaret Hospital by enrolling medical and administrative staff in the "need-serving" development process.

A deep dive with a broad lens in Gear One helps to reframe the challenge, define criteria for innovation, and open up new opportunities to create value.

Gear Two: Concept visualization. This phase of development begins with the broad exploration of possibilities for serving the unmet needs discovered in Gear One, and moves through multiple-prototyping and concept enrichment, ideally with users. The most important mindset in this phase is to look beyond what is to what could be, using imagination to generate solutions that are altogether new to the world. At this stage, there are no constraints, only possibilities.

All the radical breakthroughs of our lifetime that now seem so necessary started out as "crazy," "impossible," or at least "out of reach." This is true whether they were products, services, or systems. Think of the heart pacemaker (invented by Earl Bakken, inspired by Frankenstein), Federal Express (conceived by Frederick Smith as his "interesting but impossible" university thesis), or Starbucks (who would have ever imagined an essential $5 coffee?). The designers of these products, services, and businesses had the ability to imagine and, more important, envision new possibilities.

On a more modest level, one can appreciate the new product and marketing model envisioned through the Dove Real Beauty initiative, which connected the company's expertise in skin care products with emerging consumer and social needs. At the level of the consumer, the need filled is an underlying desire for self-esteem—for women to feel beautiful, on a deep level, for "who they are." At a more societal level, there has been mounting pressure to look like media models, which has triggered loss of esteem as well as contributed to eating disorders among young girls. By paying attention to these needs and issues, Dove successfully integrated social good into commercial success through its promotional support for the National Association for Self-Esteem (to combat eating disorders among young girls) and its Real Beauty campaign. The program reframed beauty by challenging emotionally damaging media stereotyping and boosting self-esteem among young girls through an integrated program of events, exhibits, and other awareness and fundraising initiatives to support the association. This platform has been extended to women of all ages behind product line extensions and an advertising campaign. The company has successfully connected new activities to their existing competencies to create new possibilities for addressing important market needs.

To envision new possibilities, development teams need tools to unleash their collective imagination and explore new concepts in concrete form. How can a team get to bigger ideas faster? Inspired by a deeper understanding of human needs, the first step in the strategic planning process should be to openly explore the broadest set of solutions to meet those needs. This is the time to explore beyond the current enterprise model and competencies, considering the broadest range of solutions—from people and products to spaces and services. (This is not the time to say, "We can't do that. We aren't in that business.") Ideation and prototyping capture the creativity of an organization and help generate possibilities for creating user value in a more imaginative, compelling, and concrete way than the best-crafted document. Pictures and props are more powerful than words in this case.

To make the process even more fruitful, involve end users in feedback and concept enrichment early on to find out what works and what doesn't, and move on to a better iteration without fussing over mediocre or incremental ideas. I have witnessed business teams create, role-play, and refine breakthrough, multidimensional ideas in two days with this process, spending $18 on supplies for low-resolution prototypes of breakthrough experiences versus $200 thousand on fancy mock-ups of incremental product ideas in concept testing.

These experiences demonstrate that rapid prototyping and iteration is an effective and efficient thinking and communication tool for enhancing and accelerating the strategic planning process. It's a creative, energizing, and risk-free way for teams to explore big ideas, stimulate healthy dialogue around possible strategies, and quick-test ideas with users as the basis for new value-creation strategies.

Most important, engaging all functions and disciplines on the business team in Gear Two brings a richer infusion of ideas into the process, fortifies team alignment, and creates traction in locking down and activating strategies later in the development process.

With well-defined, user-inspired solutions in hand, the team is positioned to ask and assess the answers to such questions as: How would that better serve our users' needs, and what would that mean for our business? What would we need to do in order to bring that to life, in terms of our capabilities and our organization's activities? This leads into the third gear of business design.

Gear Three: Strategic business design. The next step is to align broad concepts with future realities through strategy formulation and design of the business model itself. In this third gear, we explore and define what it would take to make the "big idea" commer-

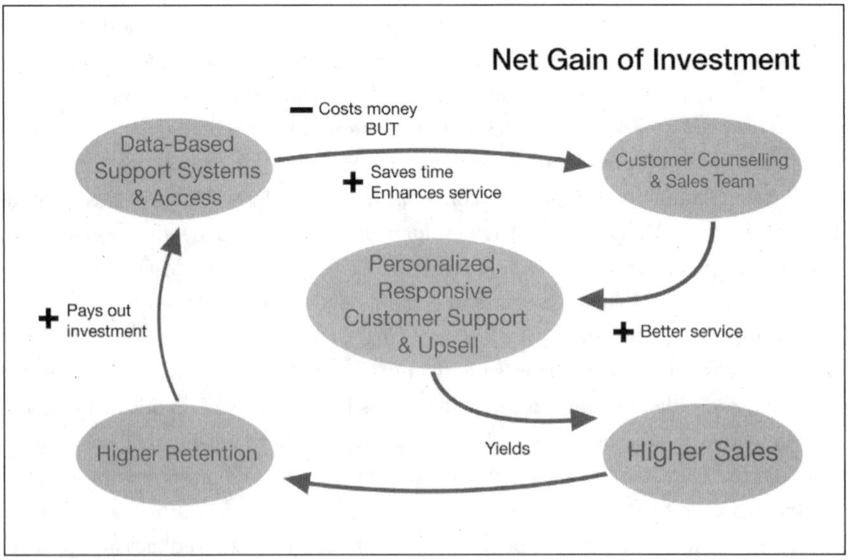

Figure 2

cially viable. We do this by articulating the strategies and capabilities required. What is most important is the identification and design of interrelated activities; this all adds up to a net commercial gain and competitive advantage for the enterprise.

As an example of one component of a broader solution, a company may decide that its customers need more personalized and responsive support. In order to deliver that in real time, it may conclude that a significant investment in database systems, access, and management is required. This will also affect organizational structure and operating procedures. Each of these components will cost money, save money, or generate stronger revenue and retention—all at the same time. Although at first, the investment may appear prohibitive, through iterative integration it can be designed to be a net gain for the enterprise (figure 2).

Like the prototyping process in Gear Two, this phase entails prototyping the business model to integrate the parts and assess the evolved activity system as a whole. It is critical at this stage to identify which strategies will drive success, to prioritize which activities an organization must undertake to deliver those strategies, and to define the relationship of those parts strategically, operationally, and economically. Ultimately, this will determine what net impact the new model will have.

There are a number of tools that can be used to integrate business strategies and assess the sustainability of a business model. Visualization is as powerful in expressing strategy as it is in expressing product and service ideas; in this case, pictures are often more powerful than words and spreadsheets. One way to visualize the strategic model is to map the "activity system"[2] required to bring a concept to life. This tool helps to identify the key strategic focus areas, capabilities, and tactical activities required to translate an idea into a strategy for competitive advantage. It's a good complement to other, more traditional financial analyses, such as mapping and dimensionalizing financial flows and conducting sensitivity analyses (on projected revenues, various capital/marketing investment levels, and payout).

To illustrate this point, we can imagine how the Apple activity system (post-iPod) may look (figure 3): a complex network of interrelated strategies and tactics that redefine the game rules of an industry while leveraging and extending Apple's historical equities in product design, a proprietary platform and intuitive user interface, and a brand reputation for radical innovation and high-impact marketing. With the integration of iTunes as a content portal and a multitude of peripherals to complete the iPod experience, Apple has truly created a seamlessly integrated and culturally current digital experience. In the following diagram, the larger gray hubs represent the core strategies driving Apple's success, including the equities and established capabilities from which iPod was built. Specific initiatives and supporting activities are indicated in the lighter circles.

What is critical in this particular case is how Apple advanced its competitive advantage by leveraging current equities and capabilities, and creating new activities and capabilities both within the company (iTunes and iPod) and through partnerships (content alliances and peripherals integration). So while the parts of this activity system may

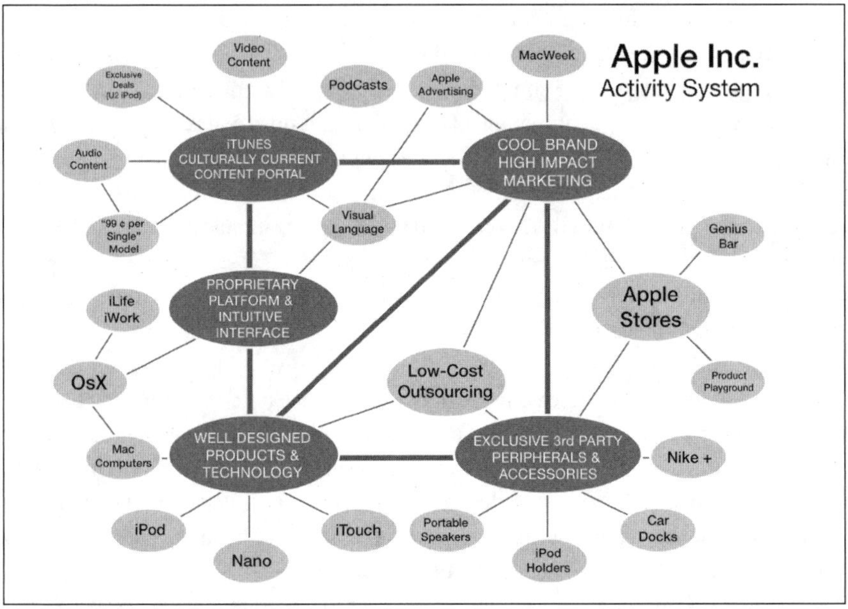

Figure 3

not be entirely proprietary to Apple, the business model is "locked" by an interrelated set of activities and partnerships that are preemptive and sustainable, because they cannot be easily replicated by competitors within the period of time required for the enterprise to gain traction and pay out the investment.

The final step of strategic business design is integrating new concepts back into the current operating model, always asking: What can we leverage in our current activity system? What tensions (barriers, issues, conflicts) must be resolved in our current activity system? For each tension point, what are possible strategies and tactics for resolution? How can we lock up this system so that it is proprietary and sustainable to our enterprise, therefore justifying the investment required to support this breakthrough strategic plan? A series of iterations, as with Gear Two, allow a new model to be defined.

Through this iterative process, prototyping (first on a conceptual solution, then on the strategic business model), and constant assessment of user value (based on the identified user needs and considerations), one can formulate a strategy for a new level of innovation and competitive advantage. By challenging the current model and exploring new ways to drive success, one can design new models that symbiotically create value for the market and the enterprise.

MINDSET MATTERS

With this as a methodological framework, the make-or-break ingredient is the mindset of individuals on the team. The following are some important emotional conditions under which design thinking can flourish.

Mindfulness. Business design is not something to be practiced on autopilot. It requires an astute awareness of the world and people around you. One needs to pay close attention to what is visible and articulated, while sensing what is below the surface and unarticulated. In the creative process, everything is relevant.

Open-minded collaboration. Everyone on the team must not only be committed to working together, but also be receptive to new insights and ideas, whether they fit one's paradigm or not. Business designers feed off new insights and effectively build off the ideas of others, embracing both the friction and fusion that comes with intense collaboration. Egos must be left at the door.

Abductive thinking. In gathering new user insights and moving from what is known to the exploration of what could be, an important capability is abductive thinking. What is critical is to allow for the leap of inference in tackling new opportunities and designing new possibilities. A product example of this: Procter & Gamble's Swiffer—a product that revolutionized the market neither as a conventional household-cleaner line extension nor as a better version of the traditional mop. It signaled a leap into a new category of cleaning and became part of the cleaning vernacular ("I'll just Swiffer that before they arrive."). To take the leap toward game-changing solutions, it is vital to think beyond what is immediately observable and provable and embrace what could be possible as a radical new solution to unmet needs. Imagine is the key word here.

Permission to risk early failure. Great design does not come without risk-taking, trying new things, and the very strong possibility of failure. There are countless stories of where a really bad or crazy idea became the germ of a brilliant concept or strategy. How often have we heard someone shut down an idea by saying, "That's never been done before. What if it doesn't work? I may get fired." For those who need to mitigate risk, this method allows for consumer needs to legitimize far-out thinking and for prototyping to provide a no-risk way of exploring new possibilities. No matter how you practice it, great design takes personal courage.

Imperfection and iteration early in the process. This is not a clean and linear, paint-by-number process; it's as messy as finger-painting. What's important early in the process is to explore lots of possible solutions, not to perfect a prototype so it becomes difficult to evolve it or even kill it. Iteration and constant change are necessary and good through every part of the process. That keeps the cost of failure low and the rewards of a possible breakthrough high.

Creative resolution of trade-offs and constraints. No great design is realized without the absolute unwillingness to give in to constraints and obstacles, and that is doubly true for business design. Roger Martin's book *The Opposable Mind* clearly defines the power of being able to embrace opposing models as the inspiration for creating new and better models.[3] Those who find ways to create new models instead of making unacceptable tradeoffs find themselves ahead of the game; this is evidenced by model-changing successes like Southwest Airlines, FedEx, Four Seasons Hotels, and Apple's iPod, to name a few. That's where the design method can help in resolving model conflicts—keeping the user at the center, and prototyping various "what-if" strategic business

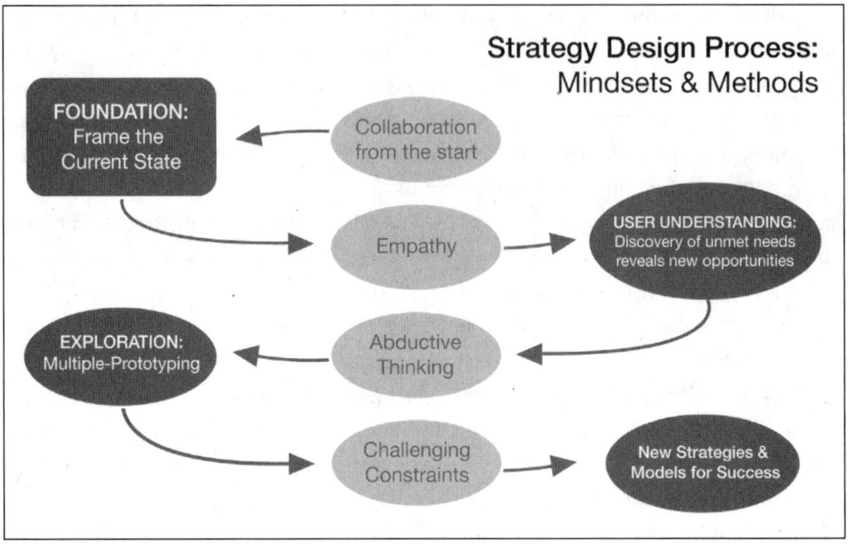

Figure 4

models to ultimately deliver value to both the user and the enterprise. In many ways, business is the ultimate creative act.

CONCLUSION

Whatever the sector or the nature of the business, any organization can benefit from the practice of business design. It taps into team intelligence, creativity, and ambition to make a meaningful impact in the customer's life, both functionally and emotionally. Embedding these methods and mindsets into strategic planning practices helps an organization to identify opportunities to capitalize on new and unmet needs, explore possibilities outside its current activity system, and set strategies to evolve the business model toward a new level of competitive advantage.

At its core, business design is about combining the essential three gears with a design mindset. A true design organization asks three questions of every opportunity: What is the need driving this initiative? Have we pushed out on the possibilities to best serve that need? How can we embed that into our business model to create a sustainable advantage? It is the power of all three gears that drives breakthrough strategies for enterprise success.

More important, a company that views design thinking not as a one-shot vaccination but rather as an ongoing fitness program for its organization will be better conditioned to stay ahead of the curve in a dynamic and increasingly competitive global marketplace. Far from static, the market demands that organizations be adaptive and agile. As the marketplace evolves, the needs of the user evolve, and thus the business model must evolve. The more an enterprise sees its business model or activity system as a living organism rather than as a fixed model, the more that company will be poised to respond to ongoing opportunities to meet new needs and to create greater market and enterprise value.

Suggested Reading

Lockwood, Thomas. "Design Value: A Framework for Measurement," *Design Management Review* (Fall 2007).

Endnotes

1. According to SportsOneSource, a Princeton, N.J., market research firm (*BusinessWeek*, November 2008).

2. Cf. Michael Porter, "What Is Strategy?," *Harvard Business Review* (November 1996).

3. Roger Martin, *The Opposable Mind: How Successful Leaders Win Through Integrative Thinking* (Boston, Mass.: Harvard Business School Press, 2008).

Chapter 5

Unleashing the Power of Design Thinking

by Kevin Clark, Program Director, IBM Corporate Marketing and Communications
and Ron Smith, Designer and Brand Experience Strategist, IBM Corporate Marketing and Communications

In this call to action, Kevin Clark and Ron Smith posit that design professionals can and should take on leadership roles in nontraditional arenas. Their own efforts demonstrate that the ways in which designers address problems—leveraging emotional intelligence, integral intelligence, and experiential intelligence—offer organizations valuable insights across a diverse range of business activities and decision-making.

DESIGN IS ABOUT making intent real.
There is plenty of unintentional to go around.
When you design, something new is brought into the world with purpose.

Unleashing the power of design thinking is about awakening design instincts and methods in business executives and organizations all around us—especially the ones we traditionally don't work with. We believe design thinking is a remarkably under-used tool for achieving strategic business initiatives that are increasingly driven by the need for innovation. The more design thinking is used to innovate and solve problems across many professions, the more design itself will be brought into significant conversations and decisions that shape our collective future in the business world.

Recognition of the gulf between business and design is well documented. For decades, there have been calls for designers to become more conversant in the ideas and language of business.

In an age of renewed interest in innovation, we suggest the cultivation of a new generation of design patrons who want to collaborate with designers in a new way—business patrons who want to move design strategy and design methods into the mainstream of business thought to accomplish business goals. These patrons would be going to designers not just to acquire the output of well-integrated design, but also to use design methods to make business itself more intentional.

Guggenheim didn't have to be an artist to be a patron of the arts.

Design methods are orderly. Design methods are inclusive. Design methods are innovative. Taking advantage of design thinking can help business leaders make their intentions real by clearly defining goals, deeply understanding customers, and getting their internal teams aligned to deliver results.

Design thinking is an established way to bring value to some parts of business, yet it remains a well-kept secret from many who could use it most. Designers tend to stay out of the domains of accounting, human resources, and legal affairs, for instance, and this is a shame.

Over the past twenty years, we have heard members of the design profession talk about learning the language of business in order to better frame design issues in business terms—initially so that our ideas would have a better survival rate, and then eventually in the hope that we would be invited into strategic discussions where big ideas have a chance to flourish. And we have seen a change in how design is embraced in many organizations, most famously today in consumer electronics with Apple, Sony, and Samsung, where design reports to the CEO.

It's time for the design leaders to reframe this conversation in the age of innovation. Design professionals need to redefine their leadership by being catalysts to help other parts of the organization use and embrace design thinking.

How do you describe design thinking to executives? It's all about innovation intelligence. Design thinking is driven by intelligence that embraces innovation and gives your organization the freedom to explore multiple ways to solve problems—and discover the option that best delivers competitive advantage.

From our perspective, design thinking also encompasses several related types of innovation intelligence. Cultivating these will help increase appreciation for, and encourage a broader use of, design approaches in many professions:

- ▲ Emotional intelligence
- ▲ Integral intelligence
- ▲ Experiential intelligence

Emotional intelligence is the ability to understand and embrace in the context of culture that moves us to act and that creates attachment, commitment, and conviction.

Integral intelligence is the ability to bring together diverse customer needs and business ecosystem capabilities into complete systems that deliver value and reflect the values of the birth organization.

Experiential intelligence is the ability to understand and activate all five human senses to make innovation tangible, known, and vibrant.

Design is about making intent real. What organization wouldn't want to have its strategic intent made real?

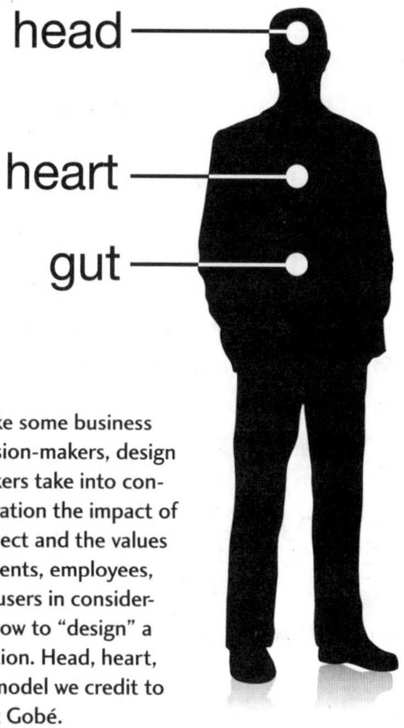

Unlike some business decision-makers, design thinkers take into consideration the impact of intellect and the values of clients, employees, and users in considering how to "design" a solution. Head, heart, gut model we credit to Marc Gobé.

ACTIVATING EMOTIONAL INTELLIGENCE

Connecting the two hemispheres of the brain, and aligning the head, the heart, and the gut: these are daily exercises for a designer.

Designers work to understand the culture of their organizations and its connection to the customers and other businesses they serve. The design process is well suited to investigate the emotional and cultural realities of doing business. F.G. "Buck" Rogers, one of IBM's most notable salespeople, famously said, "Customers buy on emotion and then justify with logic." Understanding the emotional aspect of offering appeal and transactions is pivotal to business success, and design is particularly well equipped to help in this arena of business strategy.

The Importance to Business: Emotion Drives Action

Example: IBM's corporate experience design team led a unique internal engagement with the company's human resources and communications team in India to assess the experiences of prospective employees as they apply, are hired, and are brought on board as new employees. Using design thinking to uncover underlying needs and issues, a new set of onboarding touchpoints was designed and is being used today to deliver an improved new-employee experience. First impressions frame entire careers, and design thinking helped shape an improved employment journey for new IBM India employees.

ACTIVATING INTEGRAL INTELLIGENCE

Many businesses apply a microscope to dissect all aspects of engagement into smaller and smaller pieces for improvement and refinement. While examination of detail can be valuable, design thinking reengages the imagination, encouraging it to see a more complete picture. Designers keep the big idea in mind.

This should be very appealing to many c-level executives, yet for them, design tools and processes rarely enter into the picture. To many of these executives, design is a function, not a valuable way of seeing and reframing the world for competitive advantage.

Professionals using design thinking know the details are important for success, yet also have a zoom lens to move way back and see how those details support a larger idea. Design thinkers constantly zoom in and out to keep the big idea and the details connected and meaningful.

The Importance to Business: Integral Intelligence Helps Businesses to See a Bigger Picture and to Create More and Larger Value Perspectives to Drive Revenue and Profit

Example: Corporate Experience Design and Systems and Technology Group Design formed a cross-functional team to study the out-of-the-box experience for recipients of newly delivered IBM systems. Professionals who normally didn't have an opportunity to work closely together were trained in observational research and went out in "discovery teams" to see clients receive and set up their new large computing systems. They included professionals from engineering, finance, human factors, industrial design marketing, and market intelligence. Not only did they come up with lots of recommendations, but they also continued to collaborate after the project concluded. Building community and working across professional borders is an important residue of design thinking.

ACTIVATING EXPERIENTIAL INTELLIGENCE

Experience design is one of the fastest growing parts of design and strategy practice at IBM today. The human interaction conversation has moved from ease of use for products to ease of use for IBM as a whole—and is serving to make our company more compelling and adaptive. This is a direct result of the transformation from a product company to an increasingly services and client consulting company. Design as a discipline is adapting to be relevant to a new generation of offerings and approaches to the marketplace. We see this journey of adaptation taken by many other organizations in a variety of ways.

A point of professional pride: designers have long understood and used experience elements to enhance the interactions among customers and product offerings. We are

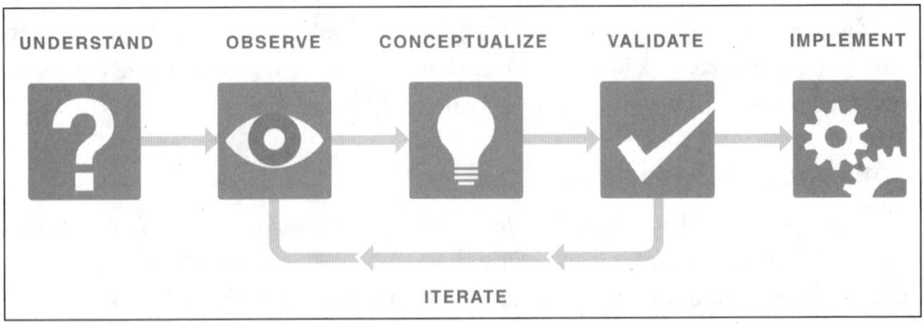

The experience design method IBM uses to explore problem solving involves observational research into spoken and unspoken client wants and needs and creating new concepts with validation and iteration phases before a product or service is released into the marketplace.

now in an age of applying this interaction knowledge to all aspects of doing business. Who should lead this effort? Clearly, it is too big an endeavor for design alone or for any other single department within the business. We need to bring more professionals into the conversation and give them the tools to engage in robust design thinking.

If you have followed the literature over the past ten years, you know that to be successful, improving customer experience must be a multifunction endeavor, including and integrating many parts of the business. A comprehensive experience strategy encompasses and then transcends the individual parts of the business, leading to customer advocates and sustainable revenue and profits.

CASE STUDY: IBM CLIENT BRIEFING CENTERS

An example of applying and transferring design thinking to the IBM business at large is the ongoing IBM Client Briefing Experience Initiative.

In 2006, IBM's corporate experience strategy and design department led an investigation into what it was like for clients to visit IBM at home. By home, we mean one of the more than 200 client centers IBM operates for hosting executives and client professionals around the world. At the centers, we offer workshops and hands-on experiences with products and services that can help make our clients' businesses more successful.

This is a fine example of the experience design method IBM uses to explore problem solving. We start by understanding what is known today about the problem to be solved. We do observational research to deeply understand both spoken and unspoken client wants and needs, and then we create new concepts with validation and iteration phases before releasing the new product, service, or experience to the marketplace. You probably have your own version of this—it has been very durable and useful in driving design solutions at IBM for half a century. It was originally intended to make products compelling and easier to use, and it has been adapted over the past five years to help make the company itself more compelling and easier to use.

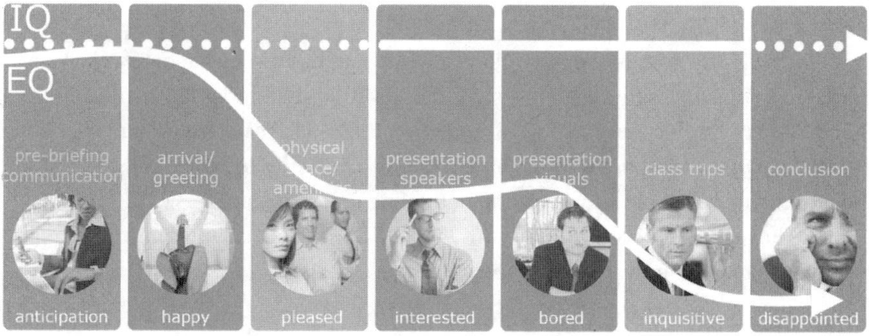

Our research showed that we were missing an opportunity to emotionally engage with our clients. A day with IBM was full of IQ, but it was also draining, and clients' "emotional quotient" dropped throughout the day. It was a clear message that we needed to innovate around how we engaged with clients that spend a day with IBM.

What did we discover about our client centers? We found that we were all too often practicing an advanced form of what information design guru Edward Tufte has famously called "death by PowerPoint": one or more days of individually excellent presentations strung together on an agenda in a university lecture format.

When we set out on our design journey, what we thought we would probably recommend were fully immersive briefing centers that would deliver a big experience to our clients. What we ultimately did was subtler than that. For one thing, turning 200 briefing centers into business theme parks is too expensive. For another, it would not have reflected the diverse nature of the centers and the clients they're serving worldwide.

The big "aha" was thinking about briefing centers not so much as places to be briefed as settings where a collaborative dialogue can take place. They became less about going to IBM University and more about clients visiting IBM at home.

We needed to move from training our professionals less in presentation skills and more in listening and leading collaborative discussions. It is a different mindset, requiring different talent.

We also didn't want to take one of our advantages—a diversity of briefing locations that were greater in number by an order of magnitude than for our competitors—and turn them toward a single unified model. This would potentially destroy the unique heritage of each location and its strengths. We embraced what the hotel industry might call a collection strategy—a collection of briefing capabilities that can clearly express IBM values, yet remain distinctive and authentic to themselves and their missions.

To accomplish this, we held a multi-day workshop with participants from our IBM briefing centers from all over the globe. This project allowed for a sustainable community to emerge inside IBM, and for a global briefing board to form across business units sponsored by corporate marketing and communications. This is a great example of integral intelligence in action. The community and the global briefing board are two lasting organization transformations that endure today and persist in driving new innovation in IBM client briefing centers worldwide.

Back to the workshop. It was held in Somers, New York, during the summer of 2006.

We heard the results of observational research we had done, shadowing clients and briefing teams in selected centers around the world. Earlier that spring, we had also visited IBM briefing locations in the U.S. and Europe, as well as selected customer-briefing centers of other companies through professional courtesies extended to us as a result of our membership in the Association of Briefing Program Managers (ABPM). We also heard the reports of several focus teams that had done research and came to the workshop with recommendations for improvements.

When the workshop ended, the team was galvanized to act and to make strong recommendations for improving the IBM client briefing experience. Several follow-on teams were formed, and the recommendation to create a global briefing board was a direct result of the work done that week.

The design team came back loaded with ideas.

Here are two things we did that have been declared as game changers by our briefing center brethren:

- *Discovering your WOW!* booklet (see sidebar) is a cookbook created to help each briefing center design its own unique and appropriate client experience.
- The IBM client experience journey map and planning tool puts the power of design into the hands of the people closest to the client. The tool uses magnetic cards to help each briefing center team explore and track a year's worth of experience planning, or map out a single high-impact visit.

The book and the planning tool together offer more than 200 ideas for client briefing professionals.

DISCOVERING YOUR WOW! BOOKLET: DESIGNING THE CLIENT BRIEFING EXPERIENCE

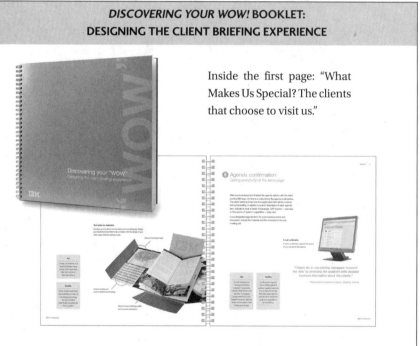

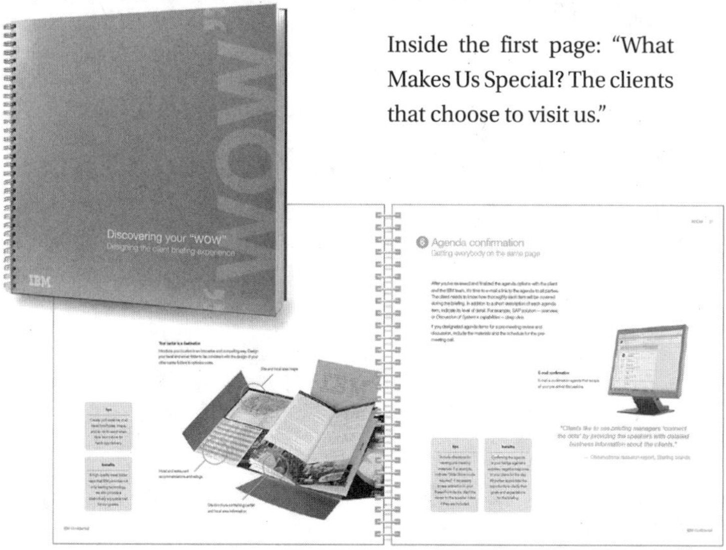

Inside the first page: "What Makes Us Special? The clients that choose to visit us."

From the opening page: "We have an unparalleled capability to deliver executive briefings with depth and skill almost anywhere in the world. More than 50 thousand times a year, clients visit one of our 200 major client center locations. The questions are: What kind of experience will we create for them? Will it just be about selling? Or will it envelop them inside something more—what it truly means to have a relationship with IBM? At no other time in the sales cycle do clients willingly invest a half-day or more with us in a setting where we fully control the experience. That's a unique opportunity for us to show IBM at its best."

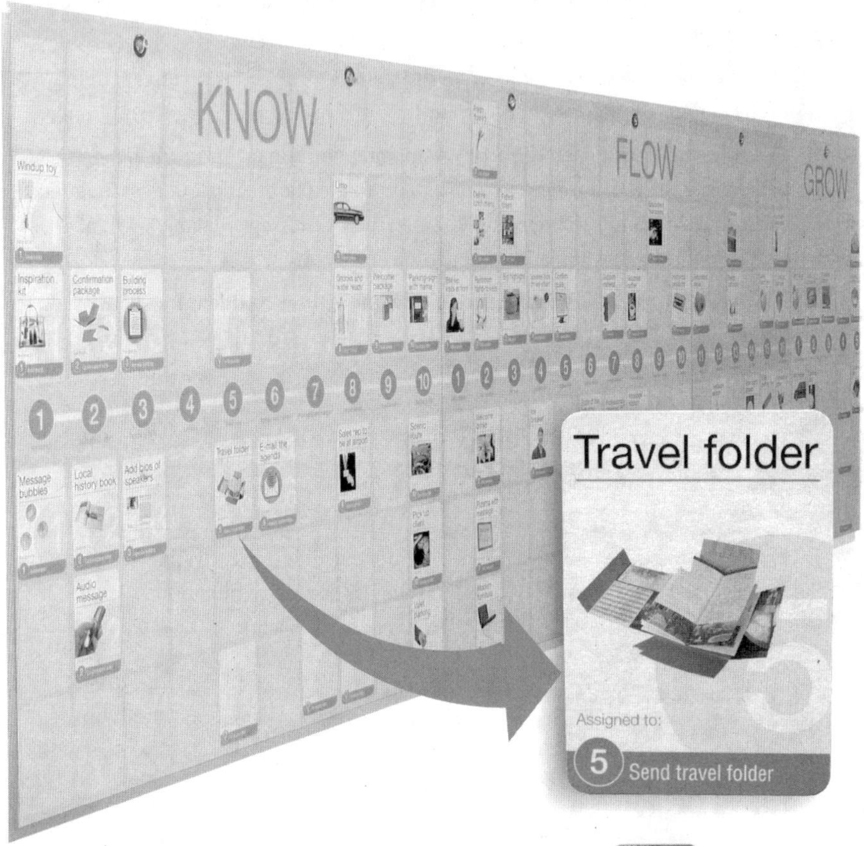
KNOW
FLOW
GROW
Windup toy
Inspiration kit
Confirmation package
Building process
Message bubbles
Local history book
Add bios of speakers
Audio message
Travel folder
E-mail the agenda
Limo
Travel folder
Assigned to:
5 Send travel folder

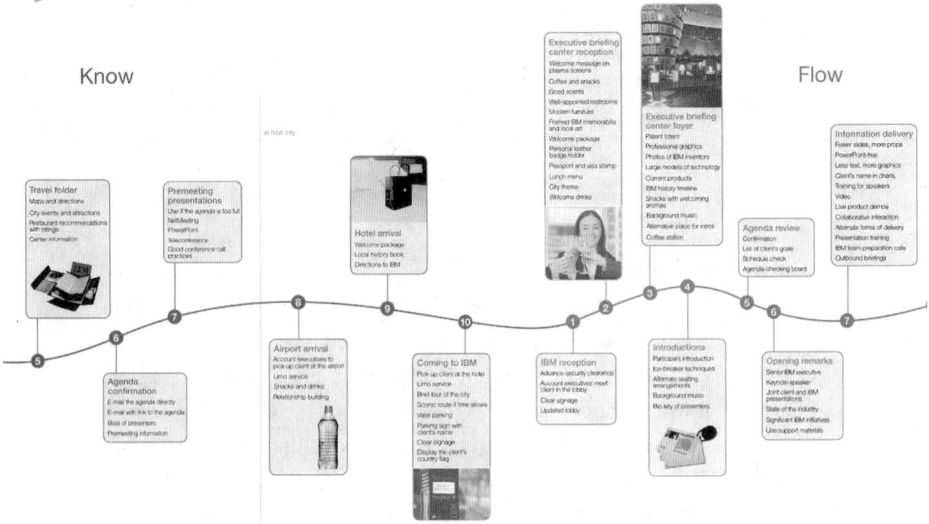
Know
Flow
at host city:
Travel folder
Maps and directions
City events and attractions
Restaurant recommendations with ratings
Center information
Agenda confirmation
E-mail the agenda directly
E-mail with link to the agenda
Bios of presenters
Premeeting information
Premeeting presentations
Use if the agenda is too full
NetMeeting
PowerPoint
Teleconference
Good conference call practices
Airport arrival
Account executives to pick up client at the airport
Limo service
Snacks and drinks
Relationship building
Hotel arrival
Welcome package
Local history book
Directions to IBM
Coming to IBM
Pick up client at the hotel
Limo service
Brief tour of the city
Scenic route if time allows
Valet parking
Parking sign with client's name
Clear signage
Display the client's country flag
IBM reception
Advance security clearance
Account executives meet client in the lobby
Clear signage
Updated lobby
Executive briefing center reception
Welcome message on plasma screens
Coffee and snacks
Good scents
Well-appointed restrooms
Modern furniture
Framed IBM memorabilia and local art
Welcome package
Personal leather badge holder
Passport and visa stamp
Lunch menu
City theme
Welcome drinks
Executive briefing center foyer
Patent totem
Professional graphics
Photos of IBM inventors
Large models of technology
Current products
IBM history timeline
Snacks with welcoming aromas
Background music
Alternative place for intros
Coffee station
Introductions
Participant introduction
Ice-breaker techniques
Alternate seating arrangements
Background music
Bio key of presenters
Agenda review
Confirmation
List of client's goals
Schedule check
Agenda checking board
Opening remarks
Senior IBM executive
Keynote speaker
Joint client and IBM presentations
State of the industry
Significant IBM initiatives
Use support materials
Information delivery
Fewer slides, more props
PowerPoint-free
Less text, more graphics
Client's name in charts
Training for speakers
Video
Live product demos
Collaborative interaction
Alternate forms of delivery
Presentation training
IBM team preparation calls
Outbound briefings

Note that we're practicing what we preach in these examples. We didn't describe a tight blueprint with guidelines for each of the 200 briefing centers to follow. We provided the education and the tools to allow each center to define and design its own authentic IBM client briefing experience. We transferred the experience bug to our client briefing colleagues, and they are now in contact with each other worldwide, and on a continual experience improvement journey. Direction, yes; dogma, no.

BEING INTENTIONAL: LINKING BUSINESS INTENT AND DESIGN STRATEGY

Business leaders can benefit from design thinking. It needs to be seen as another valuable tool to help shape business strategies and connect intentions to outcomes. Design thinking also helps to more deeply understand customers' wants and needs (spoken and unspoken) and link them to the capabilities of globally integrated enterprises.

Several years ago, we did a "sense layering" internal consulting engagement for our professional friends in IBM working on retail industry solutions. We took one of their existing client briefing locations and worked to make it even more engaging by activating all five human senses.

Visually, this center was already a world-class immersive experience in the future of retail banking. It was originally designed by the John Ryan Company and infused with IBM capabilities and technology halfway through its existence. You could walk right into the "set" and experience a retail bank prototype up close and personal. The design-led sense layering engagement added an acoustic background to the briefing location, along with aromas on arrival and more tactile sensations throughout.

This single exposure to design thinking and experience strategy triggered a multi-year exploration on the part of the IBM retail banking marketing and strategy worldwide. Today experience strategy is a key element of IBM's approach to the retail banking industry and our solutions for it. The team fully embraced experience and has been using design thinking to move the retail banking agenda forward for IBM clients around the world. We helped activate the desire for design in the strategic mix and create internal IBM client patrons for design for years to come.

We've also pioneered the Innovation Discovery program—a day set aside for our clients that offers a structured collaborative dialogue exploring ways for them and IBM to do business in new and innovative ways with each other—and to create capabilities together that are mutually beneficial and that deliver competitive advantage.

UNLEASHING DESIGN THINKING

We believe that design must move beyond its traditional boundaries to grow. We believe in unleashing design from its "private club" status so that it can become a school of thought that can solve some of the world's most pressing problems. Design thinking can help any profession solve problems in innovative ways.

To be considered a mainstream part of the business toolbox and vocabulary, design needs to reposition itself to do, as well as teach. We've shared some examples of how we've reached out to a wide variety of disciplines in IBM, applying design thinking and experience strategy to create value in human resources, mergers and acquisitions, marketing, key business units, and client sectors.

Designers can be trusted advisors in helping shape business decision-making, contributing to business strategy with a seat at the table, and cultivating design patrons who will embrace and invest in design to drive competitive advantage. We can help these design patrons innovate and create opportunities for the businesses and organizations we want to see thrive.

Designers have been in the roll-up-your-sleeves-and-get-it-done part of humanity for a long time. We see the new generation of design leaders not just as doers—we see designers as advisors, mentors, and coaches. We believe it's time to unleash the power of design thinking in every professional endeavor, not just design itself. To start, cultivate one new executive patron for design thinking today.

ACKNOWLEDGMENTS

We would like to thank all of the pioneers who are making "design thinking" real at IBM.

First, Lee Green, vice president of brand and values experience, has been a key supporter of the development of experience strategy and design and its use at IBM. Most recently, he collaborated with Maris Stanley and Kelly Tierney to create a new on-boarding experience for IBM India employees.

Key contributors to the client briefing experience case study include designers Susan Jasinski and Luis Elizalde. Other design thinking pioneers include Bob Steinbugler, Bill Grady, Camillo Sassano, Kevin Schultz, Terry Yoo, David McGorry, Missy Johnson, Maria Arbusto, Ken High, and Randy Golden.

Chapter 6

Design Thinking and Design Management: A Research and Practice Perspective

by Rachel Cooper, Sabine Junginger, and Thomas Lockwood

Design has long been about creating objects and experiences. In today's competitive marketplace, however, that perspective is too narrow. Design must illuminate a broader and more strategic range of corporate activities. The authors summarize their insights about design thinking, based on international research with educators and practitioners, and present a critical analysis.

AS DESIGN PROFESSIONALS and design researchers, we have come to a point where we feel the urge to reflect on what the recent focus on design thinking contributes to our understanding of design—and how it may inform design management. Design thinking is, of course, not a new concept or practice. It has been with and around us ever since there was design, conscious or unconscious. But some of the current interpretations offer new nuances, and that does have an impact on how we practice and theorize about design.

Our dictionaries distinguish among thinking *of*, thinking *about*, and thinking *through*. They equate the activity of thinking *of* with imagining, visualizing, dreaming up. In contrast, to think *about* something is described to mean an activity during which one considers, reflects, and deliberates. Finally, to think *through* something is to understand, to grasp, to figure it out. Design thinking seems to encompass all three of these qualities.

Design thinking is currently used in a way that tends to describe it as a key activity. Yet, when we take a closer look, it is not always clear whether we are thinking *about* design, thinking *of* design, or thinking *through* design. It appears that each of these is a different kind of activity, with direct consequences for the practice of designing—and the design of business itself. If we take these common definitions as a starting point, we might say that design thinking as the activity of thinking *about* design allows us to reflect on questions of "Who can design?" and "What can be designed?" In this reflective mode, design thinking offers us ways to study the perceptions, expectations, and capabilities assigned to and associated with the theories and practices of designing. As such, design thinking offers opportunities to distinguish among particular design methods and design principles as they involve different foci (for example, human-centered or technology-driven, product-centered or system-centered). These include, for example, participatory and collaborative design methods and visualization techniques for ideation and sense making in two and three dimensions (i.e., mapping and rapid prototyping). Thinking about design shifts the perspective from an isolated product to a more system-wide perspective. It is no coincidence that service design is becoming more of a focus here.

Building on the common definitions, to think *of* design then means to imagine, visualize, and "dream up" new understandings, new roles for design, new practices, and new applications. What if an organization were a product? What will the profile of a designer look like in the future? How will this affect the profession and practice of design management?

While thinking *about* and thinking *of* design are core elements of design thinking that offer reflections on the past and, in some ways, the future of design, it is the idea of thinking *through* design that currently shapes the design discourse. Most businesses are familiar with the first two kinds of design thinking. They think *of* design when they design specific products and services; they think *about* design as, perhaps, a tool for marketing. But now a new way to employ design thinking—thinking *through* design—is emerging, and it promises to have a much more profound impact on the way business itself is being conducted.

A WIDER FOCUS

Design thinking applied to business strategy and business transformation involves the visualization of concepts and the actual delivery of new products and services. The role of design is thus broader and more comprehensive than the role it is assigned in traditional product development. Increasingly synonymous with "thinking like a designer," thinking *through* design has the greatest potential to establish the activities involved in designing as a core capability, one that goes beyond its traditional boundaries. But what exactly does it mean to "think like a designer"? While many practicing designers still find themselves hard pressed to give an articulate answer, scholars in business and management have made some astute observations.

Roger Martin[1] has pointed to design's characteristics of integrative thinking and, in this sense, followed an earlier exploration by Peter Senge, whose *Fifth Discipline* emphasized the importance of system thinking. Senge's latest work, *The Necessary Revolution*, links even more with design thinking and design methods. Among design theorists, Richard Buchanan[2] brought the wicked nature of design problems to our attention and highlighted the values of design inquiries and systems thinking. The interesting aspect here is that we actually get a pointer to how designing is actually "done." We could elaborate on these aspects of design thinking for a full paper, but we feel a more urgent sense to reflect on what the recent focus on "design thinking" has already achieved and contributed to the practice and theory of design management.

We should, however, in this context not forget the work and the people who laid the early foundations of what is now the area of design management. This list includes Bruce Archer, Michael Farr, James Pilditch, Mark Oakley, Peter Gorb, and Angela Dumas, among many, many others. Revisiting some of these early works, one can often find a quest for design thinking and its role in the organization as the motivation of these authors. The DMI, as a nonprofit organization, has played a lead role in advancing the ideas around design management. Founded by Bill Hannon in 1975, the DMI has since published seventy-four issues of the *Design Management Journal* and the *Design Management Review*, a total of 850 articles dedicated to the problems and practices of design management. Along with thirty-two DMI case studies (now being distributed by Harvard University), these works document our changing understanding of design thinking. In particular, we can detect a shift in our notion of the product and a shift in the tasks and challenges managers face.

The way in which the term and concept of design thinking is now taking hold in management is paving the way for design to address new problems in the organization. With that, design thinking frees design activities from the product and allows design thinking to be applied outside of the traditional realms of design and to different kinds of problems (those of organization, strategy, mission, and so on). Indeed, the phrase "design thinking" has created excitement among many people previously untouched by design, and this has generated new opportunities for designers to engage with business, management, and other functions and levels within the organization. The current focus of design thinking, particularly as applied in the U.S., centers on innovations and business transformations that begin with people: it involves the discovery of unmet needs and opportunities as well as the creation of new visions and alternative scenarios that can reorient an organization around the people it serves. It is part of the "fuzzy front end" of idea generation and is also being adopted to solve "wicked" problems and help reinvent business.

On the other hand, design thinking has challenged us to inquire into the design process itself. At first glance, it appears that the current design and management discourse on design thinking contributes to our understanding of the design process. But this is not always the case. In fact, it is here that the potential problems and challenges for design thinking lie. Since design thinking and design methods always go hand in hand—that is, in design the thinking is informed by the doing, and vice versa—there is concern among some designers that the emphasis on *thinking* might overshadow the importance of *making*. Some worry about splitting the design process into two separate activities, when design research is about the active engagement between the two. This concern might be unwarranted, as most current approaches to design thinking do involve design methods.

A more valid concern is the term's currency as a buzzword. While the global popularity of design as a business tool is undeniable, design thinking could well end up being the business process "flavor of the month," if design research fails to establish itself on its own terms. Design thinking clearly coincides with the popularity of design at large, but there is more. One could point to influential management books, such as Malcolm Gladwell's *The Tipping Point*, Tom Kelley's *The Art of Innovation*, Richard Florida's *The Rise of the Creative Class*, and Daniel Pink's *A Whole New Mind*. All of these are relevant to the development of design thinking, or thinking like a designer, as a valid business tool.

IMPLICATIONS OF DESIGN THINKING FOR DESIGN MANAGEMENT

Design management is the ongoing management—and leadership—of design organizations, design processes, and designed outcomes (which include products, services, communications, environments, and interactions). Generally, design management has been more concerned with individual design projects and with incremental developments and improvements, whereas design thinking represents a more radical shift in an organization's overall way of doing business. Design thinking addresses the fundamental assumptions, values, norms, and beliefs that make an organization what it is. Design management, like most areas of design practice, is experiencing the shift from managing the design of tangible products to managing the design of innovation and services. This poses new problems for managing and for designing. There are some who see new opportunities as design moves from lower-level product-centered design strategies to the complexities involved in designing business processes and customer touchpoints on an organizational level. Not surprisingly, this shift is accompanied by some anxiety about what design management is and is not, what it should or should not be. It is clear, however, that design thinking in all its guises has been a contributing factor in the activity of managing design and the delivery of new processes, products, and services.

One might view the rise of design thinking as a way forward for design in the organization, one that can only benefit the practice and research of design management. There will be a need for design management to serve different managerial and organizational purposes. We would like to argue that the rise in design thinking has helped to raise awareness of design management at different levels in the organization and, with that, has contributed to perhaps a clearer picture of design management. Indeed, the impact on how we perceive design management is enormous, if we consider, for example, recent writings on "managing as designing," which offer some of the most useful illustrations of design thinking to date.[3] Managing as designing can be viewed in some ways as a direct response to design management, which for some seems to have focused too much on "designing as managing." This is, of course, an oversimplification, and much of the research conducted as part of design management will continue to inform these new practices. What we are likely to see is the emergence of a clearer picture of what design management can be in a given organization in a given context.

WHAT CAN WE LEARN FROM THE DMI EDUCATION CONFERENCE?

In many ways, the two DMI conferences in Paris last spring provide the first evidence that this clarification is already happening. At the international DMI Education conference, we could see the full spectrum of design management as it directly relates to design thinking. The papers and case studies presented there point to an increasing consensus that the challenges for a design manager include the ability to 1) explain the values and roles of design for a specific organizational setting; 2) define what design means for this organization; 3) communicate these roles internally and externally; and 4) create the space for design in this organization to assume and fulfill this role.

At the subsequent DMI professional conference, "Design as the Linking Force," practicing design managers shared their views on design thinking as a means to strengthen the role of design in the organization. Both practitioners and researchers emphasized the ability to visualize concepts and ideas early on and to guide an emerging rather than deterministic inquiry as one of the key characteristics of design thinking.

Figure 1 reflects the different interpretations of design thinking evident in the presentations given at the DMI Education Conference. This mass brainstorm of the entire

Figure 1 reflects the different interpretations of design thinking evident in the presentations of the DMI Education Conference in Paris. This brainstorm of the entire audience of international delegates illustrates how the notion of design thinking is broad, and as such reflect the need to further define design thinking, or indeed categorize it as we have done above. It also clearly illustrates a ladder of maturity in terms of our understanding and implementation of design thinking.

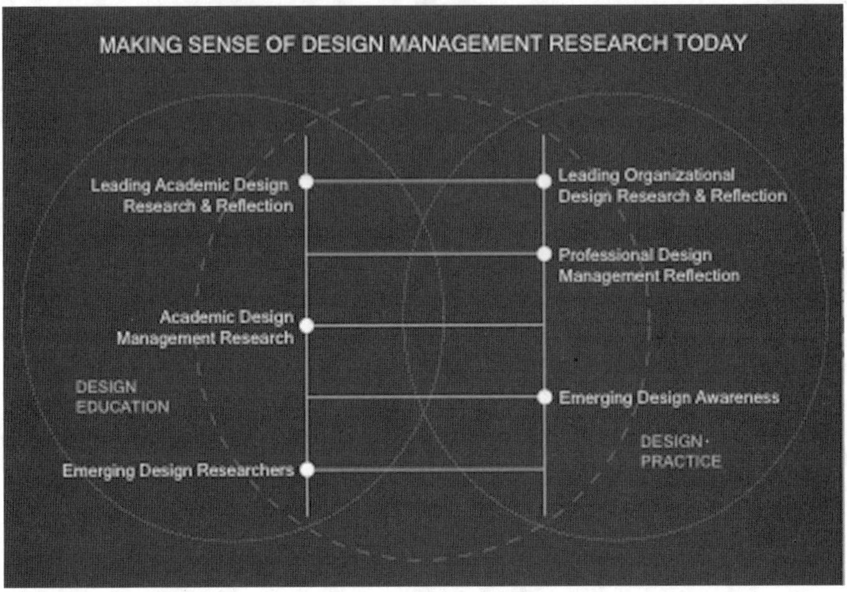

Figure 2. We found that in regions where design management is just emerging researchers tend to follow classic design management approaches based on products, technology and brand. In regions where design management is well established and has a tradition, academic research begins to inform these practices, complemented by professional reflections. However, the design thinking underlying these design management practices and research tend to remain product-centric. This changes in those regions where design has been established as part of an organization. Here we can see how design thinking is "freeing" itself from these previous traditions and emerging as a practice independent of "the product." Instead, design thinking focuses on the characteristics of a problem (i.e., a design problem as in "wicked problems"). At the lower rungs of the ladder, research tends to center on traditional design practices and the study of products and brand. Further up on the ladder, the system theories, nontraditional products and thus, thinking through design are being explored.

audience of delegates illustrates how broad is the notion of design thinking, and as such reflects the need to further define that notion, or indeed categorize it as we have done above. It also clearly illustrates a ladder of maturity in terms of our understanding and implementation of design thinking. For instance (see figure 2), in regions where design management is just emerging, researchers tend to follow classic design management approaches based on products, technology, and brand. In regions where design management has a tradition, academic research begins to inform these practices, complemented by professional reflections. However, the design thinking underlying these design management practices and research tends to remain product-centric. In turn, this begins to change in regions where design has been established as part of an organization. Here we can see how design thinking is freeing itself from these previous traditions and emerging as a practice independent of the product. Instead, design thinking focuses on the characteristics of a problem (i.e., a design problem, as in "wicked problems").

CONCLUSION

If we consider design thinking as an activity that is key to developing products, then design thinking has been around ever since design has been around. What is different today is that it has been discovered by more people as a valuable tool with which to address problems and issues that do not necessarily involve a product to manufacture for sale. There are multiple ways in which design practitioners and design researchers have made use of the term. It appears that design thinking provides managers with a new way to think of new products and services and about ways of designing them. The imperative now is for business schools and design schools alike to open new paths for students to acquire design skills that allow them to think *through* design. This involves the ability to quickly visualize problems and concepts, the development of people-based scenarios, and the design of business strategies based on design research methods. In this new way, managers are able to see how design methods and design principles can help them navigate the uncertainties and complexities they now face. Moving beyond its traditional role, design is establishing itself as a tool with which to address a wide range of issues, from strategy to social change.

Suggested Reading

Archer, Bruce. "Systematic Method for Designers," in *Developments in Design Methodology.* Cross, N. (ed.). (Hoboken, N.J.: Wiley, 1984).

Brown, Tim. "Design Thinking," *Harvard Business Review* (June 2008).

Cross, Nigel. "Designerly Ways of Knowing: Design Discipline Versus Design Science," *Design Issues* 17:3 (Summer 2001).

Dewey, John. "The Pattern of Inquiry," in *Logic–The Theory of Inquiry* (New York, N.Y.: Henry Holt and Company, 1938).

Dumas, A., and Mintzberg, H. "Managing design, design management," *Design Management Journal* (Fall 1990).

Farr, Michael. *Design Management* (London, U.K.: Hodder and Stoughton, 1966).

Gorb, P. "Design and its Use to Managers," *Royal Society of Arts Journal* (November 1979).

Pilditch, James. *Talk about Design* (London, U.K.: Barrie and Jenkins, 1976).

Endnotes

1. Cf. Roger L. Martin, *The Opposable Mind* (Boston, Mass.: Harvard Business School Press, 2007).

2. See R. Buchanan, "Wicked Problems in Design Thinking," *Design Issues* 8:2 (Spring 1992): 5–21. R. Buchanan, "Design as inquiry: the common, future and current ground of design," DRS Futureground International Conference, Melbourne, 2004.

3. See, for example, R. Boland and F. Collopy, *Managing as Designing* (Stanford, Calif.: Stanford University Press, 2004).

Chapter 7

The Four Powers of Design: A Value Model in Design Management

by Brigitte Borja de Mozota, Professor, Management Science, Université Paris X, ESSEC France; DMI Life Fellow

This analysis proposes a framework to bridge the gap between the world of designers and the world of managers. Illuminating her thesis with examples from Steelcase, Decathlon, and other companies, Brigitte Borja de Mozota parallels design's ability to differentiate, integrate, transform, and contribute to the enterprise and bottom-line results with a corporate focus on markets, processes, talent, and finances.

IN SUMMER 2005, *BusinessWeek* published a twenty-page special report on building innovative companies."[1] The report celebrates the emergence of a "creativity economy" in which managers are starting to discover "design strategy." In addition, Innovation 2005, Boston Consulting Group's second annual survey of 940 senior executives, ranked two icons of the design community, Apple and Sony, in the top five of the world's twenty most innovative companies. Taking their cue from the creativity economy, universities and business schools from Toronto to Paris are taking up new collaborations with design schools.

Although the trend in favor of design can be seen as a way to promote design as a qualified partner for innovation and management, it's a trend that tends to forget about design management—a simplistic view that risks relegating design skills to the vague realm of creativity and the development of "wow" products, conveying the idea that merely collaborating with designers is enough.

Instead, business managers should know about design management's power to create value in companies, which has been proven through research and can also be demonstrated through management concepts such as Michael Porter's value chain. In this article, I hope to describe to design professionals a research-based value model for design management and to convey to them how this model can be implemented using Robert Kaplan's and David Norton's Balanced Score Card (BSC) decision tool[2]—a guide that should be familiar to all kinds of business managers.

THE FOUR POWERS OF DESIGN

My research on design-oriented European SMEs became the basis of a value model for design as differentiator, integrator, and transformer.[3] It also introduced the concept of the four powers of design, in the context of management science. These four powers are:

1. **Design as differentiator:** a source of competitive advantage on the market through brand equity, customer loyalty, price premium, or customer orientation.
2. **Design as integrator:** a resource that improves new product development processes (time to market, building consensus in teams using visualization skills); design as a process that favors a modular and platform architecture of product lines, user-oriented innovation models, and fuzzy-front-end project management.
3. **Design as transformer:** a resource for creating new business opportunities; for improving the company's ability to cope with change; or (in the case of advanced design) as an expertise to better interpret the company and the marketplace.
4. **Design as good business:** a source of increased sales and better margins, more brand value, greater market share, better return on investment (ROI); design as a resource for society at large (inclusive design, sustainable design).

DESIGN IN THE VALUE MANAGEMENT MODEL

Design is thus fairly easily integrated into the value management model. So, what is the problem? Why are designers still suffering from lack of recognition and support from managers? Our insight is that there are two missing links:

1. Designers' lack of knowledge of management concepts and of management as a science
2. Designers' difficulty in implementing a value model in their everyday practices

In addition, the scope of design management has changed. This is the result of business's changed understanding of the place of design in an organization, as well as of designers' changed understanding of the scope of business management (figure 1). In this

DESIGN AS STRATEGY	Controling design ROI & business performance and brand value.	Design leadership. Coherence of the design system and driving the future "advanced design."	Design as resource for the challenges of contemporary managers—socially responsible enterprise.
DESIGN AS PROCESS	Design research methods—ethno design, etc. DM as managing the design function.	Integrating design in other processes: brand, innovation, TQM. DM as improving the performance of processes.	Integrating design in management decision processes. DM as inventing the future and "sense building" in a changing environment. DM for the quality of staff.
DESIGN AS STYLING	Integrating design in marketing, R&D, corporate communications. DM as managing a design project.		
	MANAGEMENT AS COMMAND & CONTROL	MANAGEMENT AS ART OF COLLECTIVE ACTION	MANAGEMENT AS MANAGING CHANGE

Figure 1. Design management is defined by what you think of design (vertical axis: the "learning ladder" of design), and by what you think of management (horizontal axis).

way, design management spreads from project design management to strategic design management in a dynamic process.

Before the value of design to a firm can be measured, it is crucial to measure that firm's efficiency in relation to the efficiency of its industry. Each market sector has its specific growth potential and its norms in terms of profitability. In other words, the first question to ask a design manager is whether the superior product or service achieved through design brings profits superior to the mean in the industry.

Designers should keep in mind that there are more differences among companies in the same industry than among companies across industries. In every industry, technology, distribution, and marketing tend to be similar. A company competes through inventing a combination of these resources that make its offer unique and its EVA (economic value added) superior. Value in management science happens by achieving a result superior to that of the competition, not just by making a well-designed product. And a superior result is defined as a greater ratio between the profits realized and the capital invested.

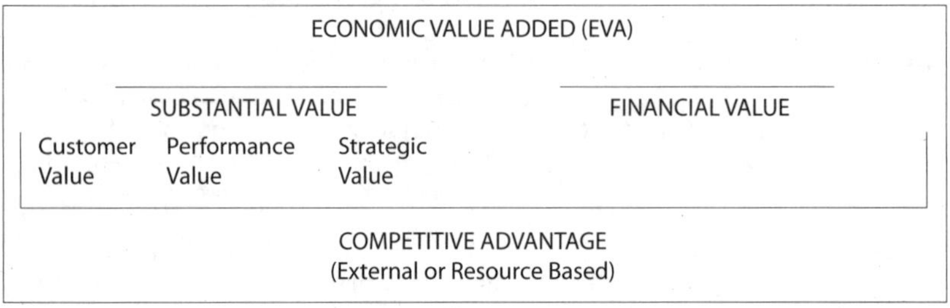

Figure 2. A competitive advantage brings economic value added if both substantial value and financial value are created.

Let us assume that your organization has a result that is close to the mean of your industry and that you think design can bring better value to your organization. Or perhaps you want to invent a new business unit that boasts a superior EVA. How do you teach managers and CEOs to be better at their jobs because of the input of design?

You can explain that through design they can develop a competitive advantage that will be valued by the market—truly, an objective of any manager (figure 2). But how do you build that advantage?

First, consider that competitive advantage can take two forms:

1. **Design as differentiator.** External, market-based advantage derived from the design-based differentiation of the company's product or service (design of products, design as perceived value, brand design value, corporate image)
2. **Design as coordinator or integrator.** Internal competitive advantage that comes from a unique, invisible, and difficult-to-imitate combination of organizational processes and resources (that is, a resource-based view: design as process, design as knowledge, design science, design as resource, advanced design for new business)

Companies in the first camp are really thinking of design in a reputational, or brand, context. Companies in the second camp understand design as a core competency.

Now, consider that EVA comes from two types of value: financial and substantial.

Financial value is the value created for the company shareholders, partners, or investors—or even society at large, in the case of companies that practice sustainable development—through finance, investment, or mergers. Designers often forget this financial perspective or think of it only in terms of economic value (sales, margin, costs, market share)—forgetting the stock-market power of shareholders and the political forces of stakeholders and laws.

Substantial value is the value created for the company's suppliers, customers, and employees following two rationality schemes:

1. **Competitive rationality:** The company portfolio represents a value perceived by the market (value chain, customer relation, competitiveness, future cash).

2. **Organizational rationality:** The company structure is the base of the value created and shared by all human resources—that is, process improvement, individual creativity, knowledge management, performance of projects.

In summary, there are many paths by which a competitive advantage can be built, and the same variety applies to design-driven value.

IMPLEMENTING DESIGN AS VALUE USING THE BALANCED SCORE CARD TOOL

Although they know design brings value, designers and design managers still understand that one cannot manage what is not measured. So measuring the impact of design value is a key success factor for designers who want to successfully implement their design strategy—and for design managers who want to present design as a tool for value management.

In other words, designers and design managers make a bigger impression on business managers when they use a value-based model to measure the impact of design. I suggest that designers and design managers use the Balanced Score Card (BSC) methodology mentioned earlier. For designers, the BSC is also easy to appropriate, because it is vision-based as well as holistic (figure 3).

The four perspectives of the BSC model neatly coincide with the four powers of design, or the four design values system: customer perspective (design as differentiator); process perspective (design as coordinator); learning perspective (design as transformer); and finance perspective (design as good business).

As noted earlier, the BSC model is widely known by MBAs and often used by audit and strategy consultants. It is a common language shared and understood by most executives, whether they occupy the CEO's office or work in finance, marketing, procurement, or research and development. This model is strategic and long-term-driven, which aligns it well with design thinking and design coherence, also based on long-term thinking. It offers help in asking about the four issues that are key to every design project: that is, client, performance, knowledge management, and finances. It is also simple to apply to any design decision, design policy, or design project.

But more important, the BSC tool is a cause-and-effect model, in that each perspective has an impact on the other three. Employee quality, for example, drives customer value and financial value; process improvement affects financial value and customer value, and so on. Just as a designer working on a project is used to thinking holistically, the BSC indicators are meant systemically—improving the quality of product design improves employee satisfaction and creates new knowledge that can generate better production process performance (and vice versa). In the same way, the BSC shows how each design discipline is linked with other design disciplines in a system based on a common, central vision.

The cases starting on page 72 are examples of the implementation of this model in three companies, each of which focuses on a different design discipline: Attoma (information design); Decathlon (product design); and Steelcase (workspace design).

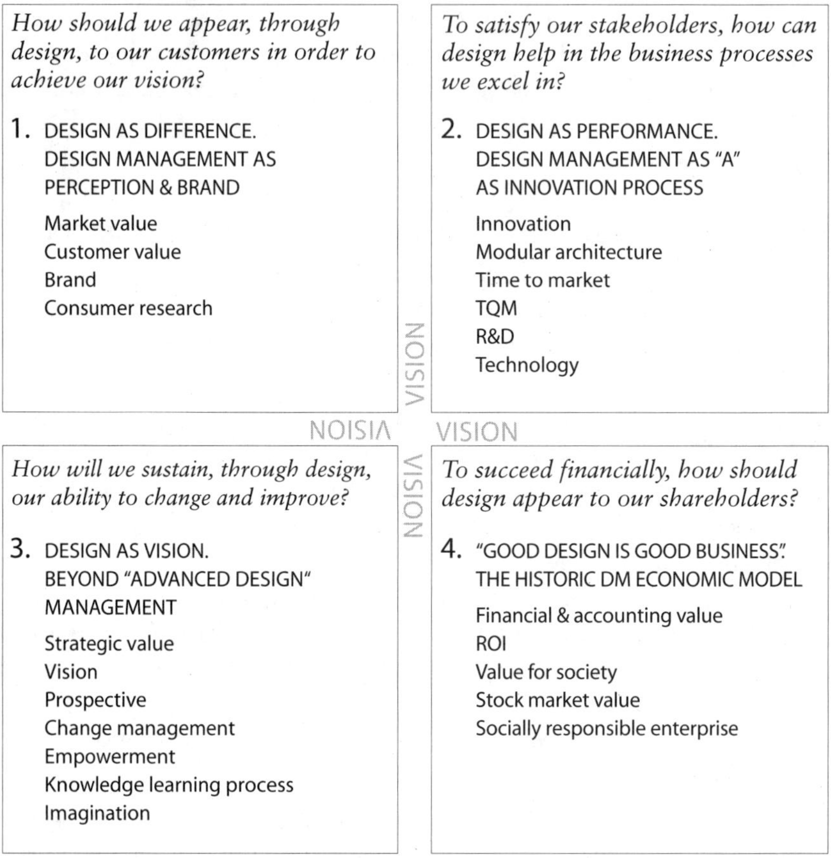
How should we appear, through design, to our customers in order to achieve our vision?
1. DESIGN AS DIFFERENCE.
DESIGN MANAGEMENT AS PERCEPTION & BRAND
Market value
Customer value
Brand
Consumer research
To satisfy our stakeholders, how can design help in the business processes we excel in?
2. DESIGN AS PERFORMANCE.
DESIGN MANAGEMENT AS "A" AS INNOVATION PROCESS
Innovation
Modular architecture
Time to market
TQM
R&D
Technology
VISION
VISION
VISION
VISION
How will we sustain, through design, our ability to change and improve?
3. DESIGN AS VISION.
BEYOND "ADVANCED DESIGN" MANAGEMENT
Strategic value
Vision
Prospective
Change management
Empowerment
Knowledge learning process
Imagination
To succeed financially, how should design appear to our shareholders?
4. "GOOD DESIGN IS GOOD BUSINESS".
THE HISTORIC DM ECONOMIC MODEL
Financial & accounting value
ROI
Value for society
Stock market value
Socially responsible enterprise

Figure 3. It is crucial to explain in any design brief, and to measure in any design project, how design creates value from the four perspectives of the Balanced Score Card model. Source: R. Kaplan and D. Norton, "Linking the Balanced Scorecard to Strategy," *California Management Review* 39:1 (1996).

THE BALANCED SCORE CARD FOR RUNNING A DESIGN DEPARTMENT OR A CONSULTANCY

Now, how shall we apply the Balanced Score Card to measure the performance of a design consultancy or a design department?

Imagine that you are a design manager or a CEO. What issue faces you both when you come in to work each morning? Company performance. What is design's responsibility in improving this performance? What indicators should you measure on a continuing basis? How could that goal be expressed with the design value model or the four BSC perspectives? Figure 4 offers an example.

For each of the four BSC perspectives, we chose indicators that are easy to measure and easy to link with company performance indicators. Some indicators are used by many functions of the organization; some are specific to the design function. It is important that design managers link their own indicators with the BSC indicators of

1. THE CUSTOMER VALUE PERSPECTIVE

How should we appear, through design, to our customers in order to achieve our vision?

Increase market share/% products or services above mean price.
Improve brand image/% products or services sold under our brands.
Improve customer satisfaction/User oriented design: customer satisfaction survey.

2. THE PERFORMANCE VALUE PERSPECTIVE

How does the design department improve the process we excel in?

Improving innovation process/more projects conducted per year.
Improving production process/fewer defects.
Implementing CRM/
Design in information systems management: fewer complaints.

VISION

3. THE LEARNING PERSPECTIVE

How does the design department sustain our ability to change and improve?

Recruit high potential profiles/ Recruitment design.
Competent staff/Improving learning abilities through design.
Motivated and empowered staff/ Working through design on transversal multicultural teams.

4. THE FINANCIAL VALUE PERSPECTIVE

To succeed financially, how should design appear to our shareholders?

Increase turnover/% sales of new products or services.
Improve intangibles/Number of licensed and protected designs.
Improve ROI/Improve results versus capital invested in design projects.

Figure 4. The Balanced Score Card for a design manager. Create your own BSC for measuring the performance of your design department or your design consultancy in a dynamic way. In each quadrant, choose for a company objective the pertinent indicators for the input of the design activity. And check your BSC results regularly.

the company's performance, as well as with design briefs, as a measure of the everyday performance of design staff.

CONCLUSION

Design offers four powers or directions through which to create value in management, and these four directions can be seen as a system with the vision in the center. The design value model and its application through the Balanced Score Card toolkit provide a common language for designers and managers and this can help the design profession effect a change from project-based to knowledge-based.

Hence, this value model gives a conceptual framework to the emerging trend toward design leadership and explains the potential of design thinking for analyzing the challenges faced by managers (such as, sense building, complexity, user-oriented innovation, building a socially responsible organization, and so on). In this way, it facilitates the convergence of design and management.

CASE STUDY 1: ATTOMA: THE VALUE OF INFORMATION DESIGN FOR BUSINESS PERFORMANCE

Companies are facing increasingly complex environments. Models for managing complexity are needed, and mental visualization models can help. With its horizontal and systemic approach, information design is capable of bringing concrete answers to an intelligent management of complexity. Attoma Design is an information design consultancy based in Paris, founded by Giuseppe Attoma Pepe, board member of the IIID (International Institute for Information Design).

One of Attoma's recent projects was done for RATP, the Paris Métro subway, which was implementing a contactless smart-card system called Navigo. If Navigo was to be successful, it would be vital to humanize the technology. Attoma was

Graphic User Interface (GUI) for a Ticket Vending Machine: Four Perspectives of the BSC Method

Value for the customer • Learning to cope with teleticketing as a seamless experience through an intuitive interaction ***Measure*** • Customer satisfaction survey	***Value for the process*** • Accompanying a multidisciplinary project group through the building of a common mental model using visualization tools for decision making ***Measure*** • Minimizing change during the project • NPD project members' satisfaction
Value for the employee • Gaining knowledge of user-oriented design methods ***Measure*** • Capacity to develop future versions using the knowledge gained in this project, eventually developing a distinctive sign for the RATP brand	***Value for the stakeholders*** • Facilitate and support teleticketing in the general public as a strategic issue for the Paris region; develop expertise in the Paris population, with no class distinction ***Measure*** • Exponential growth of customers using the digital interface of Navigo system

CASE STUDY 1: ATTOMA: THE VALUE OF INFORMATION DESIGN FOR BUSINESS PERFORMANCE

asked to design the graphic user interface for the Navigo vending machine. Chief among the methods Attoma used were visualization tools for prototype, test, and reduced time to market. The whole project was a success in sales growth and customer satisfaction, but also in the way it helped to spread the new technology among the general public. It also changed the way in which RATP viewed new product development.

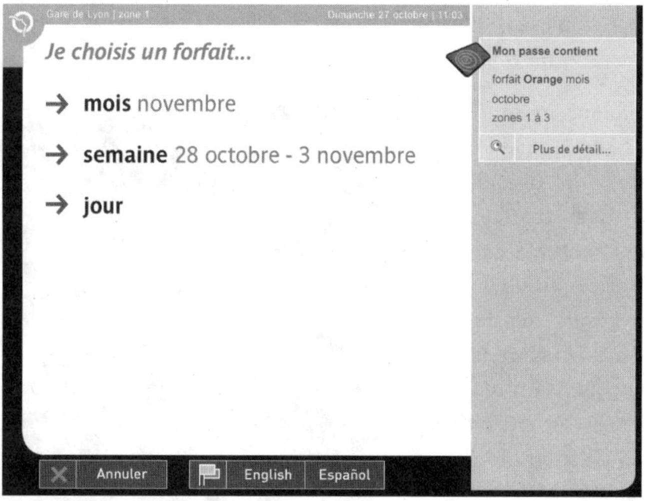

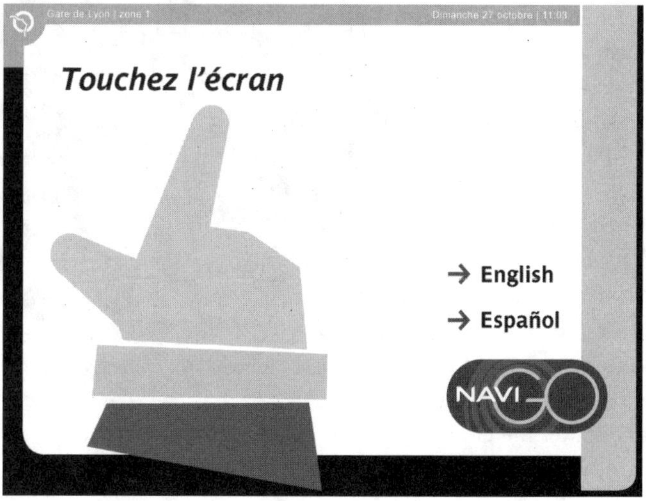

CASE STUDY 2: DECATHLON: DESIGNING VALUE INTO THE PROCESS

Since its founding in 1976, Decathlon has always had a very clear goal: make sport more enjoyable for everyone. In every corner of the globe, this purpose is expressed through two complementary areas of expertise:

1. The design and manufacture of in-house brand sporting goods covering about sixty-five sports
2. Retailing sporting goods (350 stores worldwide, twenty-two thousand store employees, thirty-five thousand different articles on average per store, and 100 million customers every year)

Decathlon's in-house design team is made up of ninety multidisciplinary designers sharing the same values: honesty, fraternity, and responsibility, all used toward making the pleasure of sport accessible to all. Many of these designers are practitioners of the sport for which they design.

Decathlon's Tribord Inergy surfing wetsuit for women.

Nine Decathlon products received International Forum design awards in 2006. One of these was the Tribord Inergy wetsuit for surfing. The Inergy was designed for women. It suits the female morphology and enables women to surf more comfortably and easily. In doing so, it also invites more women to discover the pleasures of surfing. This was a strategic approach for Tribord, and is currently being duplicated in other products.

CASE STUDY 2: DECATHLON: DESIGNING VALUE INTO THE PROCESS

The Tribord Inergy Woman's Wetsuit for Surfing: Four Perspectives of the BSC Method

Value for the client

- Surfing is a question of balance. A rigid structure reduces unwanted movements that spoil the balance. The Tribord design actually reduces elasticity in certain directions, making balance much easier.
- The chest area of the Tribord is designed to support each breast independently. This area is similar to a bra, but the two cups are visually integrated in the wetsuit pattern.

Measure

- Value of Tribord brand

Value for the process

- Staying true to a user-oriented innovation process, Tribord as a Decathlon brand has moved its research location close to user practice areas on the French Côte Basque, in Hendaye, where nautical sports are practiced.
- Technology value: Use of silicone on neoprene to control movement; matte areas and shiny areas visually differentiate the functional areas.

Measure

- Number of new products launched

Value for the employee and knowledge management

- Empowering female employees and improving knowledge management in understanding women's needs and desires. Well appreciated by Emmanuel Joly, five-time Olympic gold medal winner and technical partner for Tribord, as well as by female design team members.

Measure

- Employee satisfaction, especially among female employees
- New market positioning for all Decathlon brands

Value for the shareholders and society

- Design as a resource for shareholder value through the democratization of sports
- Innovation provides exclusivity

Measure

- International Forum design awards improve the company's intangible value.

Another award-winning Decathlon product is the Quechua 2 Seconds tent, which radically reduces the time needed to erect a tent. This tent can literally be thrown into the air and will open on its own before it reaches the ground. The idea was to preassemble the tent's various elements (room, double roof, hoops) to simplify the camper's life as much as possible. Once the tent is up, the camper has only to put six tent pegs in the ground to secure it. Roomy enough for two, the 2 Seconds Tent is reasonably priced at 49€, offering everyone the chance to go off and camp, even if he or she has never put up a tent. At the same time, it is a real tent, with all the technical features of, for instance, a coated double roof with waterproof seams and anticondensation, or breathable, fabric.

CASE STUDY 2: DECATHLON: DESIGNING VALUE INTO THE PROCESS

Decathlon's Quechua 2 Seconds tent literally pitches itself.

Quechua 2 Seconds Tents: Four Perspectives of the BSC Method	
Value for the client • Spring hoops allow this tent to be thrown into the air and to open up on its own before it reaches the ground ***Measure*** • Customer satisfaction in Quechua brand; product used in television campaign	***Value for the process*** • Better integration of marketing and design upstream in focus groups • Process innovation: the (patented) process that allows the automatic opening of the tent to include a room and a roof ***Measure*** • Fuzzy-front-end NPD process and expertise in design research • New process for development of future range of tents
Value for employee and knowledge management • Development of new innovation processes and progression in the capacity to develop prospective designs ***Measure*** • Growth of new concept development in the company (new business opportunity)	***Value for shareholders and society*** • Sustainable design (longer lifespan; no packaging—the cover acts as carrying pack) • Enabling Quechua to move up on the range of 10-inch little dome tents ***Measure*** • 78 percent growth in number of tents sold and 51 percent revenue growth in tent sales in the first year • Patented model of tent peg • Design awards in 2006: International Forum and Red Dot design awards, Annual Design Review (USA), Observeur du Design (France)

CASE STUDY 3: STEELCASE: THE VALUE OF WORKPLACE DESIGN FOR BUSINESS RESULTS

As businesses experience new dimensions of competition, more organizations see how workplace design affects bottom-line results. Using the workplace as a leverage point, organizations can better facilitate structural realignment; implement new technology; redesign business processes; and reinforce the organization's values, culture, and image.

Measurements related to the workplace have typically focused on cost per workspace, space efficiency, reconfiguration costs, and energy use—the cost side of the cost/benefit equation. The workplace, however, significantly affects an organization's people, processes, and technology. In the business results model shown below, the workplace is one of four key factors that drive business results. Efforts in all four areas must be integrated, balanced, and measured. Using the balanced scorecard model, let us take two examples:

Steelcase

Steelcase logotype

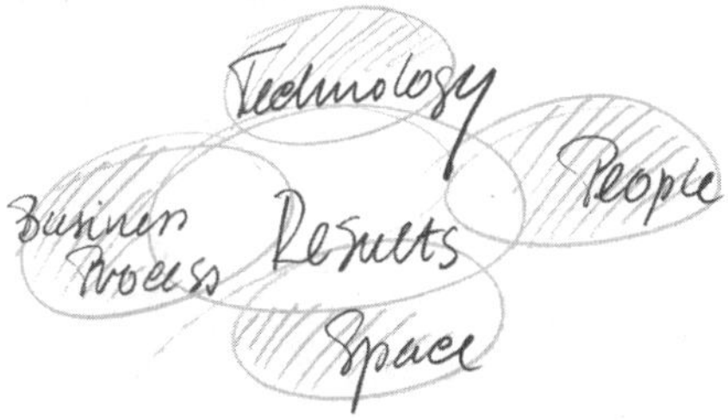

Steelcase business results model

Steelcase Workplace A: Improve worker interaction and workplace flexibility. The workspace at this high-tech electronics firm was allocated on the basis of hierarchy, status, and rank. As the firm reengineered and moved to a more fluid, team-based work process, the design of the workplace impeded progress. Team members were located on multiple floors; conference rooms were unavailable on short notice; and moving a person took as long as twelve weeks.

CASE STUDY 3: STEELCASE: THE VALUE OF WORKPLACE DESIGN FOR BUSINESS RESULTS

When the firm redesigned the workplace, members of each team were co-located to encourage informal communication. Collaborative space was integrated into the teamwork setting to facilitate interaction. Freestanding furniture within panels cut the time required for personnel moves from twelve weeks to twelve hours. A modular network and lay-in cabling sharply reduced changes to network connections.

Using the four categories of the BSC method (financial value and value for market position, personnel, and process) gives us the result seen in the chart.

Steelcase Workplace A: Four Perspectives of the BSC Method

Value for the market position: • Increase market share ***Measure:*** • Percent of market share contributed by new products	***Value for the process:*** • Accelerate product development process • Implement self-directed work teams ***Measure:*** • Time to market (before and after)
Value for personnel and knowledge management: • Increase worker interaction within product development teams ***Measure:*** • Workplace flexibility to support frequently changing work teams	***Financial value:*** • Move people and equipment, not furniture and cables ***Measure:*** • Time and costs required for workplace moves, adds, changes reduced by 72 percent. • ROI in five years (i.e., in five years, the company will have recouped its investment in design)

CASE STUDY 3: STEELCASE: THE VALUE OF WORKPLACE DESIGN FOR BUSINESS RESULTS

Steelcase Workplace B: Implement new technology and improve the balance sheet.

The leaders at an international building products firm were on a mission to expand their overseas markets through the improved use of technology. Goals for the new workplace were simple but radical—reshape the workplace to align with a flatter, more horizontal organization and provide ready access to a global communications network. There was one catch. With an existing multi-million-dollar investment in systems furniture, it had to be accomplished with intelligent redesign and reuse.

In the new environment, multiple hoteling workspaces support mobile workers who carry computers instead of briefcases. Teleconferencing rooms connect workers from all over the globe. Every workspace, from lobby to private office, features plug-and-play capability and modem access.

Steelcase Workplace B: Four Perspectives of the BSC Method

Value for the market • Increase revenue for international customers *Measure* • International sales volume	*Value for the process* • Implement global communications network *Measure* • Number of laptop connections to network
Value for personnel • Allow easy connection of laptops to power and data *Measure* • Speed acceptance of new technologies	*Financial value* • Will contain operational costs *Measure* • Minimize new capital expenditure and maximize existing furniture investment

ACKNOWLEDGMENTS

Thanks to Giuseppe Attoma of Attoma Design and to Yo Kaminagai at RATP. Our warm thanks also go to Philippe Picaud and Philippe Vahé at Decathlon Design and to Catherine Gall and Thierry Coste at Steelcase, Inc.

Suggested Reading

Borja de Mozota, B. *Design Management* (New York, N.Y.: Allworth Press, 2002, 2003, 2006 [Turkish, Chinese, and Spanish translations]).

Kaplan, R., and D. Norton. "Linking the Balanced Scorecard to Strategy," *California Management Review* 39:1 (1996).

Endnotes

1. Bruce Nussbaum, "Get Creative! How to Build Innovative Companies," *BusinessWeek* (August 2005).

2. For more information on the Balanced Score Card methodology, see R. Kaplan and D. Norton, "Linking the Balanced Scorecard to Strategy," *California Management Review* 39:1 (1996).

3. Brigitte Borja de Mozota, "Design and Competitive Edge: A Model for Design Management Excellence in European SMEs," *DMI Academic Review* 2 (2002).

Chapter 8

Transition: Becoming a Design-Minded Organization

by Thomas Lockwood, PhD, President of DMI; Author; Visiting Professor, Pratt Institute

Building a design-minded organization goes well beyond the design itself. Whether innovating new products, services, interfaces, brands, or entire business transformations, embedding design requires an alignment with corporate culture, business processes, and customer values. Thomas Lockwood presents ten steps for integrating design thinking into the organization, supported by first-hand experience, and summarizes the key processes, systems, and operations.

THE ROLE OF design in business has shifted dramatically over the past few years, and it is now being recognized as a key business asset that can add significant value. Yet few business professionals—or design professionals, for that matter—know how to develop a design-minded organization.

This chapter presents an overview of the key concepts and methods involved in developing a more design-minded organization. Any organization can develop these competencies, either by growing internally or by partnering with external experts. Although both paths can be successful, in general it is most effective to build a combination of internal and external resources. The key is to create a clear strategy and plan of action to integrate design and design principles into business. Becoming a design-minded organization is challenging and takes time, but with the right planning and a little nurturing and patience, it is not as difficult as it may first appear. This chapter presents ten principles to help make the leap toward embedding design thinking into your business.

MOVING FROM STATUS QUO TO DESIGN-MINDED

First, let me state that becoming a design-minded organization is not about proprietary processes and techniques; it's about empowerment and transparency of methods and ideas, and being open minded to change. As a starting point, let's first consider what Richard Buchanan[1] outlined in 1995 regarding the "four orders of design":

1. *Communication*—the creation of signs and symbols to be used in mass communications
2. *Construction*—the creation of objects via traditional industrial design
3. *Interaction*—the actions and behaviors of people, as affected by design
4. *Organization*—design considerations in the context of organizations, environments, systems, and cultures

The first and second orders are about design as an outcome, a resource. They're really the baseline—every corporation applies this level of design, with the only difference being the degree of innovation and effectiveness. The third order moves into the interaction arena—also commonplace, and also handled with varying degrees of effectiveness. But the fourth order is the sweet spot—the point at which the organization can involve design more integrative and holistic, building design methods into some of the internal systems and processes, and moving design towards a core competency. This is the desired end state because the real value of design is in discovering and solving all manner of problems.

Why make this change? Well, for one thing, according to business media pundits like *BusinessWeek*'s Bruce Nussbaum,[2] our businesses and institutions aren't working any more. Corporations, financial systems, the environment, healthcare, education—all are basically broken, says Nussbaum. The upshot of this is that we don't need innovation in increments; that would be inadequate to deal with the complexity of the changes needed. What we really need are business transformations. And that's where design and design thinking come in.

The role of design is now being recognized as a process as much as it is an artifact, communication or environment. What many now call "Design 3.0" is integral to business success. Because it's not what design is that matters, it's what design does. And the role of the designer has shifted from solving simple problems to solving complex problems, and from working independently in a single-discipline focus to working collaboratively with cross-functional teams. Design is everywhere. Everything made by human beings is designed, and in today's world of sophisticated business competition, this has to be managed.

In addition, design is not only integral to developing new processes, products, and services, and to enabling innovation, but it can also add significant value to the "triple bottom line." The social, economic, and environmental—or people, profit, and planet—areas are more crucial than ever. The value of design is incredibly powerful, versatile, and far-reaching. Design is now being viewed as a way of knowing through thinking and doing, from giving form to ideas to a way of doing things.

Here are just some of the shifts in social and economic areas that are affecting the role of design in business:

- Globalization
- Web 2.0
- The "triple bottom line"
- Innovation drives business, and design enables innovation
- Seeking meaning in an "experience economy"
- From mass media ads to brands as stories and relationships
- From manufacturing-centric to consumer-centric
- The integration of customer touchpoints

It is clear that creativity and design drives innovation, and that innovation drives new business growth. But concentrating just on what's new does not give a business true sustainability or long-term viability; what we really need is the kind of innovation that drives transformation. Brigitte Borja de Mozota (see chapter 7) is an early adopter of the idea of using design for business transformation—now a hot topic in popular business and innovation blogs. It seems we've reached a tipping point, as writer Malcolm Gladwell would have it;[3] design in business has now achieved the three "distinguishing factors of epidemics" that Gladwell likes to cite:

- Contagious behavior
- Little changes that had big effects
- Changes happened in a hurry

When these are coupled with Richard Florida's *The Rise of the Creative Class* and Daniel Pink's *A Whole New Mind*, we begin to see a new picture. We are in the midst of a sea change about the role of creativity and design in business, which is driven by micro and macro factors. This is why change is here to stay, and it is crucial for organizations to become more design-minded.

UNDERSTANDING TERMINOLOGY

Now that design is "hot" (recognized as adding value), there is no shortage of catchy new terms to define the various processes, functions, and attributes. I love the simple definition of "strategic design" by Marco Steinberg: "'Regular design' is giving sense to objects; 'strategic design' is giving sense to decisions."[4] I like this idea, because it describes what organizations do when they embed design into their very culture: they use design as output, but also as a means of making better business decisions.

I am often asked to help people understand the differences between *design thinking* and *design management.* Design thinking is primarily an innovation process—part of the "fuzzy front end," and a great method with which to discover unmet needs and create new product and service concept, not to mention transforming businesses through solving "wicked" problems. Design management, however, is broader in scope and involves the ongoing management and leadership of design processes, organizations, operations, and design outputs (i.e., products, services, communications, environments, and interactions). These points are further discussed in chapter 6.

Essentially, design leadership and design strategy can be viewed as outputs of effective design thinking and design management. Generally, design management and design leadership lie in the areas of integrating design into business and in continuous improvement. Design strategy sets direction and road map, and design thinking is more involved in the front-end innovation process. However, all are critical to helping an organization become more design-minded. Figure 1 outlines my point of view regarding several of these terms.

Profile of Terminology

	Objective	Scope	Process	Typical Players	Thinking Style
Design thinking	Innovation, clarifying fuzzy front end, direction finding	Concept of objects, services and processes	Collaborative, conceptual, iterative, idea formulation and demonstration	Designers, reseachers, managers, individual contributors, anyone	Abductive* thinking
Design strategy	Clarify design attributes and design policy	Define use of design and design style, including look and feel	Define and guide. A continuous process	Designers, design managers, brand managers	Inductive thinking
Design management	Direct design organization and operations, processes, resources, and projects	Project, business unit, or corporate level	Management of people, processes, projects and budgets	Design manager, brand manager, project or program manager	Inductive and deductive thinking
Design leadership	Connect design to business. lead design operations and collaborations	Design and business integration, top-level advocacy	Influence and guide top management decisions	Chief design officer, design council, expert consultant, CEO, VP	Deductive thinking

**According to Darden professor Jeanne Liedtka, abductive thinking is "the logic of what might be." Inductive thinking is proving through observation that something actually works; deductive thinking is proving through reasoning from principles that something must be.*

Figure 1

Figure 2, whose initial concepts I attribute to conversations with Alto Design's Alan Topalian and design manager Raymond Turner, attempts to define the differences between design management and design leadership.

Scope and Roles of Design Management Versus Design Leadership	
Design Leadership	**Design Management**
Enable corporate strategy	Solve specific problems
Envision future scenarios	Organization and people
Business planning	Design sourcing
Enable innovation	Financial resources
Design strategy	Design process
Affect corporate reputation	Design work

Figure 2

The role of design in business can further be viewed by where it takes place—at the corporate level, business-unit level, or project level. Figure 3, whose initial concepts I attribute to University of Lancaster Professor Rachel Cooper and others, outlines these differences.

Levels of Design Management Integration		
Corporate Level	**Business-Unit Level**	**Project Level**
Design as part of corporate strategy	Design for new products and services	Design organizations and operations
Strategic advantage	Secure new markets and new customers	Design resources
Can influence the focus and direction of the organization	Competitive advantage	Effectiveness and efficiency of the design process
Holistic customer experience	User benefit	Project level
Corporate strategy	Process for product and service development	Operational and creative advantage
Design vision	Implementing and monitoring design strategy	Design activities
Strategic direction	Creating management structures	Managing projects
Creating supportive environment	Developing projects	Improving skills
	Evaluating outcomes	Implementing, monitoring and evaluating design work
Having and intent and a plan for design	Design process	Physical outcomes of design
Strategic	Strategic and operational	Operational
Embedding Design		
Planning Design • Organizing Design • Implementing and Monitoring • Evaluating		

Figure 3

As an innovation process, design thinking crosses all of these three levels. Integrating design into corporate culture also, of course, includes embedding design thinking into business processes.

As noted in the foreword and in chapter 6, design thinking is an innovation process. The key steps in design thinking processes are generally identified as developing deep consumer insights and rapid prototyping, as well as seeking innovation rather than incremental change and empowering teams to be innovative. In my experience, design thinking is most effective when it involves using field observations and ethnographic methods to go beyond the limitations of traditional market research. The goal is to first understand what is meaningful to consumers and discover unarticulated needs. Next, the use of rapid prototyping using mock-ups, storyboards, storytelling, user testing, and even acting out concepts and services can bring clarity to concepts. The intent is to reduce the risk of failure and accelerate organizational learning as an iterative process. I had an interesting discussion with creative teams at Pixar and learned that one of their ten core operating principles is to "fail quickly" so that they can move on to the best solutions as soon as possible. The design thinking process involves a team approach, and the goal is to unlock the creative potential of the organization and its partners. The power of interdisciplinary teams is undeniable, and the ability of design teams to see both the big picture as well as the details is important and rather unique.

Researchers like Michele Rusk have identified common personality traits that have been attributed to design thinkers:[5]

- ▲ broad curiosity
- ▲ ability to employ tacit knowledge
- ▲ ability to develop awareness and foster insight
- ▲ ability to understand complex problems and ability to identify root causes of problems
- ▲ ability to anticipate and visualize new scenarios
- ▲ ability to invent ideas and synthesis
- ▲ ability to problem solve

Rusk notes that creativity is the thinking, that innovation and design are the doing, and that the ability to shift from divergent to convergent thinking styles and, when necessary, suspend judgment, is crucial. Similar, yet more recently, Tim Brown, the CEO of the design consultancy IDEO has also identified a "design thinker's personality profile,"[6] which includes skills and capabilities in empathy, integrative thinking, optimism, experimentation, and collaboration. These are important attributes of becoming a design-minded organization, as well.

TEN PRINCIPLES TOWARDS BECOMING A DESIGN-MINDED ORGANIZATION

As we've seen, to get the full benefits of design, firms must embed it into their business and processes. Here are ten principles or areas of focus to build in your organization:

1. **Develop empathy for the customer.**

   It all starts with caring about customers, and design must be an advocate for the customer. Every company prides itself on giving customers what they ask for, but the problem with listening to customers is that when companies ask customers what they like, customers are sure to answer by naming products and services that already exist. This form of research is really just being an order taker, not an innovator.

   Instead, we need to develop a deep empathy and understanding of customers that will better discover their unarticulated needs. Dev Patnaik argues in his book *Wired to Care* that companies prosper when they learn to reach outside of themselves and connect with their customers, and the best way to do so is to essentially imagine the world from a customer's perspective—thereby beating the problem of "assumed similarity." This taps into our natural tendency to care, and our gut-level intuition. By seeing through the customer's eyes and using design to create and prototype concepts, we increase the possibility of discovering new opportunities. The point is that it takes the development of real-world experience and human connection to really understand customers and determine their needs and desires.

   Developing customer empathy also requires the need to evaluate trends in order to get a view on what customers may want next. It is important to be observant of the world around us, and to practice trendspotting. Recognizing and reacting to trends involves reading, observing, learning, exploring, and doing. So, get out and be aware, and hang around with customers and prospects in order to link design to value for consumers. Coming to an understanding of what customers *value* is far more beneficial than asking them what they *want.*

   The process of innovation begins with understanding what customers want to achieve, and ends with the creation of what they will buy. The role of design thinking is to guide the research process to focus on desired outcomes, and identify unarticulated (and unmet) needs. Embedding design begins with identifying customer needs through the eyes of designers—working in the field, hands-on, not by desk research—and compiling statistics and spreadsheets.

2. **Engage unique design processes.**

   Embedding design requires unique processes. Yet these processes need to be integrated with other key business processes, or they won't get traction. It's a tricky balance—you must be independent enough to use the best design processes, yet embedding design into the business means embedding it into processes that already exist.

   In my PhD thesis, I developed a model of "integrated design management" based on in-depth discussions with fifty-two design managers at Caterpillar,

Kodak, Levi Strauss, Microsoft, Nike, Starbucks, and Sun Microsystems, and subsequently with BMW, Braun, British Airways, Samsung, and Sony. I have also worked with and looked closely into the processes of some of the world's leading design consultancies. In summary, the best design processes are iterative—less like a series of stage-gates, and more like driving a car through a congested roundabout intersection. I visualized my model as an inward spiral that permits a continuous process of discovery, shaping, and forming, and that allows team members to enter and exit when needed, as the design process iterates closer toward a final design solution in the center.

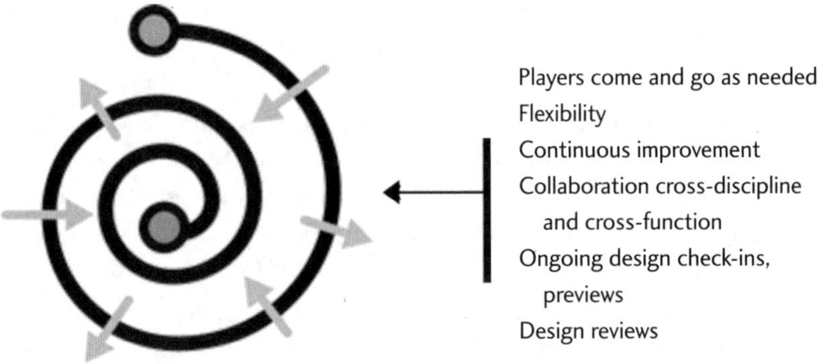

Integrated design management process

This diagram demonstrates a process that is continuous and iterative, and does not start and stop, but rather allows for interaction and collaboration. The gray arrows indicate various team members coming and going, collaborating as needed throughout the project. These interactions include many types of frequent design reviews, design check-ins, and consumer feedback loops.

Basically the model begins by defining the problem, but as is often said, sometimes what's manifested is a symptom, not the real problem. Use the technique of "asking why five times," and soon you will discover deeper problems to be solved—perhaps a root cause. The next step is to develop insights into customers' behaviors and motivations through careful observation, interviews, and analysis. Looking beyond the surface of an environment or situation can reveal much about consumer behavior and preferences.

The next step is to sort the findings to discover opportunities. Look for patterns and connections. (Post-it notes abound!) The goals are to identify clusters and to get closer to consumer needs and desires. Next is the ideation phase, where the task is to design quick concepts using very rough sketches, prototypes, storyboards, or stories to communicate the findings and explore alternative solutions. (This phase should include customers and other team members—it's not about designers working alone.) Hopefully the ideation phase leads to innovation, with another round of showing the prototype concept to consumers, this one leading to further developments. The ideal result is process improvements, new products and services, new partners, and hopefully a transformation for the business itself.

As noted, this process must include cross-functional teams and, frequently, both internal and external participants. Designers are great at mixing and matching with other designers and cross-functional ad hoc collaborative teams to solve specific problems. Given the collaborative atmosphere and the iterative nature of the work, the process needs to be adaptable and allow for ambiguity. Be flexible. Embrace creativity. But remember that designers typically appreciate constraints, because constraints serve to focus scope of the work and increase its challenge, so clarify what is inbounds and what is out of bounds early, but be prepared to change new parameters as needed. Remember, the key is to solve the right problem, and the right problem often is not the first one identified. If the organization needs to solve those wicked problems, it needs designers on the team from the start, and it needs design-oriented processes.

3. **Connect with corporate culture.**

Here is something to consider: It's not about putting design into corporate culture, it's about putting corporate culture into design. So many times, people say to me that getting design recognized is like pushing a rope—but that's often because they are challenging the corporate culture and norms. We need to support them.

For example, when I managed design at Sun Microsystems/StorageTek, I wanted to redesign the entire storage product line. As a result of legacy issues, we had separate industrial design styles for each of our business units—servers, mainframe storage, network hardware, and so on. This did not make any sense from a brand or efficiency point of view. But I knew the executive team would not support a full product redesign for many reasons, so I set project goals to 1) decrease product cost, 2) decrease new product time to market, and 3) improve the expression of the brand; all goals I knew the team members would find appealing. The design solution involved creating a common platform system for all our hardware products, which could be done by developing a shared chassis design, a common user interface, and shared design of components across the business units. This accomplished the project goals and demonstrated the value of good design, and the CEO released funding for a full redesign of the entire product line.

Here are seven simple steps to integrate design into corporate culture:

1. Determine cultural norms and drivers.
2. Determine how design can support the norms.
3. Build awareness about the value of design.
4. Set appropriate design organization and partners.
5. Integrate design processes within corporate business policy and practice.
6. Measure the value gained by design.
7. Train and empower others in design thinking methods.

Aligning design with corporate culture is a strategic imperative. Culture is a key element of the way in which collaboration occurs within workgroups and teams, across organizations, and between corporations and the marketplace. I think that culture and design are interdependent. As a result, design leadership can be more intentional and proactive in its approaches to creating and implementing more aligned strategies, processes, and design methodologies. According to organizational leadership expert Edgar Papke, it is important to interpret culture and consider the motivators of human behavior —the needs for inclusion, competency, and openness—that will best embed design into the organization.

4. **Set design strategy and policy.**

One broad definition of design runs along the lines of "a plan to make something." This is actually quite informative when you think about it, because the key words are *plan, make,* and *something.* This involves an understanding that would help identify challenges and frame opportunities (in other words, *plan*) in order to create (*make*) new solutions (*something*).

It is also important to recognize that every activity and output of an organization is dependent upon design. Design is what makes corporate strategy a reality—the reason being that even strategy is a series of activities, and all activities have to be designed. So the proper design of all activities can influence the effectiveness and internal adoption of strategy. Design is the process and the output to bring innovation to the market, by aligning the organization and enabling corporate strategy to succeed.

Research informs design concepts that develop and support corporate strategy, and this also involves developing a design strategy, so the organization creates propriety design "look and feel," or trade dress. First, develop the design vision and road map, and then establish design principles, visual language, and signature elements. This also involves setting up appropriate organizational structures and sourcing of design resources. One way to embed design-mindedness is to team up with others, because open innovation is a shared process and purpose. (By the way, forget the gigantic slide decks with animated type builds and data intense spreadsheets—just communicate clearly by using visual language and simple stories.)

5. **Align (and help define) business strategy and design strategy.**

   Strategy is a way to accomplish objectives. A dictionary might define it as "a careful plan or method" or as "the art of devising or employing plans." It's not too difficult to see the similarities between design and strategy; however, in most large corporations the strategy department and the design department are worlds apart. As Hartmut Esslinger, the founder of frog design, recently noted, "Businesspeople are from Mars, and designers are from Venus." While this may not be far from the truth, our challenge in building design strategy is to bring these two disparate worlds into alignment. They share a common ground in the desire to accomplish business objectives. So, the strategist and the designer, each with a clear understanding of business goals and objectives, can be a powerful force if they work together. This is one of the roles of design-mindedness—to bring design and design thinking into organizations in support of the development of corporate strategy.

   Design gives us a new way of approaching strategy—from a user perspective. Strategy is meant to obtain a desired outcome. It should bring clarity, but often it brings confusion instead. Design can help to *define* strategy as well as to clarify it. The trick is to get those involved in strategic planning to add design thinking to their mindset.

   Probably the broadest overlap in strategy and design comes when a business is evaluated in light of the "triple bottom line": from an economic, social, and environmental viewpoint. I would argue that no other business discipline or function has greater potential to affect that triple bottom line than design. And obtaining that result is the true value of design strategy. As I've already said, when one considers the contribution of design to processes as well as products or services, its benefits are virtually unlimited. That's why design strategy is so important.

6. **Design for innovation and transformation.**

   A fundamental criterion is to integrate design and design thinking with other processes in order to achieve successful innovation. Adopt and integrate key methods of design and customer research, with an emphasis on observational processes and customer empathy, and you may find new solutions to difficult business problems, leading to transformation. Use design thinking as an open-out method of innovation, as opposed to the traditional funnel-down method or simply applying design as styling near the end of a process. Apply design methods and processes to issues of systems and complexity and watch the realm of possibility and business solutions expand.

7. **Design for relevancy at each touchpoint.**

   Embedding design involves coordinating all touchpoints, including brand identity and imagery, products, services, environments, interfaces, and communications. All customer touchpoints should be integrated, or at lease proactively coordinated, to influence the appropriate customer perceptions. Design influences perception, perception influences purchase, therefore design influences purchase. All touchpoints influence perception, including:

   Product design. Products are generally the most visible aspect of a company. They are often the reason we know the company, and they drive our attitudes toward it as well.

   Communication design. Equally important, communication design affects all touchpoints that rely on visual communications—from symbols and corporate identity to packaging, advertising, instructions, and directions.

   Information design. We have all come to rely on the importance and functionality of information design, from Web interfaces to product interfaces, from signage to wayfinding, from information architecture to customer invoices.

   Environment design. Affecting everything from branded retail environments to showrooms, from exhibitions to our workspaces, the design of our environments can be extremely influential in our professional as well as our personal lives.

   Service design. This is emerging as a discipline unto itself. Consider that all services, from bank-teller processes to restaurants, from hospitals to governments, from hotels to travel carriers, are designed. The question is whether they are well designed or simply a reflection of the status quo.

8. **Focus on the customer experience.**

   Becoming design-minded involves understanding consumer behavior and decision-making, with the objective of turning consumer insights into meaningful brand experiences. By truly understanding consumer motivation, companies can make their designs more effective. As experience expert Dave Norton pointed out in a recent DMI seminar, the right way to think about consumer motivation is that people want to accumulate two types of "capital" in their life: economic and cultural. Cultural capital helps people create meaning from their experiences, and if designers take this into account, it can help them design better solutions, ones that matter to the consumer. In addition, designers should identify the key "moments of truth" for their customers—when they make the decision to purchase, or repurchase a product or service—and strategically design those moments to increase the cultural capital associated with the experience. This often involves all of the customer touchpoints and requires design coordination across all disciplines.

Therefore, becoming a design-oriented organization involves not only all design disciplines but the accumulated customer experience as well.

9. **Empower creativity.**

A key objective for nearly every organization is to innovate, and in doing so to create meaningful value for its stakeholders and its customers. To that end, the successful organizations of the future will be those that make the most of the creativity of their employees and their partners. As Marty Neumeier so simply observes in *The Designful Company*, "Creativity in its various forms has become the number-one engine of economic growth." Similarly to innovation, creativity is often inspired through methods of open design—by codesigning with end users. Today's open source systems—from Linux to the whole universe of wikis and social networking sites—make it all the more possible to arrive at new solutions and answers to problems.

Creativity is a mental activity, but it can also be part of a systems model. In fact, because it challenges traditional management processes and styles, creativity requires adaptive dynamic systems. The domains of creativity lie in action and experiment, because creativity is a journey, not a destination. Developing your inner resources is part of the very fabric of creativity. Learning to think creatively in one discipline opens the door to understanding creativity in other disciplines. The approach to creativity should be integrative and multidisciplinary; in this way it can solve everything from small design challenges to complex systems problems, thus relating back to the holistic customer experience.

In this age of innovation, business requires a creative spark, stimulated in many ways, from "creative abrasion" to "informed play" and the blurring of disciplinary boundaries. Design is the perfect discipline to engage creativity. Jeff Mauzy argues that creativity can be divided into three categories; creative thinking, climate, and action.[7] Consider the dynamics of personal and team creativity, how creativity works, and the process of reinvigorating creativity in organizations, and the climate and environment for innovation increases. Empowering creativity is a core component of embedding design.

10. **Be a design leader.**

Design leadership is twofold; first, it involves developing personal leadership skills. Design managers are expected to drive and deliver sustainable value that reinforces key business strategy. A common characteristic is that an effective leader knows how to develop proper function of all parts of the group being led and how to mobilize resources to make the most of opportunities. In general, the design leader is involved with the planning, processes, resources, and staff, in building a culture for design. Obtaining a design leadership position often requires both internal and external design resources.

Design leadership also means developing a competitive advantage for the organization through the use of design. Companies that measure customer satisfaction, usability, or brand value often attribute part of their success to superior design; think of brands such as Apple, Dyson, OXO Good Grips, BMW, Audi, and Target as demonstrating leadership in design.

SUMMARY

What is the added value of design in business? Design solves problems, and businesses have many problems. The trick is to determine which problems are the right ones to solve, and then focus on the task of designing the right solutions. The added value of design in business is simply to discover the key problems, and solve the problems of both the customers and the business. A great definition of good design is: good design solves the right problems. And good design is for everyone. It can provide benefits throughout the "triple bottom line," and we all need to help organizations understand how this can be accomplished. It is as much about the process as it is about the final solution and design outcome. Embedding design can take an organization well beyond "posters and toasters" to create meaningful experiences, solve wicked problems, and add value at social, economic, and environmental levels.

Businesses need metrics for measurement, and design can create value based on four categories: more profit, more brand equity, more innovation, and faster change. Design must have a close and supportive relationship with the organization's objectives, and must be managed in a manner consistent with this relationship. Here are ten categories[8] by which to evaluate the performance of design:

1. Purchase influence or emotion
2. Enable strategy and new markets
3. Enable product and service innovation
4. Reputation, awareness, and brand value
5. Time to market and process improvement
6. Customer satisfaction
7. Cost savings, ROI, and IP
8. Developing communities of customers
9. Usability
10. Sustainability

Embedding design is particularly relevant in the current economic climate, because design is not decoration or cost; rather it is part of the essence of business and an added value. It's what helps us add meaning to our lives. What is more, the very fluidity of economies, corporate cultures, and complex systems presents challenges that design leaders can help solve.

Endnotes

1. See R. Buchanan, "Rhetoric, Humanism, and Design," in *Discovering Design*, ed. R. Buchanan and V. Margolin (Chicago, Ill.: University of Chicago Press, 1995).

2. Cf. Post on the "Nussbaum on Design" blog in *BusinessWeek*: "Is 'transformation' a better concept than 'innovation' to guide us forward?"

3. Malcolm Gladwell, *The Tipping Point* (Boston, Mass.: Little, Brown, 2000).

4. From Steinberg's comments at the 2009 Design Management Institute conference in Milan, Italy.

5. C. Michele Rusk's comments (as part of a panel on intercultural business communication, headed by Francesca Bargiela) at the Fifth ABC European Convention on Communicating in Business, held in Lugano 2003.

6. Tim Brown, "Design Thinking," *Harvard Business Review* 84 (May 2008).

7. See Jeff Mauzy, "Managing Personal Creativity," *Design Management Review* 17:3 (Summer 2006).

8. Adapted from Thomas Lockwood, "Design Value: A Framework for Measurement," *Design Management Review* 18:4 (Fall 2007).

SECTION 2

BUILDING BRANDS, BY DESIGN

STRATEGY

INSIGHTS

BRANDING

EMOTION

COMMUNICATIONS

INNOVATE

CONNECT

Chapter 9

Building Leadership Brands by Design

by Jerome Kathman, President and CEO, Libby Perszyk Kathman

Jerry Kathman articulates four timeless principles companies can embrace to establish powerful and enduring brands. Richly amplified with examples, these tenets speak to the content and characteristics of effective brands, the ways in which they are communicated and nurtured, design issues, the necessity to innovate, and the types of relationships compelling brands have with consumers.

WHY ARE SOME brands more successful than others? How is it that some brands can extend themselves around the world, as well as into other product categories, while others fail? Are brand life cycles inevitable, or do brand builders make choices that determine their destiny?

These questions are posed at an unsettled time for businesses. The process of brand building continues to undergo dramatic change. Conventions that seemed timeless only yesterday are being retooled or abandoned altogether. New ideas and process models are entering the discourse. For practitioners, separating the verities from the vagaries isn't easy.

After thirty years of partnering with various clients, such as Procter & Gamble, Hershey, Valvoline, and IBM, in their global branding efforts, I have observed commonalities among leadership brands—attributes I believe have made these brands the best in their class. To that end, I have identified four principles that brands need to embrace to achieve and maintain global leadership status.

PRINCIPLE 1: ARTICULATE AND INCULCATE THE BRAND STRATEGY

Leadership brands have self-knowledge and an uncanny ability to anticipate. This ability, however, is not a result of good fortune; rather, it is the result of passionate commitments to understanding the strategic framework of the brand, as well as to planning ahead. Further, when the framework is understood and the plan is articulated, it is understood and embraced throughout the enterprise. The successful transference of knowledge is as critical to leadership brands as the creation of the knowledge itself. No brand-builder is an island.

Developing brand strategy involves understanding the meaning of the brand. The meaning includes dimensions of brand insight, brand differentiation, and brand elasticity.

Foundation Built on Insight

Whether developing a new brand, evolving an existing brand, or extending a brand into new opportunities, the foundation must be based on deep consumer insight. The process of creating and managing the brand foundation defines strategic equities and creates desire by understanding this insight.

Leadership brands are deliberate in identifying and articulating aspects of insight that are expected, yet compelling, within their category. Points of category parity, such as "great taste" within a food category, serve to establish critical must-haves in order to be credible within a particular competitive set. Consumers tend to purchase confectionery products, for example, as a treat within a hectic lifestyle. Consumer insight

In-depth consumer research reveals that Reese's success is based on dimensions of personal reward, not just taste.

reveals that a Reese's Cup or Hershey's Kiss represents time saved for oneself, a small indulgence that is satisfying not just on the intrinsic dimension of taste, but also on a deeper dimension of personal reward. The more brands understand that it is not just the features of a brand that create consumer pull but the benefits as well, the more leadership they will attain within their categories. Leadership brands build a foundation that leverages this deep consumer insight.

The Differentiated Brand Promise

Establishing core covenants of brand meaning that serve to differentiate a brand on both rational and emotional grounds is also critical to creating and maintaining a leadership position. The process of building leadership brands includes the assignment of strategic equity components that serve to separate the brand from competitive offers, while leveraging key motivational insights.

In the case of Pantene, the brand has created an identity presenting itself as the authority on healthy hair. Its leadership position has been achieved by delivering a benefit tied to beauty through health. This approach leverages not only the established category mandate based on promising beautiful hair but has also stretched beyond this meaning to include a strategic health benefit, which is a much more powerful and proprietary position in this high-involvement category.

The formalization of both features and benefits within a distinct personality is the cornerstone of successful strategy and serves as the compass for all marketing activities

Pantene's promise of transformation is based on a strategic health benefit—a differentiated promise in a crowded category. The global Pantene plan is infused with regional cultural knowledge.

for leadership brands. While the fundamental foundation of a brand is consistent even across diverse world markets, it is through regional tailoring that true global leadership may be attained. Insight and differentiation, with an infusion of regional and cultural knowledge, build leadership.

Elasticity of Leadership Brands

The ability of a brand to capitalize on emerging business opportunities by extending a relevant strategy in areas beyond the original product is the hallmark of elastic brand architecture. Leadership brands stretch their influence in a way that is believable to the consumer on the basis of a framework of consumer benefits that deliver a fundamental human value.

In the case of Pampers, the world's leading diaper brand, what began as a product focused on absorbency and containment has now emerged as a global mega-brand with a portfolio that extends beyond the product. By creating a strategic meaning that is focused on the experiential relationship between mom and baby, the brand's equity umbrella is now much broader and relevant beyond narrow product features.

Although (as any parent quickly learns) the amount of liquid a diaper can hold is important, that rational, feature-based argument isn't likely to enable a brand to extend itself. But if a diaper brand is positioned on the basis of the joy of parenting and the needs of parents and their babies, a case for the brand based on "we understand babies" may be made. Once this level of trust is established with consumers, it becomes very easy to expand into all sorts of baby needs, including wipes, lotions, diaper bags, apparel, and other items never before imagined for a brand that stood only for diapers.

The Pampers brand foundation is far more elastic than a concept based on product features alone.

This philosophy drives the brand-building process for leadership brands and gives the franchise far more elasticity than any concept based solely on a set of rational attributes.

PRINCIPLE 2: LEVERAGE THE DESIGN FRANCHISE

Once you understand the meaning of the brand, you can create compelling brand expressions. Brand expression for a leadership brand is the visual manifestation of the desired brand experience. A self-evident design strategy that is expressed across time, media, and geography builds leadership.

Design is a new frontier for many companies. Manufacturers are beginning to understand the role of design in the image-based global culture that has emerged in the last decade. Leadership brands leverage the design franchise because they understand that design not only expresses the desired brand experience but also creates a visual repository of the goodwill the brand has earned over time. Design triggers stored memory.

The link between memory and design is a particularly active area of current research. Late last year, a study was released at Baylor College of Medicine in Waco, Texas, that suggests the role of design and memory in the famous Coca-Cola debacle—the launch of New Coke. Though Pepsi was preferred to New Coke in blind taste tests, when the logo was shown three out of four participants preferred Coke. At the Brown Foundation Human Neuroimaging Laboratory at Baylor, researchers scanned the brains of the participants during the test. The Coke label triggered physical reactions in the part of the brain associated with memory and self-image. Pepsi did not trigger the same activity. P. Reed Montague, the director of the laboratory, noted when the research was released last October, "There is a huge effect of the Coke label on brain activity relating to the control of actions, the dredging up of memories, and self-image."

The concept of neuromarketing is already being discussed as a potential tool for business. I suggest that we may soon be entering the age of neurodesigning—measuring physical reaction to design stimulus.

Even without the involvement of neuroimaging science, however, the business case for design strategy is clearly in its ascendancy. Leadership brands have discovered the value of managing their design franchises.

Procter & Gamble took an important step in giving design a voice when the CEO, A.G. Lafley, appointed Claudia Kotchka the company's first chief design officer at the beginning of the new millennium. In the 1990s, P&G had seen some brands losing share to competitors. These competitors were not always offering superior products; arguably, they were out-designing and out-emoting P&G brands. Aesthetics, rather than utility, were being rewarded. P&G has been able to regain its share in critical businesses by leveraging design in all aspects of the brand development. Although product innovation remains essential, design strategy is now part of its innovation strategy. Design is brought in at the "fuzzy" front end, when conceptualization and planning are taking place, as well as at the point when a go-to-market plan is conceived. Although scents

The Valvoline design franchise leverages color, shape, and imagery to create an atmosphere of power and performance. The benefit of the brand's association with global racing circuits is enhanced by the strategic management of the design franchise.

and sounds can play an important role in the brand experience, behavioral research shows that most of what we retain about a brand is experienced through our visual sense. Therefore, brand builders must attend carefully to design equity to ensure it is consistent with the desired brand experience.

Leadership brands understand that every expression leads to an impression, and that brand identity franchises are created and strategically managed to deliver desired impressions and thereby capitalize on market opportunities. Leadership brands create and deploy assets within integrated systems of expression in order to reflect their overall meaning and positioning. This holistic approach to brand communication establishes valuable brand equity through design, helping to shape consumer behavior and delivering maximum business impact for the brand.

Design and the Brand Experience

Valvoline is an example of a global brand for which design has played a major role in delivering the desired impression across multiple touchpoints. Through a robust visual design language, design assets such as color, shape, symbol, and imagery have been developed and managed to create an atmosphere of power and performance established through the brand's association with global racing circuits.

As is evident in the industry saying, "Race on Sunday, sell on Monday," the deployment of these design assets in this context represent the tangible artifacts that consumers experience on their path toward embracing the brand.

Leadership brands leverage design choices, bring the strategic visual equities of the brand meaning to life, and establish valuable brand-building and experiential equity over time.

Design for Self-Selection

A critical aspect that leadership brands have in common is the understanding of the role of design in the self-select selling environment. The designers of leadership brands are keenly aware that selection is a critical moment in a brand's journey. Although design must first break through the static of a cluttered selling environment, it must also deliver an image that is engaging, compelling, and proprietary.

With an understanding of the role of design in self-selection, leadership brands manage the design franchise at the purchase event to enable shoppers to locate and navigate the brand effectively. Disseminating information in an appropriate hierarchy to facilitate the purchase is essential to the brand-building process in the store.

Fully Leveraged Brand Identity

Leadership brands reinforce their position in the marketplace by fully leveraging all aspects of brand communication. The product, packaging, print communications, and digital interface all collaborate to deliver a total brand experience, reinforcing strategic and experiential equities through every exposure. With discipline and constancy of purpose, equity-building opportunities are identified and design strategies are articulated and managed through technical and logistical excellence.

Leadership brands leverage this holistic approach to equity stewardship, creating sustainable momentum through repetition and context and, integrating verbal and visual elements that serve to establish a brand's image and personality over time—by design.

The in-store experience for Herbal Essence goes beyond facilitating the purchase to deliver an image that is engaging, compelling, and proprietary.

PRINCIPLE 3: INNOVATE

There is no longer a thing known as a mature business. Therefore, the first two leadership principles are not enough. Leadership brands are committed to innovation as a fundamental component of their culture. They are moving targets.

At one time or another, coffee, disposable diapers, skin care, and many other consumer-goods categories were deemed mature. Today's dynamic marketplace is different. Either the leading brand innovates or an upstart joins the competition and reinvents the category. Witness Starbucks's reinvention of coffee as a vivid example of a category that was void of innovation for decades and then its sudden shift into a new direction because of a new brand concept.

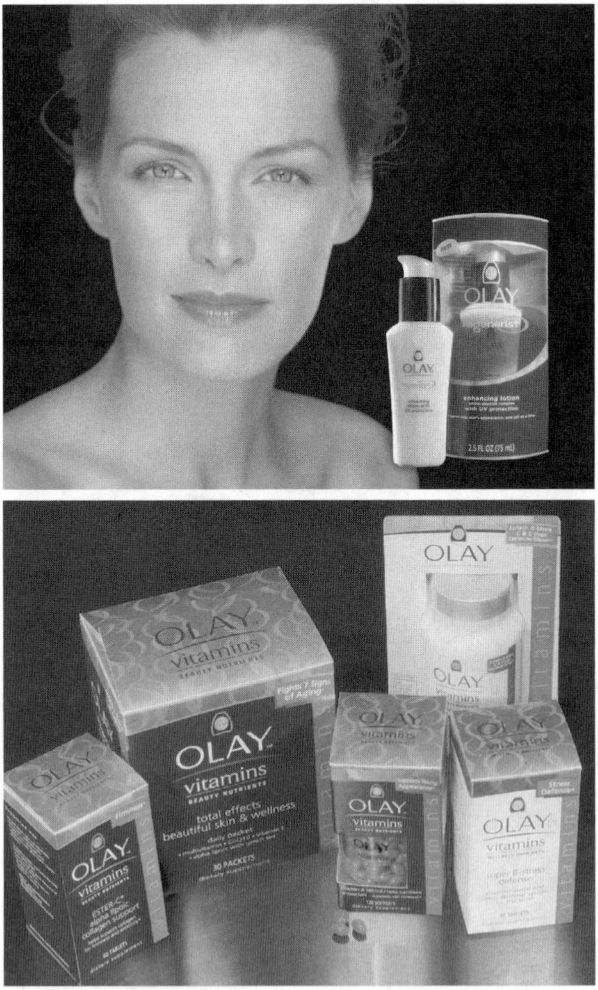

Innovation has allowed Olay to evolve into many product categories. Successfully communicating both science and beauty, the design franchise supports the brand's culture of innovation.

Innovation is, therefore, the lifeblood of leadership brands today. The Olay brand, competing in another category that seemed staid and mature, shows the commercial value of innovation. Innovative thinking and technological advances have allowed Olay to evolve into product categories far beyond the product once known as Grandma's pink beauty fluid.

Olay's introduction of a new formula under the name Total Effects repositioned Olay as a brand that promises a lifetime of beautiful skin. The benefits of Total Effects went far beyond moisturizing and into the realm of repair. With its recent introduction of Regenerist, Olay ventured into yet another area of skin care, improving skin through a serum that regenerates the skin's production of collagen and elastin.

As technological advances offer the possibility of new product innovation and as attitudes toward skin care continue to evolve, it becomes possible to consider additional areas of growth. Asian women and many women in the American and European markets believe that beautiful skin is primarily a byproduct of proper diet and a healthy lifestyle. By repositioning Olay as a brand that fights aging, it is possible to consider offering dietary supplements such as vitamins and other products that support a healthy lifestyle under the Olay name.

The design franchise reflects this combination of technological enhancements, while establishing a beauty aesthetic that is inspirational. Structure and graphics combine to deliver an authoritative yet elegant presence. Successfully communicating on dimensions of both science and beauty, the design franchise supports the brand culture of innovation.

A culture of innovation has allowed Olay to extend the brand into many new areas. From a humble beginning, the Olay business is approaching two billion dollars in annual revenue. Bringing new ideas to a brand builds leadership.

PRINCIPLE 4: CONNECT EMOTIONALLY

Leadership brands have empathy. They connect with their consumers not simply by meeting their rational needs, but by addressing the emotional context of the need, as well.

Emotion is the single most influential aspect common to all leadership brands today. Indeed, it's a component of all the principles mentioned above. Whether it relates to developing brand strategies that are meaningful, design expressions that are inspiring, or innovation strategies that deliver enhanced value, emotion is a powerful component leveraged by leadership brands across a spectrum of business categories.

Although highly emotive and sensorial categories, such as beauty care and confection, have traditionally relied on emotion to motivate, categories such as technology have increasingly recognized the power of emotional pull. There is a place for emotion in all brand-building practices today.

Telecommunications is a prime example of a category that is faced with the challenges of differentiation. Faced with today's convergent feature sets, all mobile phones struggle to break through this increasingly homogeneous category. What the industry calls "feature creep" does not drive meaningful differentiation; in fact, it annoys consumers who find technical complexity tedious. By tapping into the emotional power of branding and design, visual and verbal communication cues can be leveraged instead

The Samsung design franchise establishes an image consistent with intuitive navigation and personal style.

to deliver a unique sense of personal style. Functionality is no longer enough. Consumers now have many choices, and leadership brands understand how to leverage emotion to facilitate consumer choice.

Samsung successfully achieved this by establishing an image that spoke directly to intuitive navigation and innovation. By establishing a provocative aesthetic that celebrated the handset as a statement of personal style, the overall impression of the brand was one of leading technology and an accessory to one's personal taste.

Brands have the ability to influence and enhance people's lives. They provide a means of personal association—of internal reflection, as well as of outward projection, of self-image. Emotional brands not only support who we are, but also provide a tangible means of transformation into what we aspire to be.

By leveraging emotional power, leadership brands build enduring relationships among consumers and their products. By identifying and delivering on the most compelling aspects of consumer needs and wants, these brands provide maximum emotional relevance to consumers, fostering a context of empathy, personal trust, and loyalty. Leadership brands connect best through the heart, and are supported with the mind.

Leadership Principles

Over decades, these principles have served a spectrum of brands in my caseload. I observe the same characteristics in other leadership brands I study. Leadership brands work against a well-articulated and inculcated brand strategy. That strategy fully leverages the power of design. Further, a leadership brand establishes a culture of innovation and, most important, it connects emotionally with consumers.

The result for a leadership brand is a winning proposition the market readily understands, embraces, and rewards.

Chapter 10

Let's Brandjam to Humanize Our Brands

by Marc Gobé, President, Emotional Branding, LLC

Using jazz as a metaphor, Marc Gobé explores how the instinctive nature of creative processes and design can generate powerful brand solutions that resonate with consumers by connecting a valued product with a person's senses and emotions. To support such outcomes, Gobé advocates the establishment of interdisciplinary "brandjam centers" and research that reveals why people make purchases rather than what they purchase.

"In a century rife with the predictable, the dehumanizing, the dispiriting, jazz affirmed the fresh, the human, the hopeful, and it came to represent humanity at its best."
—JOHN EDWARD HASSE, JAZZ: THE FIRST CENTURY

DESIGN IS TO branding what jazz is to music: a new language of wonderful emotional experiences that unites brands with audiences. Design humanizes brands, stimulating our senses and feelings, and celebrates the power of collaboration and improvisation. But this was not always the case. The marketing of the twentieth century celebrated factories, rationality, and homogeneity. "You can have my cars in any color, as long as it is black," declared Henry Ford, while more recently, Theodore Levitt saw a world that would be overtaken by "a confident global imagination that sees the world as a single marketplace entity."[1] Paul Rand, one of the most influential designers of the last century and creator of the IBM logo, claimed that "modernism ... means integrity, it means honesty, it means the absence of sentimentality and the absence of nostalgia."[2] People then were perceived as a subservient mass of consumers that could easily be manipulated and their consumption habits regulated to fit a business production model. Design in that world had a functional role—to facilitate production. It was not thought of as a brand-building tool, required to inspire people's senses and emotions.

We are living in a world of commodity.

Welcome now to the postmodern "emotional economy," in which people are clamoring for more interaction with their brands. It is a new world of opportunities for marketers, but also a complex world, one to which branding has been slow to respond. Most corporations are still operating under the old paradigm, forgetting to take the new consumer into consideration. We can still see corporations managing their brands through disconnected departments offering splintered communications that weaken a brand's message. My new book, *Brandjam,* addresses this issue by proposing that, unless branding professionals and consumers start thinking together, the opportunity to truly innovate—by creating products that satisfy unmet emotional needs—will be missed. In *Brandjam,* I support the theory that it is critical to bring these diverse teams together to leverage their strength: for marketers to bring out their inner designers, for researchers to probe deeper and unveil the emotions and feelings that make people happy, and for advertisers to celebrate good products that sell themselves.

The legacy of the industrial age needs to be reversed. It has led to the generic sea of sameness that tends to characterize most products in the marketplace; it illustrates the vast cultural divide between the business world, which craves certainty and mass productivity, and the world of consumers, who seek emotional and individual experiences. As part of the heritage of the Industrial Age, the world of business is still generally averse to

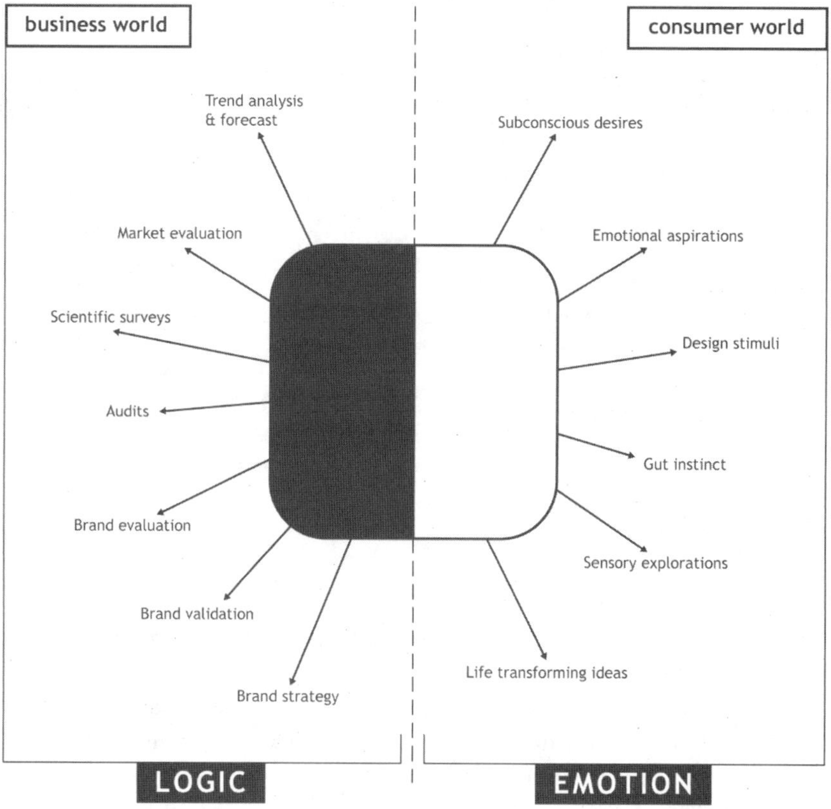

The business world needs logic, while the consumer world is driven by emotion. Brandjamming is the powerful idea that reconnects both worlds.

risk and innovation. It relies on what has worked in the past to benchmark strategies for the future—a sure way to miss an evolving consumer. It has surrounded itself with strategic tools, such as market evaluation, brand validation techniques, and brand strategies, that reflect the logical culture of the corporate ethos and miss the greater emotional understanding of customers' aspirations. The reality is that brands no longer belong to corporations but to people who vote for them with their wallets in a new consumer democracy. A new language needs to be created to link brands with people's more intimate needs. A new emotional engagement ought to become the new contract between marketers and their customers. And this language is design. Design, not unlike jazz, is innovation in action; it stimulates people's senses and emotions to create preferences.

COCA-COLA'S NEW WAVE

In 2000, Coca-Cola selected Desgrippes Gobé to redesign the Coca-Cola brand with visual graphics inspiring to a new generation of untapped cola enthusiasts. Our

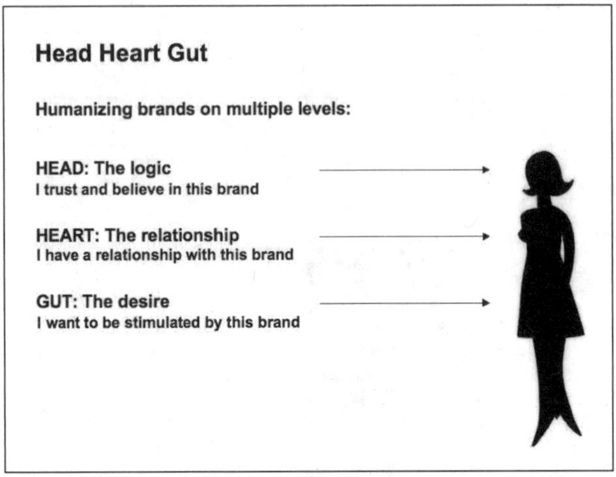
Head Heart Gut
Humanizing brands on multiple levels:
HEAD: The logic
I trust and believe in this brand
HEART: The relationship
I have a relationship with this brand
GUT: The desire
I want to be stimulated by this brand

Humanizing brands means humanizing the process by which we look at brands.

challenge was to humanize the product's iconography in new, more powerful emotional ranges.

Our new emotional model dictated a design that responded uniquely to consumers' life moments. We recognized and leveraged the way consumers respond to brands differently at different times throughout their lives, and also at unique sites. Vending machines, billboards, delivery trucks, blogs, sporting events, beach placement, retail environments—each elicits unique matrices of expectation and engagement. Graphics would be tailored for consumers according to our now famous emotional lens: an emotional need to be reassured (head), the desire to be socially and culturally involved (heart), and the craving for visceral engagement (gut). Enhancing the gut aspect of the brand was one means of reconnecting it to youth in a refreshing way. To that effect, we worked with Synovate Censydiam, a consumer insight group from Antwerp, Belgium, that probes consumers' motivations and satisfaction in relation to specific products within the context of human emotions.

In evaluating the brand's visual assets, we realized there was a powerful but abandoned icon that emotionally trumped all others—the Dynamic Ribbon. This powerful, abstract visual icon, created in the 1970s, was truly a brilliant idea; it almost suggested the action painting of a Jackson Pollock in its sprawling, dynamic flight, and was a predecessor to the Nike "swoosh." We recommended bringing back this icon but evolving and energizing it to sensually and emotionally connect with today's youth markets across the globe, particularly with the addition of effervescent bubbles to enhance the connotation of refreshment.

We were also spending countless days in Coca-Cola's Atlanta archives reviewing libraries of the brand's history. Tracing out the brand's myriad visual iterations, the color yellow kept dancing before our eyes. It appeared on delivery crates in the 1930s, promotional materials in the 1940s, and even actresses' dresses in the 1950s. Instinctively and intuitively, the team became excited about the idea of bringing yellow back into the visual narrative.

How That Little Bit of Yellow Jazzed Up the Brand

The new "Coca-Cola yellow" was used to highlight the brand's packaging, making it more energetic but also reframing and foregrounding Coca-Cola's "full red." Yellow helped to differentiate the dominant red and made it more inspiring. Moreover, the touch of yellow brought a surprising energy and optimism that enhanced the imagery and packaging. Though it was difficult to measure or demonstrate objectively, our design team felt the color's power and believed it might have found the "gut" translation of the brand we were looking for.

The new design had a far greater impact than anticipated. Because consumers responded so well initially, the new design also helped shift the internal culture at Coca-Cola, opening doors for people to innovate within the company. That little bit of yellow, backed by a floating ribbon, unleashed the energy native to the brand. This emotional design did not reinvent the brand; but it released the latent potential within its image, its audience, and its company. In short, the emotional energy of the brand was brought to life.

The new design had a greater impact than we had ever imagined.

I never felt at any point that we were designing a new packaging system; instead, I felt that we were leveraging the design process to see how much potential for innovation was inherent in the brand. The process helped the company's management team to articulate its belief that Coca-Cola was not fully leveraging its emotional capital and to rethink how to connect the brand with the youth market in particular.

From Yellow to Fashion Hero

Less than a year after the new can's launch, I was bowled over to receive a copy of *Vogue Australia* featuring a model on the cover holding the new Coke can. She was wearing the yellow and red colors of the can. The design had itself become a fashion statement! Inside the magazine, a four-page pictorial featured this same model with yellow and red fashion accessories, likewise modeled after the new can.

Model at John Galliano ready-to-wear fashion show. It was the ultimate fashion statement.

Three months later, the fall 2004 ready-to-wear collection runway show by John Galliano featured the new Coca-Cola can design decorating the hair of at least three of the models. Likewise, the color scheme for the makeup and accessories was Coke yellow and red! In this fleeting moment, my mind swam with delight. This was the ultimate consecration of Coca-Cola as a fashion statement and a lifestyle brand. It was now up to the rest of the organization to capitalize on this exceptional event.

A huge error in traditional marketing research is believing that consumer response and taste are fixed targets. Instead, they constantly evolve and respond to other cultural changes. Something like Vogue's designers picking up on the new design is, of course, good for the brand, as it serves to both recognize and amplify its design power. But more importantly, this kind of exposure helps cast a new aura around the brand that comes in the wake of its design. These kinds of changes, and in fact most of the important but subtle changes that create design success, can't be anticipated in advance, which is why intuition, emotion, and the designer's sensibility are, at the end of the day, the most promising resources one can have.

This was an unprecedented event for the Coca-Cola brand and the Desgrippes Gobé team. It revealed again the fundamental shifts and attitudes that connect a brand to culture, and it led me to the following conclusions:

- Design cuts through the clutter to reach people emotionally in the most powerful and transformative way.
- As the dominant form of communication, there is more to branding than advertising. This is because people seek a physical and sensory manifestation of a concept.
- Design is an emotional vocabulary that transcends words. It not only connects with consumers but also becomes the only brand language that matters.

The Coca-Cola cans on Galliano's runway are the product placement everyone dreams about. Those ideas, those connections can only be found through imaginative and intuitive thinking; the entry door to the world of the unconscious is only possible through the creative mind. In a world that is overstimulating, design might give consumers the ability to assimilate those changes, as well as the power to choose.

It is More Than Design Aesthetics

That color yellow in the Coke packaging unleashed one of the most exciting experiences of my career as a designer. The endorsement of this new design in the fashion world was the proof that Coca-Cola was reawakening people's admiration for the brand. Even given the powerful impact and buzz design can create with people, billions of dollars will be spent on broadcast media, overshadowing a new kind of message: design, still considered a minor investment for the success of the brand. So, is design just a fleeting part of branding, or is it a more robust way to build a more financially sound communication program?

WHY BRANDJAM?

The answer suggested itself to me during the writing of Brandjam. I had called Michael Francis, the executive vice president of marketing at Target, to ask him if that company's design culture saved the "brand" money on broadcast advertising. His answer was, "In a word, yes. Buzz [from their design commitment] or media attention has had a critical role in defining our brand with consumers. Far from mere fluff, buzz has had an astonishing amplifying effect on our marketing mix. It has helped us to level the playing field with competitors who may outspend us. It has also added a credibility factor that marketing dollars would have never delivered."

Advertising Expenditure (US) in 2005

FORD	$1 billion	TOYOTA	$776 million
SEARS*	$770 million	TARGET	$602 million
MCDONALD'S	$742 million	STARBUCKS	$36 million
MICROSOFT	$463 million	APPLE	$155 million
COCA-COLA	$426 million	RED BULL	$51 million
KOHLS	$401 million	IKEA	$86 million
BUDWEISER	$230 million	CORONA	$52 million
CADILLAC	$225 million	BMW	$137 million
EXPEDIA	$168 million	TRAVELOCITY	$85 million
EBAY	$129 million	GOOGLE	$8 million
UNITED	$78 million	VIRGIN ATLANTIC	$7 million
AQUAFINA	$27 million	FIJI	$2 million

Does spending more money in traditional media buy results?

Source: TNS Media Intelligence, copyright 2006.
Figures rounded to the nearest million; includes TV, radio, print, outdoor, and Internet (display only).
**Includes Sears and Kmart.*

Advertising spending outweighs its real impact and efficiency.

Still, upwards of $90 billion per year will be spent on advertising over the next four years in the U.S. alone and, according to industry sources, 30 percent of that money will be wasted each year. Moreover, it seems the brands that have made design a driver of their corporate and marketing culture, toward the ultimate objective of enhancing consumer satisfaction, spend fewer advertising dollars for the simple reason that their brand message is supported by the desirability of their products. The desires created by TV commercials often fall flat when people face the reality of unexciting products and the uninspired environments in which those products are sold. Clearly, the solution is to broaden the way we communicate with consumers and probe their emotions.

It is more than focus-group research. It is probing the why instead of the what.

The almost-exclusive reliance on a narrow and limited form of research focus groups as the major outlet for communication is failing to engage consumers in a more sensorial and surprising way. (In general, surprise is a brand's best friend when it is evocative of newness.) This type of research has had a role to play in fostering commodity products while reassuring marketing staff. Research that asks consumers to select innovation or judge design is a sure path toward the abandonment of the most promising ideas. We all know that Absolut Vodka and Red Bull were dismal failures in focus-group research. "People didn't believe the taste, the logo, the brand name. I'd never experienced such a disaster," said Dietrich Mateschitz, the creator of Red Bull, the energy drink now worth billions in sales.

"Only if you take people out of their comfort zone will you get meaningful answers," says Anne Asensio, director of advanced vehicle design for General Motors, and previously one of the designers behind Renault's vastly successful Megane[3] in Europe. In her career, Asensio has seen marketers making plans for cars they had not yet seen, mostly relying on focus-group input to help sell those products. "How could you have designed a car in the shape of an egg if you had to rely on research?" she asks, referring to the unique shape of the Megane.

If, according to industry sources, more than $7 billion a year is spent on research in the U.S., then we ought to revise how we probe our consumers' desires. "Why are there so many marketing failures if market research is so compelling and insightful?" muse Jan Callebaut, Hendrick Hendricks, Madeleine Janssens, and Christophe Fauconnier, principals of Synovate Censydiam, in their book, *The Naked Consumer*. Their answer is to stop asking people what they buy and focus instead on why they buy it.

Design is about consumer satisfaction. It is the insight and the message.

As I worked on *Brandjam*, I interviewed some leaders in the design industry to better understand the role of design in the success of their brands. From these interviews emerged this powerful idea: Design connects emotionally, but even more important, a void exists in knowing how brands should envision their new roles in an emotional economy. Design is about satisfying consumers' unmet needs through soliciting their senses, and that might be the key to its success. It challenges and stimulates marketers while wowing consumers.

Chris Bangle, director of group design for BMW, likes to say that great ideas are not always understood at first. He believes that "people need to feel your conviction." What else but design can convey such a conviction in the most authentic way? Design might be the proof of the human touch people are looking for behind brands, as well as the conviction that celebrates a company's vision.

Veronique Gabai, senior vice president of designer fragrances at Estée Lauder, claims that "the main hurdle to branding innovation is all those ideas people can't see; concepts that are not fully realized to be truly appreciated; research that informs on the wrong emotions and creates resistance to change." What Gabai means is that there is no live connection today among consumers and marketers, researchers, brand consultants, and advertisers. The human and sensory factor is nonexistent; ideas are not visualized to be brought to their full expression; everybody moves arrogantly to his or her own beat in a dissonant and disconnected fashion, creating loud messages but little brand harmony. The consumer suffers.

THE BRANDJAM CENTER

Great ideas don't happen in a vacuum. Brands, like jazz musicians, need to engage in some serious jam sessions, bringing together all the players to humanize their brands. Consumers, marketers, branding professionals, research organizations, and creative visionaries need to work in unison to connect brands with people emotionally. We need to pull together all those groups and disciplines around new techniques and vocabularies that integrate the science of branding with its creative and inspirational spirit. By bridging the gap, we reconcile both the logical and the emotional aspects of a brand message. We have to get to the point where the design process is recognized as strategic thinking; we have to bring out the inner designer in businesspeople to challenge the way we create and communicate brands. But brandjam requires a physical place; we need to create incubators for new ideas, ways to look at branding strategies in a more intuitive fashion. I call these creative centers brandjam centers.

- Brandjam centers validate the theory that the creative process is stronger when it is part of the corporate process and thrives when supported by top management.
- Brandjam centers encourage the process of brand innovation through a new vocabulary— the visual language—on an ongoing, long-term basis.
- Through a participative process, brandjam centers become stimulating centers and bonding places for executives willing to make change and ideation an important part of their jobs.

These brandjam centers could be internal operations or outside communications firms that operate fully under this model. Connecting the Coca-Cola brand with one of the most revered fashion designers in the world was the result of the passion of a select group of decision-makers on the brand side—visionary researchers and inspired designers coming together around a new process of emotional insight and visual discovery. Those breakthrough discoveries were only possible when great minds got together and brought them to life through the interaction of all the players. This process opened up the team's minds to opportunities they would not have considered before, ideas you can't get in focus groups.

Sometimes, this process starts with something as simple as jazzing up a can with a new color. In the right context, with the right brands, these kinds of ideas could influence the world, even if it is sometimes only the world of fashion. The role of post-modern brands is not to dominate but to stimulate. They are the impetus and inspiration to motivate people who then, in return, interpret the brand message to make it their own.

Believing that design is a shared inspiration, a "new media," and the most powerful new brand language is the central idea I developed in *Brandjam.* It makes the product the starting point of the connection with people. With the atomization of the media landscape, where technology plays a greater role, the product needs to be at the center of the message, as well as its inspiration. Inherent in the product offering, its look and feel, there needs to emerge a consistent visual and sensory manifestation of the brand's character. The product then becomes the starting point, the basis on which every communication program needs to evolve. The product is the idea and the experience, the truth well told and the best manifestation of an emotional message. When designed for an enhanced experience, the product also becomes the realization of a corporate culture, its vitality, innovative spirit, and ethics. If inspiring, the product will be a powerful voice, a brand's statement, and its commitment to bringing satisfaction to an audience and financial success to marketers.

Let's start brandjamming.

Interviews and quotes in this article excerpted from *Brandjam* (Allworth Press 2007, copublished with the Design Management Institute).

Endnotes

1. Theodore Levitt, "The Globalization of Markets," *Harvard Business Review* (May/June 1983).
2. "A Paul Rand Retrospective" (lecture, Cooper Union, October 3, 1996).
3. Quotes from design and industry leaders in this article are taken from personal interviews with the author.

BRANDJAMMING WITH BANANA REPUBLIC

Retailer Banana Republic hoped to launch a new line of personal care items, including perfumes, and the company tapped Desgrippes Gobé as its designer. Beauty company Interparfums was put in charge of business development. This meant there were three entities working on the project—located in San Francisco, New York, and Paris. We needed to come together around a shared concept, a shared language, and brandjamming was the way to do it. All in all, seven decision-makers held seventy-one bicoastal meetings over a period of eleven months.

We began with a designer-driven workshop to help all of us brandjam around imagining the most seductive ideas. These collaborative sessions looked at the brand from a sensory and emotional perspective; they were the dialogue that nourished the creative process. An image would create an idea; a piece of material would reveal a name; sketches would provoke the intuitive intelligence of the group.

Words were used in the positioning work, but only as part of the poetry or the texture, not to rationalize the process. They were an additional note to the effort, a magical expression of people's emotions. All of us felt engaged—knowing that our contributions helped or that our involvement in the process would make our future responsibilities to the new product line more meaningful.

Brandjamming helped us look at the brand from a sensory and emotional perspective.

BRANDJAMMING WITH BANANA REPUBLIC

The result was a unique collection of products that combines rich textures, innovative ideas, and sensory appeal. From this brandjamming engagement, a creative richness that I had not seen in much of our previous beauty work seemed to coalesce into a brand narrative that reflected the rich heritage and the spirit of adventure that characterizes the Banana Republic brand. Fragrances with names such as Alabaster or Jade for women and Black Walnut or Slate for men emerged from this participatory creative discovery.

Although it was never tested with focus groups, the line is a huge success. Maybe there is some kind of universal wisdom that runs beneath our conscious minds, and it is design that helps reveal it. Innovation has a way of emerging when inspired by people's emotional states. Only by combining the logical mind of marketers with the intuitive nature of designers can such magic happen.

Chapter 11

Bringing the Future into Global Brands

by Tony Kim, Professor of Design Management, IDAS, Hongik University, Korea

In a competitive environment where product cycles are growing shorter and shorter, design managers need to identify "opportunity gaps"—unmet needs and attributes that can be translated into an innovation or a next-generation project brief. Tony Kim describes how this can be done and cites several Korean companies that have profitably implemented this type of forward-looking investigation.

WHAT DO BILL Gates of Microsoft, Jeff Bezos of Amazon, Byung-Chul Lee of Samsung, and other successful business people have in common (besides hefty bank accounts)? They were all looking for a share in future opportunities. Bill Gates was a Harvard student and thereby practically guaranteed a good job after graduation. He had an instinctive feeling, however, that there was an untapped opportunity lurking around software for personal computers. Gates quit Harvard and started Microsoft with Paul Allen, his long-time friend. The rest is history. Jeff Bezos was a rising star on Wall Street, a young vice president for D.E. Shaw & Co., the well-known and technically sophisticated hedge fund. But he, too, anticipated a great potential opportunity in the new Internet and quit his prestigious job to start an online bookselling business. Samsung founder Byung-Chul Lee was successfully running Samsung's Cheil Sugar and Cheil Textiles division in the 1960s. After years of long discussions with business friends in Japan, however, he saw the possibilities in the semiconductor industry and invested a huge amount of the company's capital in its semiconductor division despite considerable resistance from his fellow executives, who worried that this was too risky a move. That foresight and action have made Samsung Electronics a world-class electronics company.

Of course, all three entrepreneurs were also interested in increasing market share for their companies. Increasing market share is a visible effort. It brings practical profits and is predictable, whereas securing a share of an opportunity is invisible and visionary. The future is by definition not really predictable, and neither are future sales and profits.

Even if you don't think of it this way, designing a new product brand is all about trying to secure a share of a future opportunity. To achieve an "opportunity share," a new brand should be designed and developed with an eye to trends and consumer lifestyles that are just on the horizon.

OPPORTUNITY SHARE IN BRANDS

The best products are designed in a way that connects with the lifestyle and values of intended customers. However, the services that product brands provide to their current customers were designed and developed to satisfy the lifestyle and values of their past customers. Although these customers are still using the product brands and have become accustomed to the services they provide, life does go on. Consumers are daily exposed to social, economic, and other changes, and though some of these changes are probably barely noticeable, they make a difference, spurring trends that motivate customers to make changes in their lifestyles and to expect a different level of service. This split between current and expected service levels is defined by Jonathan Cagan and Craig Vogel as the product opportunity gap (POG),[1] in recognition of its possibilities for creating new brand and market segments.

PESTE FACTORS

Trends are formed by changes in political, environmental, social, technological, and economic (PESTE) factors. Understanding changes in PESTE factors provides better clues to future trend and future customer values and, thus, brand futures. Savvy companies can then use the product development process as a way to close the product opportunity gap. Figure 1 demonstrates how PESTE factors drive emerging trends and, subsequently, changes in consumer values that are then reflected in their future buying habits.

Political PESTE factors focus on global and local issues such as:

- The growing power of militant Islam
- China's desire to secure the oil shipping route through the Indian Ocean, and the U.S.'s and India's attempt to block that effort
- North Korean nuclear proliferation and the U.S.'s effort to hinder it

Environmental factors include such issues as:

- Water shortages

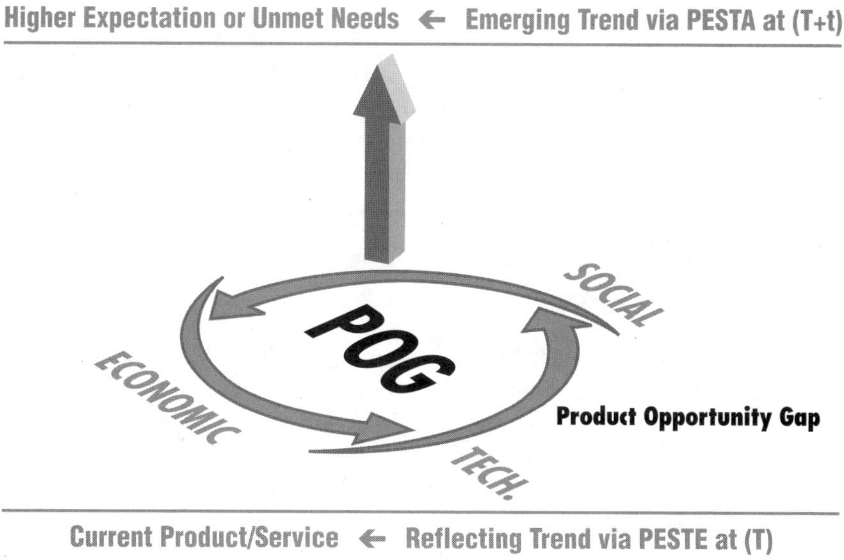

Figure 1. A product opportunity gap (POG) is a void between what is currently on the market and the as yet unproduced new or significantly improved products that may result from emerging trends. These trends are driven by changes in PESTE (political, environmental, social, technological, and economic) factors. Current products were designed reflecting emerging trends in a time (T) that has passed. However, consumers are already expecting a higher level of service or an improvement in product design at some time (t) in the near future.

- The need for waste reduction
- Global warming
- The rapid depletion of oil and other natural resources

Social PESTE factors include:

- New family and work patterns
- Health issues
- The aging of the population in advanced countries and the population explosion in underdeveloped countries

Technological factors include:

- Nano- and biotechnology
- The discovery/invention of new materials
- Robotics
- The explosion in digital media

Economic factors focus on:

- The discretionary income people perceive they have, or expect to have

- Psych-econometrics
- Widening gap between rich and poor
- Retirement of baby boomers

Where the development of consumer products is concerned, the influence of political and environmental factors on trend formation is less important than the influence of social, technical, and economic factors. The case studies that follow involve only social, technical, and economic factors.

CONSUMER VALUE OPPORTUNITIES

Customer value systems change as time goes by. For example, in the 1960s and '70s long hair was popular, perhaps in emulation of the Beatles and other celebrities. Now (conveniently, for many balding baby boomers), Michael Jordan and other sports celebrities have made shaved heads popular.

Here was an example of a gap between the service level of current products and the service levels customers expected as the result of a new trend. When Philips saw this product opportunity gap, it introduced the HeadBlade, which became an immediate success in the market.

Spotting future trends as they emerge is the province of such organizations as the World Future Society, which recently published a report offering up fifty-three trends that can be transformed into design attributes that could successfully affect future product development.[2]

To analyze consumer value systems, Cagan and Vogel developed a value opportunity analysis (VOA) that breaks down consumer value opportunities into seven categories: emotion, aesthetics, identity, ergonomics, impact, core technology, and quality. Let us look at the attributes of each category in detail.

Emotion

All the attributes listed below support a product's ability to contribute to the user's experience. However, emotion defines the essence of that experience, including:

- Sense of adventure, excitement, and exploration
- Feeling of independence, freedom from constraints
- Sense of security, safety, and stability
- Sensuality—a luxurious feeling
- Confidence, self-assurance, motivation to use the product
- Power—authority, control, feeling of supremacy

Aesthetics

Aesthetics focus on sensory perception. The five senses (visual, tactile, auditory, olfactory, gustatory) are all important attributes.

Product Identity

Product identity supports the user's statement about his or her individuality and personality.

- Personality: The ability to differentiate from the competition; connection to the rest of the products produced by the company
- Point in time: For a product to be successful, it has to capture a point in time and express it in a clear and powerful way
- Sense of place: Fits into the context of use
- Ergonomics
- Usability is the main focus of the ergonomics attribute
- Ease of use: The ergonomics of the size and shape of the components a person interacts with should be logically organized and easy to identify, reach, grasp, and manipulate
- Safety
- Comfort: A product should be comfortable to use and should not cause physical or mental stress during use

Impact

As was seen in the Enron case, corporate social responsibility becomes more and more important because it is connected with the customer's personal value system.

- Social: Product effects on the lifestyle of a target group, from improving the social wellbeing to creating a new social setting
- Environmental: Effect on the environment is becoming an important issue for consumer value; green design prevalence is one example

Core Technology

This must enable a product to function properly and to perform to expectations, and it must work consistently and reliably.

- Enabling: Core technology should be appropriately advanced to provide sufficient features
- Reliable: Technology should work consistently and at a high level of performance over time

Quality

The precision and accuracy of manufacturing methods, material composition, and methods of attachment is the focus.

- Craftsmanship: Fit and finish
- Durability: Performance over time

FORESIGHT, INNOVATION, AND DESIGN

To design a product that overpowers the competition, or to develop a new product that accommodates future needs of customers, requires foresight, innovation, and design. Foresight leads to the selection of an appropriate set of customer value attributes. Innovation is the process of lifting current value attributes to a higher level to meet the expected or unmet needs of the target consumers. Design implements that innovation.

The following case studies exemplify the use of this method.

CJ Corp.'s Het-Bahn Rice Bowls

In 1995, the design team at Korea's CJ Corp. believed they were observing a demographically driven trend in Korea—a trend toward more single people, as well as an older generation that would have a greater interest in eating healthfully. People would have more leisure time, and there would be an increased interest in life outdoors. Also, microwave ovens would be more available to the general populace.

Rice is, of course, a staple food in Korea. But single people—single men, especially—often did not have the time to cook rice. (There is also a prevailing belief that cooking rice is Mom's job.) Precooked rice was available in the marketplace, but as the CJ team knew, it was of low quality and was not particularly tasty. On the other hand, a tasty bowl of rice in a single-sized package cooked in the microwave was a possibility.

The CJ team, in essence, compared the service level of the current cooked-rice product to the service level of a satisfying bowl of rice cooked in the microwave. The new product was called Het-Bahn (fresh-cooked rice, in Korean). The core concept was "tasty and convenient rice cooked by mom." The brand concept was fresh and quality rice cooked by Mom—but with a more modern Korean image that included stylish people aged twenty to thirty. Each package contained either half a dozen or a dozen easy-open, single-size servings (figures 2 and 3).

Figure 2. CJ Corp.'s Het-Bahn single-serving microwave rice product offered a great improvement over existing versions, and filled a product opportunity gap that led to a number of product extensions.

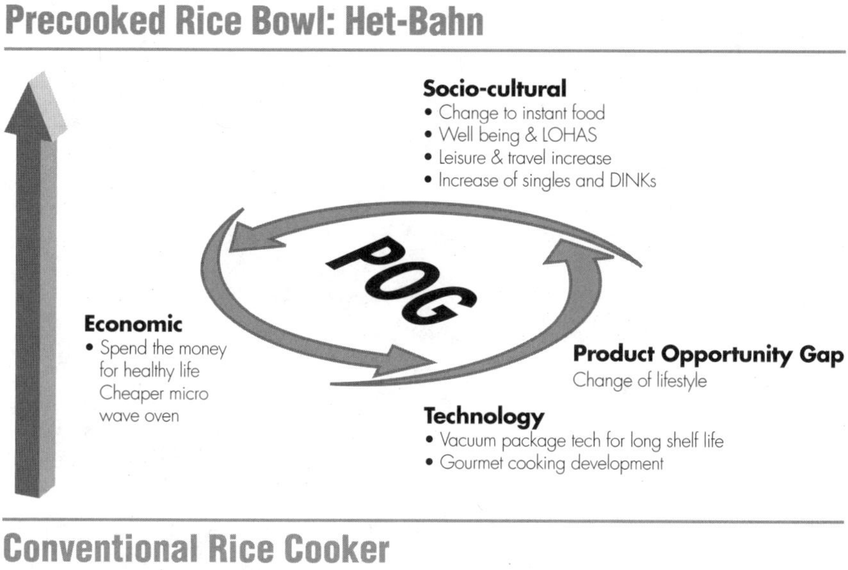

Figure 3. The POG that CJ Corp.'s Het-Bahn microwave rice filled.

The success of Het-Bahn in Korea opened up an opportunity to extend the product into different types and flavors of rice, porridge, and soup. Het-Bahn was so successful in Korea that CJ launched a CJ Gourmet brand in the U.S. in August 2005. The concept was "natural, premium, and convenient." It offered Het-Bahn with bulgogi (Korean sesame steak) sauce, as well as "crunch-oriental" and kimchi-salsa flavors. The products are now available at Gelson's and Mayfair grocery stores, and Het-Bahn has great potential to be a global brand.

Hauzen: An Integrated Brand for Samsung's Home Appliances

The market situation for Samsung Electronics's home appliances was difficult. There were as many as twenty brands of large and small "white" appliances, all of medium quality and with minimal identity. However, the Korean home appliances market was trending toward the larger and more luxurious, and Samsung's had lost their competitive advantages. A new product development team was formed. Their foresight was that the market was experiencing a new paradigm in living space, and appliances were beginning to be considered part of interior design, especially for singles and DINKs (double income, no kids) couples living in limited space. Advanced technology and convenience were very important.

Hauzen became Samsung's new integrated home appliance brand. A high-style, high-touch, premium brand, it features advanced technology, Zen-style design, and a sophisticated color remodeling system (figure 4). It featured the world's first nano cleaning technology for silver, touting 99.9 percent sterilization and a 92 percent reduction in electricity. Hauzen captured a future trend, as well as a new paradigm, for home appliances (figure 5).

Figure 4. Samsung's Hauzen home appliance line traded on the understanding that appliances were beginning to be considered part of the interior design scheme for homes and apartments where space was limited.

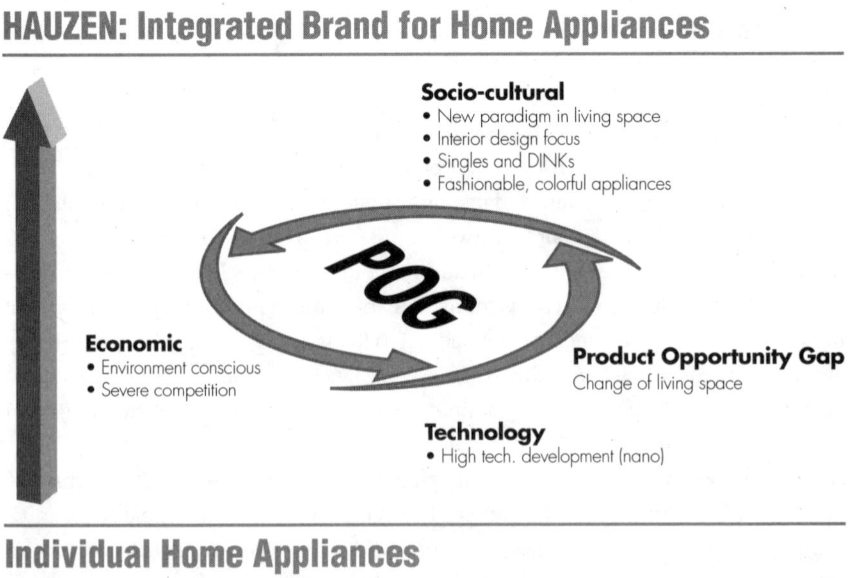

Figure 5. The POG filled by Hauzen's line of products.

STC's EI Solutions

In 2000, a Korean life sciences company called STC acquired a British high-tech cosmetics brand that offered biotech-based skin care. STC's cosmetics development team scanned PESTE factors and foresaw that there was room for improvement (figure 6). Consumers were annoyed by eye shadow that smeared when wet. Aging consumers were looking for premier anti-aging makeup and premium skin care. STC came up with Energy Water Innovative Solutions (EI Solutions), a line of products based on "energy water"—STC's patented bio-tech cleansing solution. EI Solutions makeup not only soothes skin but improves skin tone as well.

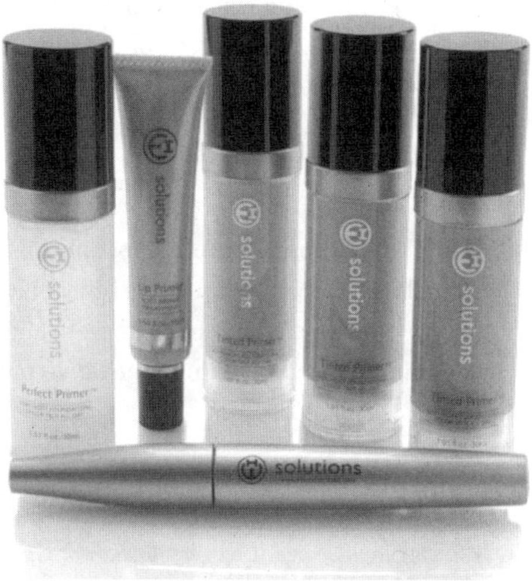

Figure 6. STC's EI Solutions Color Makeup was aimed at consumers looking for premier anti-aging makeup and premium skin care.

Initially, EI Solutions offered nineteen product lines and a consistent brand identity reflecting prestige, simple and global. The package image emphasizes advanced technology and unique skin-care solutions. Even though its technology was developed in Korea, the brand was produced and launched in the U.S., and most American consumers think of it as an American high-tech brand (figure 7). It has since gone on sale in the

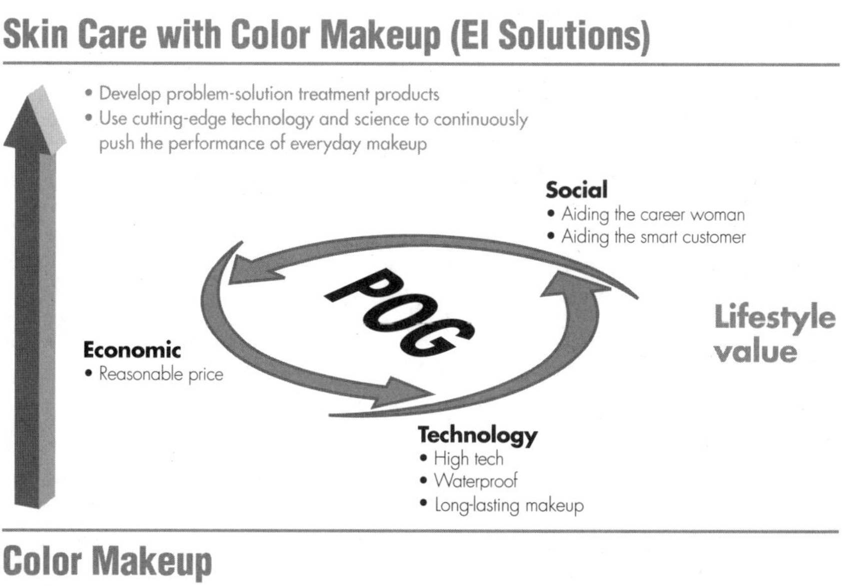

Figure 7. The POG EI Solutions filled.

European Union and will be sold in Asia, as well. EI Solutions was successful because STC grasped the unmet needs of consumers looking for color makeup combined with skin care. The company set a new paradigm in innovative cosmetics and managed the brand asset effectively.

CONCLUSION

World-class corporations focus not only on market share but also on opportunity share. World-class brands are developed by analyzing trends, done by scanning PESTE factors; interpreting changes in customer values through value opportunity analysis; and by designing and developing innovative products that transform value attributes into innovative design elements.

Endnotes

1. J. Cagan and C. Vogel, *Creating Breakthrough Products* (Princeton, N.J.: Prentice-Hall, 2002).

2. M. Cetron and O. Davies, "53 Trends Now Shaping the Future," *World Future Society* (2005).

Chapter 12

Brand-Driven Innovation

by Erik Roscam Abbing, Founder, Zilver, Rotterdam, The Netherlands
and Christa van Gessel, Consultant & Researcher, Zilver, Rotterdam, The Netherlands

As the nature of innovation shifts from the application of new technology to the delivery of meaning and value, brand and design become critical resources, as well as partners, in the development of market-leading products and services. Erik Roscam Abbing and Christa van Gessel provide an overview and case studies of this process as it moves from "brand usability" to "innovation strategy" to "design strategy" to "touchpoint orchestration."

THE ROLE OF branding for organizations and their stakeholders has changed considerably throughout its history. From its origin as a sign of ownership through the recognition of its status as a mental representation of consumer benefits, the brand has now arrived at a point where it represents the vision and strategic positioning of an organization in relationship to its environment. As such, the concept of brand has moved from being thought of as merely an addition to the offering (the logo on the product) to its acceptance as a representation of the culture, knowledge, and vision that inspires and strategically guides that offering. The brand, in its most developed form, has become a strategic asset for businesses, inspiring both ideation and action and helping them to make decisions and to frame the future in an increasingly complex world. This has significant consequences for the way brands are managed within organizations and for the role of design in bringing brands to life. We see four major shifts occurring (Table 1):

Table 1: Shifts in the way brands are managed.			
Aspect of branding	**Old branding paradigm**	**New branding paradigm**	**Implication**
Focus	Creating promises	Fulfilling promises	There is a strong new focus in brand management on touch-point design and offering innovation.
Ownership	Marketing	Entire organization	The "usability" of the brand for all stakeholders becomes increasingly important.
Place in process	At the end	At the beginning	The brand as foundation for business process has to be rooted in strong organizational and stakeholder insights.
Content	About the strengths of the organization	About the relationship the organization aspires to have with its stakeholders	The brand as relationship has to be based on insights within the organization *and* its stakeholders.

1. The focus in branding is shifting from creating compelling promises to fulfilling those promises in a meaningful and authentic way.
2. The ownership of the brand is shifting from marketing to the entire organization. It is even being shared by stakeholders outside the organization.
3. The place of the brand in business processes is shifting from the end to the beginning, especially in the processes that deal with innovation and creation of offerings.
4. The content of the brand is shifting from stressing organizational strengths to framing a vision of the relationship the organization aspires to have with its stakeholders.

The great opportunity that arises from these shifts is that the fulfillment of the brand promise has become a task for everyone within the organization, and innovation and the development and design of new products and services are great ways to accomplish this fulfillment. Brands, in short, need innovation.

Just like branding, the role and meaning of innovation for organizations is also changing. Innovation is often described as a risky process that is difficult to manage, but that is inevitable for organizations that want to stay alive in marketplaces where everything, from user needs to legislation, from technology to competitor behavior, is in constant flux. In other words, organizations are forced to innovate, but it's a painful business.

Our view on innovation is different: We believe it can be a very rewarding process, from both a business perspective and a human perspective. Just as personal growth stems from natural curiosity, the pleasure of learning, and the satisfaction derived from achieving new levels of knowledge, insight, or skill, innovation is the natural tendency of organizations to become better at what they do or to discover new areas of excellence.

Table 2: Shifts in the way innovation is managed.			
Aspect of innovation	**Old branding paradigm**	**New branding paradigm**	**Implication**
Drivers	External	Internalized	Organizations have to develop a strong and authentic vision of who they are and what they can mean to their stakeholders.
Attitude	Reactive	Proactive	In creating opportunities, organizations need a strong and shared sense of direction.
Role of design	At the end	At the beginning	Design thinking, methods, and techniques become vital parts of an organization's innovation toolbox, in both research and development processes.
Focus	Pushing technology	Creating value	Value innovation can only be based on a deep understanding of the organization's culture and potential, as well as the needs and desires of the people using its products and services.

This means that beyond satisfying external stakeholders and responding to external opportunities and needs, innovation should be driven from within. This has important consequences for the way innovation is managed within organizations. Again, we see four major shifts occurring (Table 2):

1. The drivers for innovation are changing. Where once the major drivers were external (new technologies, competitor behavior, and market metrics), now they lean more toward the internal (unique insights, vision, competence, and ideas). This does not imply that organizations in which innovation is internally driven are isolated from the outside world—to the contrary. The change we see lies in the way these organizations handle the outside world. External changes and influences are internalized and embedded in the organization's unique culture before being used as a springboard for innovation.
2. Innovation is no longer about reacting to change, but rather about proactively creating change. It is about creating opportunities rather than saving one's hide.
3. The role of design in innovation is changing from making the innovation look pretty in the end to being a source of meaningful new directions for growth. Design's function is to merge the various disciplines involved in the innovation process into a synergetic team and to combine visionary inspirational ideas with tangible and concrete solutions.
4. The focus of innovation is shifting from the application of new technology to the delivery of meaning and value.

Again, the opportunities that arise from these shifts are huge. We see innovation growing toward a discipline focused on creating opportunities for delivering value. This value is based on a strongly embedded vision and sense of direction, with design in a lead role as a source for meaningful ideas and a linking force among disciplines.

This implies that the innovation domain within organizations needs a common internalized vision of what the organization is and of how it is connected to its changing environment, in the present and the future. In short, innovation needs the brand.

And so it appears that the domains of branding and innovation need each other to prosper and to benefit from each other in a number of ways. It also becomes clear that design is taking a lead role in this convergence. The bottom line is that for brands to have maximum effect, they need innovation to fulfill their promise, while for innovation to have maximum effect it needs the brand to provide vision, focus, and direction. And in this dance of branding and innovation, design is the music that bonds the two in a shared understanding and a common goal.

A FOUR-STEP METHOD FOR BRAND-DRIVEN INNOVATION

While exploring this convergence of branding and innovation and the role of design in this process through project work for our clients at Zilver and through academic research (at the Delft University of Technology's master's degree program for strategic product design and at Eurib's degree program for the master's in design management), we started to work on a framework for managing it. We called the framework Brand Driven Innovation (BDI). BDI defines four domains of opportunity, which can be seen as separate fields, but also as phases in a process:

1. Brand usability
2. Innovation strategy
3. Design strategy
4. Touchpoint orchestration

We will explain each step in more detail in the following paragraphs and discuss what the phases mean in practice in two case descriptions.

Phase 1: Brand Usability

We approach brand usability in the same way in which product usability is researched by product interaction specialists when they acquire insights on how users interact with and feel about the product. If the brand is to be relevant for the organization and the end user, and since it is to be used by marketing and product development (figure 1), acquiring insights on how these stakeholders interact with the brand is key.

Another insight: If we want the brand to be used by designers, traditional models to capture the brand will not suffice. We want a brand format that is rich, uncut, highly visual, and authentic.

We have also learned that brand usability increases when all the stakeholders who have to work with the brand are involved in capturing it in a usable format.

Figure 1. The brand positioned in the center, connecting the organization with the end user, and marketing with product development.

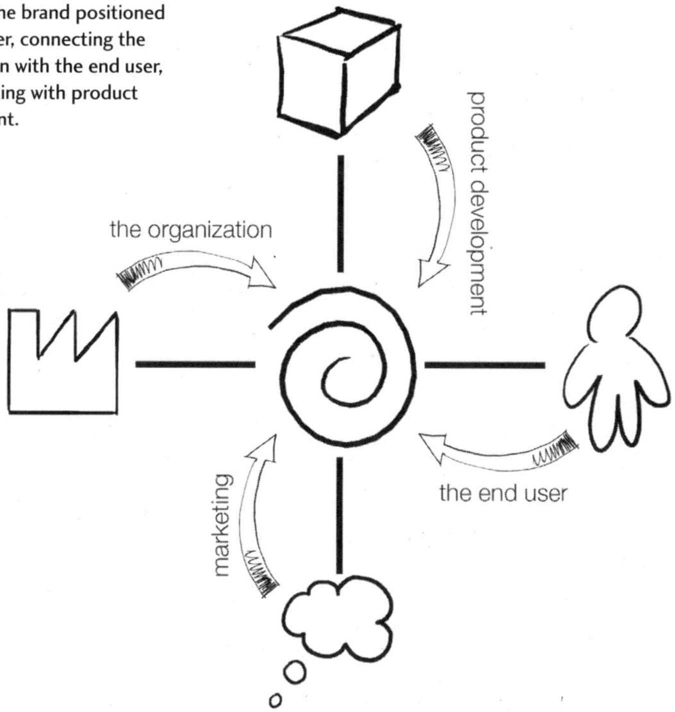

These three requirements (based on stakeholder insights, captured in a usable format, and high involvement in the process) have led us to the use of techniques from the domain of design research—that is, context mapping, ethnography, and cultural probes.[1] Note that this is research for design, as well as research by design.[2] These techniques fulfill the three requirements mentioned above, but are generally used to generate product interaction insights. We are discovering that they work equally well to generate brand interaction insights.

Phase 2: Innovation Strategy

Now that we have a brand that is understood and lived by marketing and product development alike, it is time to map out the innovation strategy that helps us fulfill the brand's promise. In this phase, the team explores desired, probable, and not-so-likely future states of the organization, its stakeholders, and the world in which it operates. It starts by looking at the brand as the relationship between the organization and its customers or end users. It then projects this relationship into the future. By using various creativity techniques, such as scenario building, storyboards, and road-mapping, we explore the relationship the organization aspires to have with its stakeholders, and how this future relationship can be brought to life through future brand interactions. The result is a common understanding of desired and possible future touchpoints, which can form the basis for short- and long-term innovation portfolios. Needless to say, this exercise needs to be repeated on a regular basis to allow for changes inside or outside the organization.

Phase 3: Design Strategy

Once we know what the directions for innovation are, we can plan how to make this strategy tangible. Using the brand as a source, we can plan a design strategy for turning the fulfillment of the brand promise into a tangible experience for the end user. We see design as "the creation of carriers for meaningful interaction." In this definition, we consider aesthetics as merely one of the pillars of effective design. To get a grip on the full scope design has to offer, we distinguish five layers in which design can play a role (figure 2). The layers correspond to the way the user comes into contact with, and experiences, brand touchpoints:

1. First the user encounters the sensorial aspects of the touchpoint—color, shape, and texture. We call this the sensorial layer.
2. Then the user interacts with the touchpoint by handling or testing the product, entering a store, or browsing through a Web site. We call this the behavioral layer.
3. By interacting with the touchpoint, the user gets a feel for what it does, how it functions, and how it performs. We call this the functional layer.
4. Next, the user is confronted with what the touchpoint is made of, how it's constructed, and what physical properties it has. We call this the physical layer.
5. In the end, after having gone through all the layers, the user distills a certain meaning from the touchpoint. A mental picture of the entire experience with the touchpoint is formed in the user's mind. We call this the mental layer.

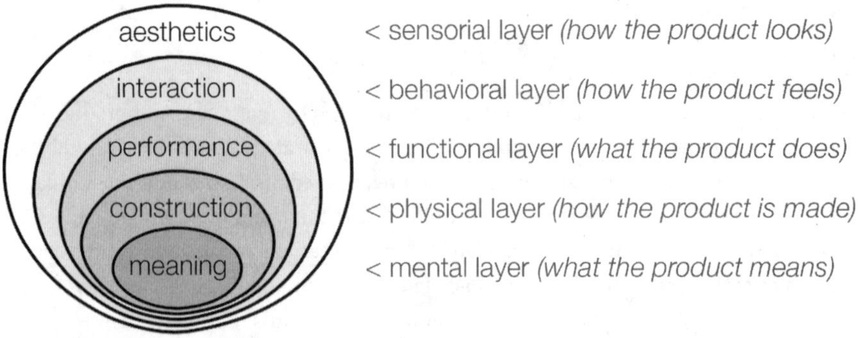

Figure 2. Layers of brand-driven design. The layers correspond with the way the user comes into contact with and experiences designed brand touchpoints. These layers are helpful in the use of design as a strategic resource because design plays a specific role for each one.

Figure 3. Touchpoint orchestration. Product design, communication design, environment design, and the behavior of employees all have to be in tune. Orchestrating brand touchpoints is an important task for design managers who use brand-driven innovation.

We think these layers are helpful in the use of design as a strategic resource, because in each layer design plays a specific role. When developing a design strategy for our clients, we define design guidelines for each layer, and we assign specific tasks to each layer as well, relating to the specific aspect of the brand it needs to convey. Next to that, we also connect design disciplines to each layer and define how each discipline can bring the brand to life in that specific layer.

Phase 4: Touchpoint Orchestration

The fourth level is the level of design tactics. The innovation and design strategy are rolled out in the actual product or service design and in all touchpoints surrounding the offering. Rather than striving for consistency, BDI strives for touchpoint harmony: Each touchpoint should convey its own version of the brand story, but it should be in tune with all the other touchpoints (figure 3).

In practice, this means we employ our design management skills to ensure that designers from various disciplines:

- Are briefed in an inspiring way, suitable to their tasks and expertise, and leaving enough room for dialogue and interpretation
- Are briefed with the brand as starting point and are given the explicit task of bringing it to life
- Are stimulated to connect to the design strategy from Phase 3 by involving them in discovering the rationale behind the strategy themselves
- Are briefed simultaneously and are given the chance to exchange experiences across disciplines, both at the kick-off and during the design process

Our task in this step is to orchestrate so that each designer exceeds expectations, and to let the resulting symphony be even more than the combination of the individual instruments.

CASE STUDY 1: BDI FOR A SMALL, HIGH-TECH B2B START-UP

One of Zilver's clients is a Dutch start-up in the domain of gas chromatography, a chemical analysis technique. The company is highly specialized and operates in an international B2B environment. Our assignment was to create a usable and inspiring brand for them and to develop the resulting innovation and design strategy. We then went on to manage the various people and agencies involved in creating the design touchpoints for the introduction of the brand to an international audience.

The Brand Usability Phase

In order to get a deep understanding of the stakeholders of the brand (the founders of the company and a selected group of lead users), we employed context mapping. The results of lab visits, the diaries we sent around, and the sessions we held were shared and interpreted with the client and developed further in a number of creative sessions. This resulted in the identity and vision of the organization and the identity and vision of the end user merging into a brand vision and a brand promise. Again, these were shared with and refined by the entire team (figure 4).

The Innovation Strategy Phase

In this step, we focused on merging the client's existing innovation strategy, which was impressively well developed, with fresh brand insights. In informal sessions with the client, we explored the future of the client's market from the viewpoint of the brand: How can we continue to build a meaningful and authentic relationship with our end users, given the choices we have made regarding our brand and given the changes we forecast in the market in which we operate? And we explored the way innovation should be organized in terms of partnerships, the use of existing infrastructure, and the ways in which different market segments should be targeted.

Figure 4. Diaries and creative sessions lead to brand insights. The company founders, as well as lead users, were involved in this project. They were asked to keep visual diaries (probes) and to take part in brand insight sessions. This created a lot of commitment to the new brand, both inside and outside the company.

Figure 5. Visual design guides for the different design layers related to product design. The collages use examples to inspire designers and to guide them in the right direction, without too explicitly specifying the end result. Left: examples for the products' sensorial layer. Middle: examples for the products' behavioral layer. Right: examples of the products' physical layer (see also figure 2).

The Design Strategy Phase

In this step, we translated the group's insights regarding brand and innovation into a design language comprising a design vision per discipline and a set of guidelines per layer (figure 5). We developed these guidelines based on our own experience with multidisciplinary design projects, but we also tested them with designers from different disciplines to ensure that they balanced direction with inspiration and that they were easy to understand and applicable.

The Touchpoint Orchestration Phase

This step entailed the briefing and orchestration of a team of designers working on the company's first flagship product, the corporate identity (including logo, stationery, presentation template, posters, brochures, spec sheets, and tone of voice for texts), the Web site, a set of promotional videos, a trade-fair booth, and even clothing (figure 6). The introduction was a success: The company won two highly coveted awards for innovation, and was complimented by many on the well-balanced and inviting look and feel of the entire offering. But what's most important, the company's founders are extremely proud of their venture, and orders come in faster and in higher numbers than anyone dared to hope.

CASE STUDY 2: BDI FOR A LARGE B2C MULTINATIONAL IN THE FASHION/LIFESTYLE INDUSTRY

Another client of Zilver is Mexx, a large internationally operating fashion brand. Our assignment was to explore innovation and design opportunities for the brand in the context of social networks and Web 2.0.

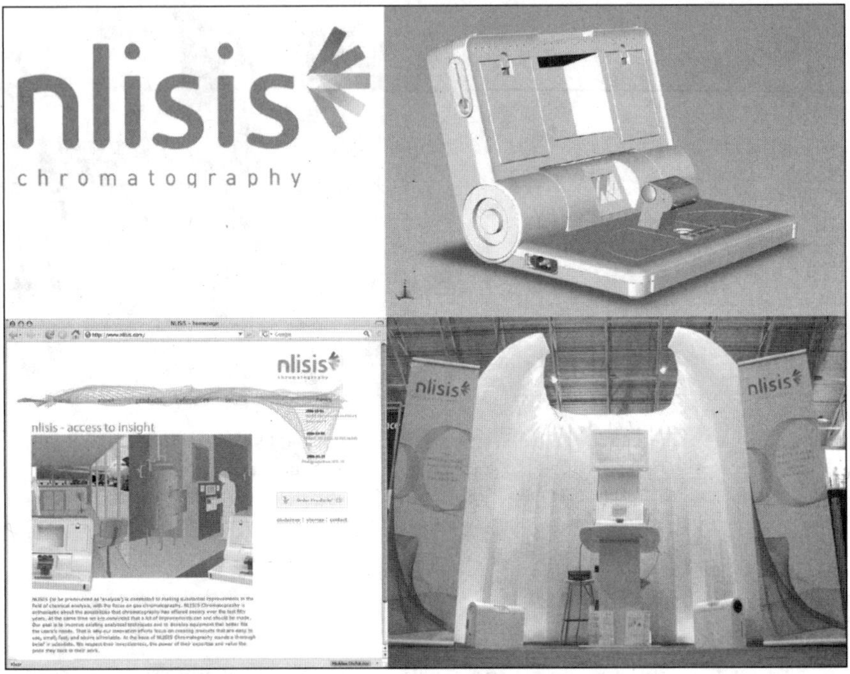

Figure 6. Various touchpoints that evolved from the NLISIS brand. Top left: the NLISIS logo, with the fan representing chromatography colors and the process of simplifying complexity through analysis. Top right: the first NLISIS product, a self-contained device for simplifying the process of coupling capillary glass tubes. Bottom left: the NLISIS Web site, with flash animation and introduction movies developed according to the design guidelines. Bottom right: the NLISIS trade fair booth travels the world to introduce the new brand and its products.

The Brand Usability Phase

For this project, we built an online design research tool (figure 7) that allowed selected end users to keep a visual online diary about their lives in the context of fashion and lifestyle. Designers working for our client get assignments that stimulate them to study and discuss the online diaries and their authors. They can post comments and react to the comments of others while browsing through the diaries. A result of this dialogue will be a rich and inspiring understanding of the brand and its end users, captured in consumer personas.

The Innovation Strategy Phase

This phase focused on the client's strategy regarding innovation in the realm of social media and Web 2.0, seen both as research for design and as marketing opportunity. With the help of Ralf Beuker (www.design-management.de), we gave structure to the opportunities for social media and Web 2.0 within the client's overall branding and innovation strategy.

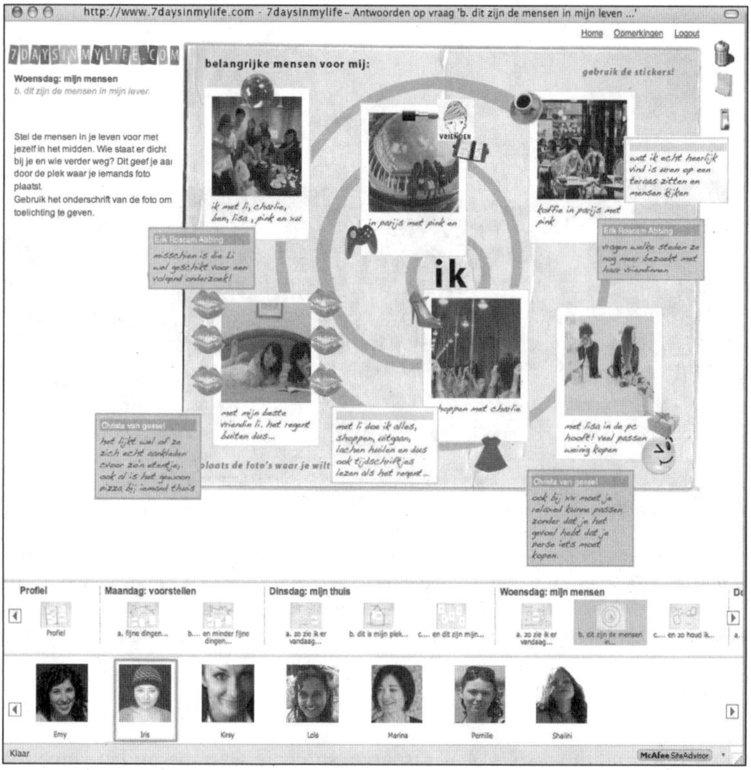

Figure 7. 7daysinmylife.com is an online design research tool for brand development. The figure shows a screen dump of the tool in operation. Participants in the research keep an online diary about their life in the context of the brand that is researched. Participants can upload images ("Polaroids") and text ("Post-its") to fill their diaries, while—invisible to the participants but with their consent—researchers and designers are allowed to comment on and discuss the content of the diaries with their own "Post-its."

The Design Strategy Phase

For this phase, we developed a tool based on consumer journeys (figure 8). With this tool, we look at the way consumers come in contact with different brand touchpoints. The tool helps to look at touchpoints as points of interaction that contribute to building a relationship. The sort of touchpoints to design, and how to design them, follow from the kind of relationship the organization aspires to build with its prospective end users.

The Touchpoint Orchestration Phase

Part of the work we do for this client is done within a multidisciplinary design venture called Designest. Designest was created with the orchestration of brand touchpoints in mind. It is formed by design management specialists and designers from product, graphical, and new media backgrounds. Most of the sessions for our client are conducted

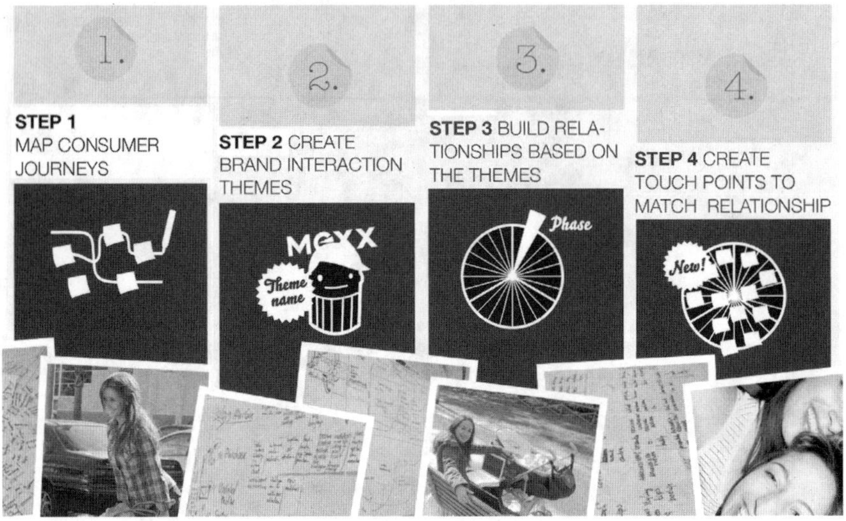

Figure 8. Our consumer journey tool. The tool uses personas and their "journeys" through the brand's touchpoints (step 1) to create brand interaction themes for each persona (step 2). These themes are used to brainstorm on the specific relationship the brand has with that persona (step 3). A brainstorm (step 4) then focuses on how new touchpoints can contribute to building that relationship.

with this group, and the results of all research, strategic sessions, and creative sessions are shared with this group. This way of working ensures that all disciplines work in sync and have a clear understanding of the brand, its strategic positioning, and aspirations with regard to innovation and design.

The result of this project is twofold: On the one hand, our tools and our approach are creating better alignment between outside design teams working for our client on various design disciplines. On the other hand, we have delivered concrete online interaction concepts that help our client to meet its end users and that help the end users connect to our client's brand in a more interactive and engaging manner than before.

CONCLUSION

In a world where organizational authenticity and end-user relevance are increasingly seen as key success factors in innovation and design, we see the brand as an inspiring and strategically solid driver for innovation. Brand-driven innovation can help you employ this driver to create a durable relationship among your organization and its stakeholders, and to forge a synergy between your marketing and product development teams. For design management professionals, there are huge opportunities in helping organizations fulfill their brand promise by offering unique and meaningful products and services to their end users. In our view, performing this task with both vision and hands-on pragmatism is what design leadership is all about.

Suggested Reading

Karjalainen, T. M. *Semantic Transformation in Design: Communicating Strategic Brand Identity Through Product Design References* (Helsinki: Ilmari Design Publications, University of Art and Design, 2004).

Roscam Abbing, E. "Brand-Driven Innovation: Fulfilling Brand Promise Through New Product Development." Dissertation for the Master of Design Management degree, 2005, Nijenrode/Inholland, available on www.branddriveninnovation.com.

Stompff, G. "The Forgotten Bond: Brand Identity and Product Design." *Design Management Journal* 14:1 (2003).

Online Resources:

www.branddriveninnovation.com

www.zilverinnovation.com

www.design-management.de

Endnotes

1. Cf. W. Gaver, T. Dunne, and E. Pacenti, "Cultural Probes," *ACM Interactions* 6 (1999): 21–29. F. Sleeswijk Visser, P.J. Stappers, R. van der Lugt, and E.B.N. Sanders, "Contextmapping: Experiences from Practice," *CoDesign* 1:2 (2005): 119–149.

2. Brenda Laurel, *Design Research: Methods and Perspectives* (Cambridge, Mass.: MIT Press, 2003).

Chapter 13

Branding and Design Innovation Leadership: What's Next?

by Phil Best, Vice President of Product Design and Innovation, Libby Perszyk Kathman

Saying the right things about innovation is one thing. Making it happen is quite another. In this concise primer, Phil Best translates his many years of experience into an innovation action plan—one that synthesizes creativity with brand and strategy. He summarizes an innovation process. He presents a list of innovation triggers. And he even includes a system of metrics for evaluating design proposals.

IN A PREVIOUS era, it was strategy, strategy, strategy. More recently, it's been innovation, innovation, innovation—throw in strategic innovation, as well. As design thinking process implications seem poised to sweep away some of today's celebrated innovation practices, we must be wondering what new provocation is on the horizon. Relax, I'm not planning to conjure one up. Also, don't expect any landmark case studies that reframe our design existence; instead, expect some relatively simple thoughts and observations from a relatively simple design farmer.

As Collins and Porras offered in their book, *Built to Last,* we need to be thinking about preserving the core and nurturing progress. When the shifts are too radical, it only serves to whipsaw us from one extreme to another—kind of like a roller coaster ride, where you get slammed so painfully into the sides of the seat and retaining bar that you forget all about the dramatic, spectacular motion and instead concentrate on making it to the end of the journey without further injury.

THE ROLE OF DESIGN

For those of us on the design consulting side of the business, it has not exactly been a smooth ride lately. But then again, I can't say that I ever remember it being all that smooth when the demand for all forms of basic design and new production capability was sky-high. Having lived one career on the corporate design side of the consumer products industry and now a good part of another on the consulting side, I've seen the ascendancy of design as a profession and the movement of design toward business competency. At the outset, we were about style and the creation of bright shiny objects, and dutifully manned our post at the last decoration station on the way to the marketplace.

Arguably, today there are only two strategies in the marketplace: You either succeed as the low-cost producer, or you successfully differentiate your offering by design in a relevant, meaningful way that is valued by shoppers, consumers, and sellers. As such, the theoretical role of design in business is relatively uncomplicated and straightforward.

The complications come with these two questions: Where does the core idea around a differentiated, relevant, valued offering come from? What is its relationship to this thing we used to call design? You know—the one with the stylish bright shiny objects. In our practice, we refer to the former as innovation strategy, and to the latter as design strategy. Somewhere in between resides the opportunity for brand strategy, and we hope to create a system in which there is a seamless flow from ideas to brand meaning and, finally, to how that brand or product or service is expressed and communicated to its target.

Putting all three aspects of this brand-building practice together provides validity in thinking about design as one of the primary idea generators for the creation of viable business platforms. Assuming for the time being that the manifestation of a business offering is realized in the context of a brand, that brand requires meaning, a defined expression, and then, given some success, a plan for continued opportunity development that sustains and grows the business.

In short: meaning, expression, vision.

INNOVATION LEARNING

Although the I-word (innovation) is everywhere in the design and business media, what I've hungered for over the long haul is a meaningful discussion about what it is and how to go about it in simple terms. I began collecting definitions, tips, and tricks a few years back, and I feel that I've amassed a pretty solid understanding about what it is and how to go about it.

Innovation is:

- Opportunity identification for sustained brand/business leadership
- An idea that delivers positive, discontinuous business results
- An idea that causes your target to think and interact differently with your business proposition

The
Brand-Building
Process
Innovation
Opportunity identification for sustained brand leadership and growth
Brand Vision
· Inspire the Future Consumer and Marketplace
- Core Innovation
- Product Innovation
- Commercial Innovation
Strategy
Unique and meaningful brand promise
Brand Meaning
· Understand consumer, shopper, market and brand
- Establish Brand Promise
- Establish Brand Positioning
- Establish Brand Architecture
Design
Express of brand strategy through experiential brand assets
Brand Expression
· Create identity interface
- Establish Individual equity assets
- Integrate through holistic execution across franchise
- Create guidelines for allegiant implementation

All three major types of innovation identify opportunities to sustain and grow brand leadership by delivering positive, discontinuous business results.

From my experience, there are also three major types of innovation to consider:

- ▲ Core innovation—the invention of new businesses or definition of the future state of a business
- ▲ Product innovation—creating new product features and benefits
- ▲ Commercial innovation—nonproduct, noncore offerings, such as framing or reframing an opportunity through positioning, packaging, promotion, and the like; exploring distribution and delivery white space; exploring competitive white space; breaking down barriers to trial and usage

Innovation can also occur as a one-off effort around a specific initiative or innovation and be part of a larger overall strategy (the S-word again). Pipeline innovation is a strategy involving multiple innovation efforts that are planned to sustain and grow a broad business base.

THE EXTRACTION OF INNOVATION PRINCIPLES

On the "how to" side, I found it maddening to digest one case study after another championing "great design leading to great business results," only to be disappointed by my inability to extract any principles that seemed to drive the innovation. By chance, a colleague sent me an article from the September 4, 2003, issue of the *Economist,*

To begin the discovery process, each workshop participant assimilates the background testimony given on the ten Triggers of Innovation.

As workshop participants process the testimony, they record and share idea fragments to generate additional thoughts and connections for the targeted ideation.

Ideation workshops that immerse a multifunctional team accelerate the innovation process.

"Expect the Unexpected." The article reviewed press and academic assessments of the success and failure rates of newly marketed innovations and why they worked or didn't. From this, I extracted a set of causal factors and added some additional context parameters. The resultant list I call "Triggers of Innovation." I have found this list to be extremely useful in generally evaluating the success or potential success of ideas. Inverting the list has also been useful in determining what background or reference information should form the basis of ideation pre-work.

The innovation triggers (listed below) should provide useful information, provoke and inspire designers and others, and help us figure out where to ideate. Insight mining highlights opportunity areas or pathways for ideation. Ideas need to be based on some relevant insight about connection to the desired outcome—otherwise they are just ideas.

INNOVATION PROCESS

So, let's start the innovation process. Pick your favorite problem or opportunity, or make it "blue-sky." I'll be focusing on the framework used in our LPK Innoventures process, which can be summarized stepwise as follows:

- Immerse for understanding
- Discover opportunities
- Create vision
- Validate with stakeholders
- Integrate and activate

Immerse for Understanding

My preference for immersion is a multifunctional ideation workshop intended to kick-start and accelerate the process of idea development. A team of experts and nonexperts, designers and nondesigners needs to assimilate summary "testimony" on the Triggers of Innovation to begin the design discovery process. Here are the triggers:

- **Brand.** What is the existing brand context (if any), and are there analogies in other categories that might inspire thinking around the idea work to be done?
- **Business.** What are the general business factors and considerations affecting the proposed development?
- **Consumer or end user.** What is known about the target consumer, and might we have potential opportunities with others? What are their rational, emotional, and primitive drivers? What is their desired life experience, and where might we fit in? How do they behave as shoppers, as well as end users?
- **Customer or seller.** What are the anticipated sales channels and motivating factors that would distinguish one channel from another and one retailer from another?
- **Competition.** What are the positioning, status, and direction of other brands and products in the target marketplace? Who are they, and how do they connect with the target shopper/consumer? How do they distinguish themselves? Are there opportunities in spaces among various competitors, or will the competition be more direct?
- **Client.** What business does the client want to be in? How might new propositions fit the client's business portfolio, and what criteria will be used to judge success or failure?
- **Problems to solve.** Are there known problems that this new product/brand/service offering might solve?
- **Technologies to leverage.** What technologies are utilized in our intended offering? Can we deliver initial or sustainable competitive advantage through delivery of proprietary technologies?
- **Trends.** What is the socio-demographic and socio-cultural context of this opportunity? What are the relevant macro and micro trends from local to global that might shape our offering and connect with our target today and in the future?
- **Connections.** This final trigger is about what we do with all the information, insight, and imagination that are generated when each of the workshop participants assimilates the expert testimony given on the other nine innovation triggers.

Since the initial immersion and ideation workshop might occur over the period of just a day or two, it is important that the expert testimony on each of the above triggers be short and to the point.

I have found that a top-line summary of each subject delivered in fifteen to thirty minutes is most appropriate to begin ideation activity. Balance the amount of time allocated to briefing on each trigger on the basis of the overall importance of the subject. (You'll probably want to spend a bit more time on the consumer as the primary target of the overall business proposition.)

In my experience, trends have historically been the most neglected area of ideation fodder. There is also a huge difference between trend information that reflects and describes what is going on in the world and where society is going and relevant, synthesized trend information that is pertinent to the specific opportunity being addressed. Trend information needs some level of synthesis and interpretation before it is useful as a basis for ideation. Showcasing trends as the final innovation trigger to be assimilated can be a great source of inspiration to the workshop participants.

Discover Opportunities

As workshop participants process background testimony on the Triggers of Innovation, they record keywords, phrases, random thoughts, sketches, ideas, and the like that they feel address some aspect of the project at hand. Posting these idea fragments for others to review and consider generates additional thoughts. Once ideas are more fully formed by connecting various fragments and targeted ideation against emerging themes, they can be initially filtered against project objectives and additional criteria that are expressed during trigger testimony.

Create Vision

It is up to the workshop participants to develop idea constructs in the form of words, pictures, stories, and experience prototypes. A good idea is not the idea of any one person, but rather the result of team synergy. In this way, we can capitalize on the diversity of long-standing expertise, as well as the newness of others seeing the problem or opportunity for the first time. We build support for leading ideas and align the workshop team around the core of each idea and how it needs to be expressed and communicated to others. The activities and exercises of a carefully orchestrated workshop encourage the attendees to "try on" and refine ideas as they hear, see, say, and teach each other the new concepts.

Validate with Stakeholders

Stakeholders refers to the shopper, consumer or end user, customer or seller. The ability to quickly make experiential prototypes and test them with stakeholders and provide them for client review is essential. Accelerated ideation warrants rapid prototyping, testing, and validation of ideas. Prototypes are often thought of as physical product prototypes; however, those fall short of need if they are not an integrated part of the brand/product/service experience. A robust experiential prototype needs to be manifest at each opportunity and intersection with target. Meaning: How does the target find out about the offering; how does he or she experience it before buying; what is the buying experience; how does the offering find a home; what is the in-use experience; how does the target remember and reflect upon the experience; how does he or she repurchase and ultimately promote the offering to others?

The client and the innovation team need to agree on realistic success criteria, understand the validation and testing of the ideas, and, perhaps most important, determine whether the brand/product/service is an appropriate fit for its business portfolio.

Consumer frustrations lead to an innovative solution in the Mr. Clean Power Multi-Surface wipes packaging structure, which features a user-friendly dispensing mechanism.

Integrate and Activate

Once ideas are validated, they enter the commercialization process. There are two primary entry points: branding and design. Sometimes, the idea has been developed in the context of a given brand or business and needs to be designed for launch. At other times, the idea also requires the development of a specific brand meaning and brand strategy prior to development of the design expression.

CASE STUDY

The landmark case study I denied at the outset is for you to discover.

Take the innovation triggers and evaluate a brand, product, or service that you deem worthy, either for its stellar achievements or for its grand demise. Take each of the triggers and assign a value, positive or negative, á la force-field analysis.

In case you don't know force-field, the scale is somewhat arbitrary, but it's a methodology for data-based decision-making. You assign each factor (in this case, trigger) a value either positive or negative, depending on its strength of influence in the overall model. On a scale of 1 to 10, let's say a strong driver is an 8, 9, or 10, and a moderate weakness is a –3, –4, or –5.

For illustration purposes, we'll use the Apple iPod.

Brand **+ 8**

Strong capitalization on the Apple brand promise . . . "everything just works" or "cool innovation" or <insert your favorite adjective here >. The iPod answers the most important brand questions: Who am I? What do I do? Why am I right for you? In addition, the Apple iPod design franchise delivers an experience that personifies the design expression principles of a brand that is engaging, compelling, and proprietary.

Business **+ 6**

Personal electronics and media market ripe for development of this technology and its capability to deliver a consumer "wow."

Consumer **+10**

First to market in delivering personal, portable media solutions behind a strongly recognizable brand name noted for excellence in consumer-oriented product design and a highly intuitive user interface. Apple's iPod delivers on the most important principles associated with life and lifestyle—an experience that is positive, memorable, and unexpected.

Customer **+2**

Available with little distinction in most mass merchandising and specialty channels. No specific retailer or channel variation offered to drive retailer differentiation. Two bonus points given for the Apple Store.

Competition **+8**

None then. None since.

Client **+8**

Although the iMac started the movement, the iPod made it a universal marketplace icon. Apple needed this type of accelerant to build upon its moderate success as the Windows PC alternative.

Problems to Solve **+ 8**

I want my music when I want it. I want it whenever and wherever, and I want a superior, intuitive user interface. I also want my iTunes music source immediately available to get the newest of the new when it's available.

Technologies to Leverage **+ 8**

Technology miniaturization and superior user interface.

Trends **+10**

Personalization, personal expression, and customization.

Extensive consumer research, cutting-edge trend forecasting, and analysis were used to create the innovative ergonomic Crest toothbrush with first-in-category gum massaging tips.

Need I say more? Okay, you might disagree with my values, but go ahead and assign your own values with whatever rationale you choose and I'll bet you come up with a winner. Now that you've got the methodology, pick a failure, a new market entrant, or simply an idea that's been floating around in your head for some time, and see what you come up with. Don't expect that every case will be as clear-cut as the iPod example, but do expect that brands, products, and services that do one or a few things incredibly well with no critical faults will also be successful. Others that do nothing particular well or manifest critical negatives will fade into extinction.

INNOVATION: CORE CAPABILITIES

After some experience and consideration, I have compiled my own short list of essential innovation capabilities, all of which we incorporate in our innovation practice. They are as follows:

- ▲ Robust process for accelerated ideation
- ▲ Holistic rationale for idea provocation and idea assessment
- ▲ Multifunctional opportunities for idea enrichment
- ▲ Trend assessment and activation skills
- ▲ Experiential prototyping methods and capabilities
- ▲ Mechanism for rapid research and idea validation
- ▲ Experience

INNOVATION—ORGANIZATIONAL BARRIERS

Here are some important "watch outs" I've encountered in my time. Note, however, that the last one on the list is the most significant. Nearly every new idea has some start-up investment requirements. True innovation requires the adoption of a belief system that sometimes must prevail in the face of other data metrics. Read up on the

Insights around consumer behavior and usage with food storage containers drove the patented interlocking lids and nesting bowls innovation for GladWare's Snap 'n Keep stackable design.

great inventions and business wins of all time and you will note that at the core of most of them lie belief, dedication, and the passion to succeed. Today's business leaders are often too afraid to move ideas forward without ironclad data proofs that they will be successful. In the end, they are the losers. Use your head, listen to your heart, and feel what's in your gut.

- Functional issues
- History and what we already know
- Internal idea competition
- Costs (start-up and ongoing)
- Accounting methods
- Politics
- Lack of guts

WHAT'S NEXT?

As long as the human spirit and the marketplace lives, I'm sure we will be inventing and innovating. Innovation is the commercial side of discovery and invention. Change is a huge driver of both discovery and invention. The world changes around us and we discover new things and we observe change and invent new things to deal with change.

What's next is that change is taking us to a critical point in human history. The tipping point of natural resources, in particular, will have dramatic effects on people, business, and society. Food, water, and energy issues will drive unprecedented change in the next few years and I'm expecting that people, business, and society will look and act very differently in the near future.

For some additional perspective, let me suggest you have a look at *Plan B 3.0: Mobilizing to Save Civilization* by Lester Brown. In the face of change, we will continue to discover and to invent and hopefully to commercialize that which serves us best. Hopefully, that which serves us best will be for the greater good, as well.

Part of our success in what's next will depend on our ability to both manage and lead design as a profession. If we are content to function as purveyors of bright shiny objects, manning the last decoration station on the way to the marketplace, we will likely fade into obscurity. On the other hand, if we step forward and deliver the orchestration of the total experience with a brand, product, or service in the context of our changing environment, we will likely succeed.

From a branding, design, and innovation perspective, scenario planning may be an appropriate vehicle to better understand who we are and where we are going. Consider opportunities to:

- Frame the system
- Understand the stakeholders
- Determine trends and directional forces

- Assess variability and uncertainty
- Look for connections and synergies among the component parts of the system
- Consider the extremes of possibility
- Express the scenarios in words, pictures, stories, and experience prototypes
- Develop research and validation methods to understand progress vs. scenarios
- Adjust scenarios and plans accordingly

Excuse me, I feel a new set of triggers coming on. . . .

SECTION 3

THE IMPORTANCE OF SERVICE DESIGN

SYSTEMS

INTERACTION

PROCESS

CREATIVITY

TOUCH POINTS

INTERFACE

INNOVATION

Chapter 14

Service Design: An Appraisal

by Roberto M. Saco, Owner and Principal, Aporia Advisors
and Alexis P. Goncalves, Independent Consultant, Business Innovation

In this thoughtful analysis, Roberto Saco and Alexis Goncalves map the landscape of service design. They define the discipline and key players and sketch its potential vis-à-vis growth and profitability. Saco and Goncalves elaborate on the multifaceted realities of this work with examples from Ritz-Carlton Hotels, Herman Miller, and Egg Banking. Then, they wrap things up with a discussion of key principles related to practice.

SERVICE SCIENCE, SERVICE engineering, service design: although not interchangeable, these are all terms for an emerging discipline that attempts to join the worlds of business, design, change management, and the service economy for a multisided approach to the introduction and sustainability of services. Though manufacturing has been the dominant logic in the business world for most of the twentieth century,[1] this panorama is changing quickly as the service sector becomes ever more prevalent, comprising 70 percent to 80 percent of GDP in many developed countries. And while there's an established consensus that "service is different" from manufacturing, practitioners and experts alike still insist on employing tools developed on the factory floor for use in a service culture. Service science, and more fundamentally service design, posits that we need to codify the language and artifacts of the world of service. In fact, we may need to create an entirely new language of service. The landscape in this arena is shifting.

While the more academic service science seems to have currency in major American universities, service design owes quite a bit of its origin to both American and British design consultancies, notably IDEO, and public institutions in England and Germany, such as the U.K. Design Council in London and KISD in Cologne. Service design not only accepts that service is different, but also acts on this premise by employing features that include cocreation, constant reframing, multidisciplinary collaboration, capacity-building, and sustaining change. A multitude of tools, many from the social sciences, are brought to bear on problems, all under the banner of design as an organizing principle and leitmotif.

For this article, we interviewed five prominent academics from the U.S., U.K., and Germany; we also met with three consultancies from the U.S. and U.K. (Engine, IBM, and Peer Insight) and looked into service design practices at three companies (Egg Banking, Herman Miller, and Ritz-Carlton). The reason for the variety of practitioners, academics, and companies was to allow us to sample the large spectrum of practices and schools of service design (for details, see Table 1).

ENTER SERVICE DESIGN

That design itself is in the forefront of public discourse is unsurprising. The extent and depth of the conversation, however, seem to be taking a greater urgency. And businesses in all their diversity are paying greater attention. Trendspotters and explicators[2] in the field of design point to a democratization of taste and to a wider appreciation of practical beauty, coupled with enabling technologies. Virginia Postrel makes the case that our society is gleefully immersed in a binge of fashion and style and that furthermore, this "prettification" is overall a good thing. For many designers, engineers, and architects, though, this claim is anathema since it counters their hard-won efforts at making design a problem-solving discipline. Moreover, interaction design and affective design[3] have

Table 1. Interviewees: Panel of Academics, Consultants, and Practitioners

Name	Title	Organization	Country
Mary Jo Bitner	Academic Director, Center for Services Leadership	Arizona State University	USA
Shelley Evenson	Associate Professor and Director of Graduate Studies	Carnegie Mellon University	USA
Bill Hollins	Senior Lecturer, Westminster Business School	University of Westminster	UK
Debbie Jones	(former) Product Development Manager	Egg Banking, PLC	UK
Oliver King	Director and Cofounder	Engine Group	UK
Birgit Mager	Service Design Director, Köln International School of Design	Cologne University of Applied Sciences	GERMANY
Paul Maglio	Senior Manager, Service Systems Research	IBM Almaden Reseach Center	USA
Fabienne Munch	Director Ideation Studio	Herman Miller Inc.	USA
Jeneanne Rae	President and Cofounder	Peer Insight, LLC	USA
Stephen L. Vargo	Associate Professor of Marketing	University of Hawaii	USA
Alejandra Vicenttin	Area Director of Quality and Productivity	The Ritz-Carlton Hotel Company, LLC	USA

come to the fore, with the first attempting to manage interface issues and a mediated world in which technology has become an extension of the human senses and the second bringing emotion and play into a rational design and engineering mindset.

But just what is service design? The Service Design Network, a loose coalition of academics, practitioners, and other interested parties, emerged precisely to explore this question.[4] Inspired by service design pioneer Birgit Mager at the Köln International School of Design, the network uses the following working definition:

Service design . . .

- ▲ Aims to create services that are useful, useable, desirable, efficient, and effective
- ▲ Is a human-centered approach that focuses on customer experience and the quality of service encounter as the key value for success
- ▲ Is a holistic approach that considers in an integrated way strategic, system, process, and touchpoint design decisions
- ▲ Is a systematic and iterative process that integrates user-oriented, team-based interdisciplinary approaches and methods in learning cycles

Service design, then, is fundamentally interdisciplinary and multipurpose. Relying on a designer's sensibility, it incorporates elements and tools from several domains to attain various and, at times, competing objectives: customer satisfaction or appreciation, designer satisfaction or sense of accomplishment, problem resolution, economic and environmental sustainability, and practical beauty ("beauty that works").

APPROACHES, TOOLS, AND PLAYERS

One of the first tomes dealing specifically with service design was Bill Hollins's *Total Design* (1991). When we interviewed him, Hollins downplayed individual tools and emphasized the organizational aspects of designing for services. In his view, the key operational question is: How do we organize for services? In other words, how do we bring people into the process of creating and introducing services? Bill reminded us that service design is more a practical craft than a formal science, with its focus on hypothesis-building and experimentation. That may explain the profusion of tools at the expense of consensual frameworks. As Stefan Moritz[5] has amply catalogued, there is no dearth of tools for the service design practitioner (see Table 2).

These tools are drawn from social anthropology, linguistics, market research, organizational design, and all sorts of quality management approaches, such as process management, customer experience, and "voice of the customer." The application of tools is situational and depends on the type of service design project, the resources available, and the objectives. While there are many frameworks, these have been developed for the most part independently by various consultancies or academics. And there is as yet no clear consensus for an overarching or unifying framework.

We have grouped service design players—institutions and individuals—into consultants, academics, and practitioners. The design consultancies serve as hubs or hives of

Table 2. Service Design Tools

Service Design Activity	Tools (sample)
Understanding (assessing)	Benchmarking Critical incident technique Ecology map Ethnographical studies Shadowing Trend scouting
Thinking (framing)	Affinity diagram Fishbone diagram Touchpoints analysis
Generating (exploring)	Body-storming Randomizer Unfocus group
Filtering (reducing)	Heuristic evaluation Personas Pluralistic walkthrough
Explaining (rationalizing)	Experience prototyping Metaphors Social network mapping
Realizing (building)	Blueprint Role script

service design activity as many have followed IDEO in the product>interface> service progression. Technology, they quickly realized, has blurred the boundary between product and service. A "product" like the iPod, for instance, is part product (device), part database (iTunes), part inventory (Music Store), and all integrated service offering. Besides IDEO, several U.K.-based consultancies stand out—for instance, Live|Work, Engine Group, and Radarstation. IBM, through its Service Science initiative, is becoming a major influence as it pools together researchers and internal consultants for an integrated look at services. From academia, KISD in Germany and IVREA in Italy took early leads in service design. Birgit Mager and her design colleagues and students at KISD are crafting a new generation of approaches and tools. In the U.S., Carnegie Mellon's Shelley Evenson serves a similar maven role by, for example, hosting the annual Emergence Conference, which brings together design students, academics, consultants, managers, and trend scouts.

Individual practitioners abound, although not many have "design" in their titles. Some practitioners may even draw blank stares should it be pointed out to them that they're in the service design business. Many are in activities having to do with innovating for services, customer experience management, service operations, quality management, or marketing services.

The design councils in various European countries, notably the United Kingdom, serve as communities of practice for product and service design.

RELEVANCE TO BUSINESS—OR YET ANOTHER MANAGEMENT FAD?

While the growing, yet informal, army of service designers is quietly preparing for the next revolution in services, you may rightly ask: Why should I care? Service design has been evolving for more than ten years; it is still a young field that seems to be on the verge of blossoming. In service design, we see the melding of the customer experience and experience economy phenomena heralded by various keen observers of changing market mores.[6] Recently, service design academics have undertaken research to address the challenges this new concept is facing. The design of intangibles and fully sensorial experiences are promising arenas being developed further. Service design practitioners, as a matter of course, have also developed other competencies, such as the integration of clients into the design process— which is especially relevant when designing services, since the clients in question are in any case already involved in production and delivery.

In our interviews with academics and practitioners, we found ample consensus that while services are central to the economy, they are not always as productive and satisfying as they should be—and, therefore, they need better design. Mary Jo Bittner, of Arizona State University's Center for Services Leadership, is emphatic on the role of service design and innovation: "To be successful in a given marketplace, a company needs to have a strong sense of service design. And while companies realize that a lot of resources go into product and service design, we still don't have strong disciplines in these areas. Companies know that service design is where their growth is, their advantage is, and their future profit is." Shelley Evenson at Carnegie Mellon's design school speaks to an integrated service experience and a journey of brands: "Think of traveling to a conference in Pittsburgh. You go through a journey of brands. There has been a tremendous amount of orchestration to bring you here: airports, airlines, taxis, beverages, food, electrical power, security, and so forth. All these services are aligned to support you in some fashion. Compare your voyage to the self-sufficiency a navigator like Columbus had to have in his day."

For those scanning the horizon, the signs are obvious. Early adopters that add service design to their mix of core competencies will have a definitive edge over the complacent and the laggards on the innovation adoption curve.

CASE STUDIES

Many well-known brands—Apple, Samsung, Pylones, Target, Shiseido—are keen on design and have made it a centerpiece of their company culture. We now look at three very different companies with an eye to how they view service and design, and consider some of their experiences.

RITZ-CARLTON HOTELS

The award-winning Ritz's perspective on service is broad in nature. Service is approached as "the total guest experience" staged before, during, and after a guest stays at any of the hotel properties. In this approach, elements like design, mood, gourmet experience, and service are all well considered.

- **Design.** New Ritz hotels no longer resemble European chateaus, as was common for those built before 1997. The modern Ritz in the Georgetown area of Washington, D.C., was built on the remains of the city's former incinerator, with an unusual meeting room at the base of the old brick smokestack.
- **Mood.** Mozart concertos no longer set the tone 24/7 in Ritz lobbies, as was the case just two years ago. Today, you'll likely hear a soulful jazz ballad by singer Lizz Wright, or the mellow backbeat from the electronic band Thievery Corporation. Ritz hotels will change playlists according to time of day to reflect the mood, a technique used by hip boutique hotels. Ritz has also moved away from huge, overbearing floral bouquets in favor of smaller, more artistic designs, another sign the chain is striving for more low-key elegance rather than old-world opulence.
- **Gourmet experience.** The chain is closing down most of the Ritz dining rooms and replacing them with destination restaurants that often involve well-known chefs such as Gordon Ramsay or Daniel Boulud.
- **Service.** Ritz can no longer justify its rates simply by offering in-your-face service. The company has retrained its employees to read guests' body language before addressing them. Staffers are now more spontaneous.

Experiments in Service and Service Design

In an effort to add flexibility to their standards, Ritz executives decided they needed a scenographer—someone who, as with a play, would help them direct "scenes" for the customer, but through customized service rather than through lighting or props. The luxury chain tapped design firm IDEO, which worked with it to create a set of scenography workbooks. Creative staffers at each property brainstormed localized service scenes and outlined the key scenes using a series of photos that told an evocative story. Scenes created by the team told stories such as a warm, personalized check-in process or a big night in, in which the executive chef might send up a handwritten note, a champagne toast, and a sample from the evening's menu for guests with restaurant reservations. At San Francisco's Half Moon Bay hotel, for example, guests are now invited to an intimate wine tasting at check-in. A key intent of the scenography workbooks was to communicate the principles driving the Ritz brand experience without prescribing the solution for individual hotels. Scenography workbooks created broad corporate alignment and encouraged local creativity all at once, a wonderful formula for effective execution.

Learning and Adapting

A critical lesson Ritz learned from service design is that in order to be effective in designing guest experiences, the following four principles need to be integrated into the design strategy:

- **Culture.** Create a customer-centered culture that identifies, nurtures, and reinforces service as a primary value.
- **Talent.** Use a rigorous selection process to populate the organization with superior front-line personnel and support staff. The impulse to care for and accommodate customers cannot be taught to people who are not predisposed to do so.
- **Development.** Constantly retrain employees to perpetuate organizational values and to help them attain greater mastery of products and procedures.
- **Measure and reward.** Systematically measure and reward customer-centric behavior and excellence in front-line personnel and support staff to enforce high standards and reinforce expectations.

HERMAN MILLER

When asked about the evolving field of services, consultant Jeneanne Rae of Peer Insight pointed out, somewhat counter-intuitively, "Looking into the range of players, I believe that manufacturers are going to develop and promote more service innovation than service companies themselves." As we look around, it seems Rae is on to something, for enlightened manufacturers certainly seem to be headed in this direction. Max De Pree, one-time CEO at Herman Miller and advocate of servant leadership, defined the first task of leaders as defining reality.[7] He could also have said that Herman Miller has been defining design in the office furniture business for several generations. Herman Miller, then, tends to approach service from a human-centered perspective, constantly assessing the problems that people face and the objectives they seek to accomplish. By focusing on a clear and concise definition of the problem or the opportunity, Herman Miller minimizes the risk associated with designing products that do not address articulated or latent customer needs.

Experiments in Service and Service Design

And yet Herman Miller doesn't define itself as an office furniture company, or even a furniture company. It has set its boundaries around people and human performance. Building on the company's historical grounding in habitats—the office, the home, educational institutions, and the healing arena—Herman Miller focuses on the performance of human beings in their habitats. Shifting the focus from furniture to habitats leads the company to new design spaces. The most recent example is Convia, a modular, programmable sub-building infrastructure system for electrical and data support that makes buildings more adaptable and changeable by the user. Convia seeks to change the way people design, build, personalize, and manage space, allowing for radically flexible habitats. Herman Miller believes that Convia has profound implications for the design and management of buildings, across multiple categories of use.

Another unique perspective about Herman Miller is that it sees itself more as an integrator than a manufacturer. In its search for solving human-centered problems around habitats, the company usually ends up exploring new materials. And because it is not vertically integrated from a manufacturing standpoint, it is able to do material explorations somewhat freely. This freedom allows designers a fairly free hand to take up new ideas and experiment with any material or process that resolves the problem in question. Examples are the Pellicle material developed jointly with DuPont specifically for the aerated seat-pan material in the Aeron chair, and the structural material that allows the Kiva screen to stand still or move freely.

Learning and Adapting

Herman Miller is not your typical manufacturer. As it moves from designing furniture to shaping habitats, it refashions and reframes product design to living or service design. From Herman Miller, we garnered several lessons:

- ▲ **A culture of risk-taking.** Although Herman Miller believes that good design results from thoughtful research into the complexities of customers' needs, exploration into materials and processes, and responding to social and economic trends, risk-taking is just as important. The company strives to maintain an appetite for risk. As it has grown larger and become responsible for more equity, the pressure to minimize risk has mounted. Getting behind promising new products and services, however, remains a risk it is happy to embrace.
- ▲ **Working with outside designers.** Herman Miller is known for having partnered with influential furniture and fabric designers and for relying on an external creative network. The company's secret for working well with them is: 1) knowing how to put the right constraints in place so that you end up not only with a unique design statement, but also with a solution that solves real problems for customers and has commercial value; and 2) being willing to follow and give oneself over to outside designers—not to lose oneself necessarily, but to be open to follow them to surprising places.
- ▲ **Refrain from quick judgments.** After giving outside designers an outline of a perceived problem, Herman Miller allows these designers to share their insights and enables them to bring their own gifts to the search for a solution. The company monitors them on their journey without judging too quickly on the basis of the first physical appearance or sketches produced. Instead, it teases out the essence or value of the communication, knowing this is but one iteration in the total design process.

EGG BANKING, PLC

The customer is at the heart of this U.K.-based Internet bank's service design strategy. Between 1998 and 2004, a multitude of customer and employee programs were designed and launched to motivate employees and refocus attention around Egg's core value proposition: the elimination of confusion, mistrust, and so-called toxic practices for banking customers. Egg was widely credited in the press for being a customer champion. Design was key to product and service development, since services were generally Web-based. Indeed, Web usability was of paramount importance. Usability guidelines were put in place, including the much-heralded three-click rule, which mandated that every customer process should be executable in just three clicks. The design team was a mix of IT and marketing employees, supplemented by the addition of the "ideas hothouse," a team of external design consultants.

Experiments in Service and Service Design

Egg Banking has applied a wide spectrum of methodologies to the design of services, including human-computer interaction (HCI), usability design methods, qualitative research, and ethnographic customer studies, as well as more traditional focus groups for customer propositions and marketing communications.

Through the use of human-computer interaction (HCI), Egg has conducted several design experiments focused on providing an effective interaction between users and the Web site, which included the following design attributes:

- Intuitive access and logical progression to key user tasks
- Clear, yet usable, branding
- Visual elements that do not compromise usability
- Terminology that relates to the users' tasks—not marketing-speak
- Appropriate metaphors for navigating from the home page
- Simplicity when interacting and transitioning across Web pages

When designing for usability, Egg considers the total customer experience (TCE), which encompasses all stages of a customer's interaction with the Egg environment: the online site, back-office systems, the delivery of the product or service on schedule, and post-sales support. The breadth of the TCE approach highlights that success in services means more than just the physical design of the Web site, the front end of the organization and its usability, and the price of the product or service. In reality, the entire purchase experience influences customer satisfaction and perception of value.

Learning and Adapting

A critical lesson Egg Banking learned was the importance of integrating a change management strategy when designing new service concepts. Being creative was not the main challenge. It was being creative and profitable and legal and "launchable." The need to address service design from all these angles sometimes conflicted with the views of the consulting partners. There were instances in which differences in internal and external approaches began to surface and disagreements about the direction of the concept hampered progress. In one account, the consulting team favored more viral, futuristic concepts, while the Egg team steered toward the slightly less innovative, more imminently marketable, revenue-generating ideas. Combining two different working cultures requires considerable effort in conflict resolution and stress management. Egg learned the hard way—that is, after the fact—that innovation and service design require the management of change and political conflict just as much as they do good ideas and expert resources.

TRENDS IN SERVICE DESIGN

Companies such as Ritz-Carlton, Herman Miller, and Egg Banking have used service design approaches and methods to challenge conventional business wisdom and deliver a compelling, branded customer experience. But what does the future bring? The future of service design is intimately linked to the affinities it has with several related topics—service science, service innovation, and sustainability.

Service Science

Scientists and researchers at IBM have now added yet another acronym to the roomy service design glossary: service science, management, and engineering (SSME). The coinage is an attempt to house all service-related research under one very large umbrella. Anchored by IBM and Oracle, and created to spur SSME understanding and growth, the service, research and innovation initiative (SRII)[8] strives to foment research budgets in corporations, the government, and academia. The acronyms are tough, but the idea is simple. A discipline, no matter how advanced, cannot be properly labeled "science" unless it meets certain criteria for cause-and-effect predictability, refutability, and hypothesis-testing through experimentation. As our economies have become increasingly dependent on services, research has not kept up with the volume and importance of services.

This logic concludes with an admonition: Further advances in productivity and standards of living are contingent on better and more thorough research in services. If we consider service design one of the SSME pillars—a notion with which designers may take issue—further collaboration and research in this arena can only help to separate the wheat from the chaff. Through evidence-based methods, SSME and service design can then reap benefits leading to better professional practice. But we shouldn't be overly optimistic. IBM cognitive scientist and researcher Paul Maglio cautions, "There's this Utopian dream: different crowds talking different languages, and then someone builds an Esperanto of sorts, and before long Utopia follows because they can now all communicate.... Right?" Possibly the best we can hope for is a rudimentary service language in which different disciplines can partake, maybe awkwardly at first. As Maglio concludes, "We need to have a common language and framework that just gets us to the point of talking."

Innovation in Services

For innovation gurus like Jeneanne Rae, the term service innovation should be reserved for a certain type of initiative—one that can produce a viable new business model, as opposed to a new service or service system that executes the current business model effectively. For Rae, successful service innovations must create a new business model that:

- Throws off enough free cash flow to justify the expense
- Meets internal hurdles and performance targets
- Occurs fast enough to stay ahead of competition
- Occurs often enough to keep the brand relevant

Take one of Citigroup's businesses as an example of a strategy geared toward developing new business models. In 2000, under the name i2i (which stands for idea to implementation), the bank embarked on a journey to drive organic growth through innovation and service design. In 2005, Citi Global Consumer Bank appointed an executive vice president for growth ventures and innovation with the mission of building a venture capital model with a portfolio of small, ethnographically derived and metric-proven innovation concepts. Interestingly, Citi's venture capital model was designed to tolerate the same levels of risk as were current in Silicon Valley. Failure was expected to some degree in order to produce disruptive innovation. While Citigroup has continued to experience governance difficulties, its innovation practice garners kudos from a wide audience. Citi's innovation program is considered to be at the forefront of contactless credit, debit, and alternative modes of payments, including mobile payments and P2P money transfers. It is the only financial services firm to be listed in the recent *BusinessWeek*/Boston Consulting Group World's Fifty Most Innovative Companies.

To be effective, service innovation systems must first identify, then deconstruct and reconstruct business models. Service design, together with strategic resources and value networks, is one of the critical capabilities required to do the job effectively.

Sustainability and Transformation Design

Economic, social, and ecological sustainability are becoming increasingly intertwined, primarily because the lag factor between an economic decision and its environmental outcome has diminished. People in various communities around the world are asking themselves if growth is the only metaphor to describe their aspirations for the economy. How about, instead, economic and social deepening?[9] Concerns over product life cycles, all the way through to disposability, have been with us for a while. But how should we consider service life cycles? In 2001, the U.K. Design Council formed RED—essentially a research and development team—to explore, debate, and research the impact of design on social issues.[10] RED projects ranged from preventing ill health, managing chronic illness, reducing home energy consumption, and revitalizing democracy to improving learning in schools. In 2005, RED Director Hilary Cottam was named U.K. Designer of the Year by the London Design Museum—quite an honor for someone who "designs" prisons, schools, and healthcare systems. RED calls its approach transformation design, but it looks like, feels like, and sounds like service design applied to social systems. Our conversation with Engine Group's Oliver King led us to the consideration that a particular energy feeds design work for services. King refers to a sense of mission: "First and foremost, there's an imperative to dematerialize the world; there's too much stuff to consume, to store, to get rid of. Moreover, designers have an obligation to help people navigate a complex world." According to Oliver, over time the designer's role has transitioned from draughtsman to choreographer, and away from the very tangible to the highly conceptual. He defines a designer as someone who makes something better for someone else.

STRATEGIES FOR PRACTICE

Can we then draw any overarching lessons or strategies from these practitioners, companies, and tendencies? From the review of both interviews and case studies, we believe that the emerging practice of service design is quite complex and dynamic, and demands, among other things, multidisciplinary teamwork, prototyping as a vehicle for dialogue, open design architecture, and negotiation between functional and emotional benefits. We offer these caveats in the form of the following lessons for service design practitioners:

- ▲ Multidisciplinary teamwork. To make a significant impact, service design practitioners must look at entire ecosystems rather than at isolated problems. The complexity of doing so requires a holistic view that unites practitioners across disciplines. The multidisciplinary approach means that the designer as "lone ranger" may not have a privileged place in a contemporary service design world.
- ▲ Prototyping as a vehicle for dialogue. Instead of protecting the design from interference in certain phases of the design process, prototypes should be transparent to all actors during the design process. In service design, the prototype is more a glass box than a black box. Practitioners should make prototypes available to discussion and dialogue, both internally in relation to teamwork and externally in relation to clients.
- ▲ Open design architecture. The fact that the service is delivered via touchpoints that evolve in time makes it important for practitioners to develop open-ended solutions that allow for gradual improvements and change. For practitioners to be successful, designed solutions need to be highly adaptable over time.
- ▲ Integration between functional and emotional benefits. In order to design a compelling service, it is important to design both functional and emotional benefits across different touchpoints and to relate the design to the company's brand and service. This implies that practitioners need to understand brand strategy and have an in-depth knowledge of key touchpoints when designing services.

We have endeavored to map out the service design landscape—and we caution that conditions are still not entirely clear. But while we currently have a fine overland mist, bright patches of blue loom promisingly on the horizon. Setting aside the weather report, we should be mindful of one additional consideration. The label service design is somewhat unfortunate. Inadvertently, we have all conspired to fuse together two twenty-first-century meta-narratives—services and design—into a heady mélange of skepticism and hope. And yet consider: Has it ever been any different for the new, the emergent, and the truly transformative?

Suggested Reading

Hollins, G., and B. Hollins. *Total Design: Managing the Design Process in the Service Sector* (Philadelphia, Pa.: Trans-Atlantic Publications, 1991).

Shostack, Lynn. "How to Design a Service." *European Journal of Marketing* 161 (1982).

Endnotes

1. For the seminal article on dominant logic in goods and services, see Stephen L. Vargo and Robert F. Lusch, "Evolving to a New Dominant Logic in Marketing," *Journal of Marketing* 68:1 (January 2004).

2. Offering different viewpoints, three books stand out from the rest: Virginia Postrel's *The Substance of Style* (New York, N.Y.: Harper, 2003); John Thackara's *In the Bubble: Designing in a Complex World* (Cambridge, Mass.: MIT, 2005); and Bill Moggridge's *Designing Interactions* (Cambridge, Mass.: MIT, 2007). The latter work features interviews with more than forty designers.

3. The Japanese, with characteristic rigor and distinction, call this application *kansei* engineering. Kansei (emotion) is the opposite of chisei (reason, or "the rational"). Helmut Esslinger at frogdesign is a pioneer of this school of design and coined the motto, "Form follows emotion." See Owen Edwards, "Form Follows Emotion," *Forbes*, November 12, 1999.

4. Reference the Service Design Network manifesto at *www.service-design-network.org.*

5. Stefan Moritz, *Service Design: Practical Access to an Evolving Field* (Köln International School of Design, 2005). This publication is based on Moritz's Master's dissertation at KISD.

6. For example, Joseph Pine and James H. Gilmore, in their book *The Experience Economy* (Boston, Mass.: HBS Press, 1999), or Lou Carbone, who recently wrote, with Leonard L. Berry, "Build Loyalty Through Experience Management," *Quality Progress* (September 2007).

7. Max De Pree, *Leadership Is an Art* (New York, N.Y.: Dell, 1989).

8. See *www.thesrii.org.*

9. For the fully developed argument, see Bill McKibben's *Deep Economy: The Wealth of Communities and the Durable Future* (New York, N.Y.: Times Books, 2007).

10. In 2007, RED's activities were absorbed by the U.K. Design Council. Several RED practitioners, led by Hilary Cottam, have formed their own independent service design firm, Participle.

Chapter 15

Bottom-Line Experiences: Measuring the Value of Design in Service

by Lavrans Løvlie, Founding Partner, live|work
Chris Downs, Managing Partner, live|work
and Ben Reason, Founding Partner, live|work

Hard numbers on quality and return on investment are important feedback for strategic decision-making and the allocation of resources. In the arena of service design, Lavrans Løvlie, Chris Downs, and Ben Reason detail "gross value added," "the triple bottom line," and "the service usability index" as techniques they use to assess the impact and success of their work.

IT IS A well documented fact that businesses that invest in design outperform the competition. The U.K. Design Council reported in its annual report for 2005 to 2006 that for every £100 a business invested in design, revenues increased by £225.[1] However, particularly in the case of the service sector, it's unclear how the value of design can be measured.

In this article, we will share some of our experience in measuring the value of our work at service innovation and design consultancy live|work. Even within the complex workings of a service organization, we believe we can explain the value of design with precision.

WHAT IS SERVICE DESIGN?

In order to show clearly how we validate our work, we first need to describe the emerging field of service design.

When the three of us founded live|work, we shared a background as the first generation of designers who went straight into Internet consultancies after graduation in the mid '90s. We had strong foundations in the values that formed industrial design as a human-centered discipline aiming to improve the material lives of ordinary people. At the same time, our engagement with networked media changed our notion of what constitutes a design object.

The design process we were taught focused on reducing the complexity of the design problem and achieving ultimate control of form, but subsequently we saw that we could design immaterial experiences that constantly change and that reach people through multiple touchpoints. A bank account, for example, changes content and functionality continually and will be experienced through paper statements, online interfaces, people, call centers, ATMs, and the like.

We knew we would need to embrace the complexity of services and think more about how an experience would flow across channels rather than how we could create one perfect interface. We came to a definition of the new discipline of service design as "design for experiences that reach people through many different touchpoints and that happen over time."[2]

Since we started in 2001, we have had some fantastic opportunities to develop our methods and techniques with some of the most ambitious service organizations in the world, ranging from telecoms companies, such as Orange and manufacturers such as Sony Ericsson, to financial service companies, such as Norwich Union (the U.K.'s largest insurer), and public service providers, including the U.K. government. We have also worked with design schools across Europe.

During our first years, our focus was on developing methods that were appropriate to the design of services. Lately, however, we have also begun to look at ways to document how design provides value and return on investment (ROI) in the service sector.

HOW TO VALIDATE QUALITY IN THE DESIGN OF SERVICES

Managing design quality in the service sector is the art of matching people's expectations with an experience that is consistent across all the touchpoints that make up the service. What makes this complicated is that a service is "manufactured" at the point of consumption and is often created by a mix of digital information, products, and people—including staff and customers.[3] For instance, the experience of train travel is composed of interactions with timetable information, ticket machines, stations, trains, conductors, and a range of other touchpoints.

The best way to ensure quality within this sort of complexity is to put the people who are going to use the service, rather than the design object, at the heart of the design process.

When users are made part of the design team, the focus shifts from the perfection of each touchpoint to the journeys of use people go through when they interact with the service. Therefore, we work with potential users from the definition of the brief through to launch in order to validate the quality of our design work. In the end, our customer-

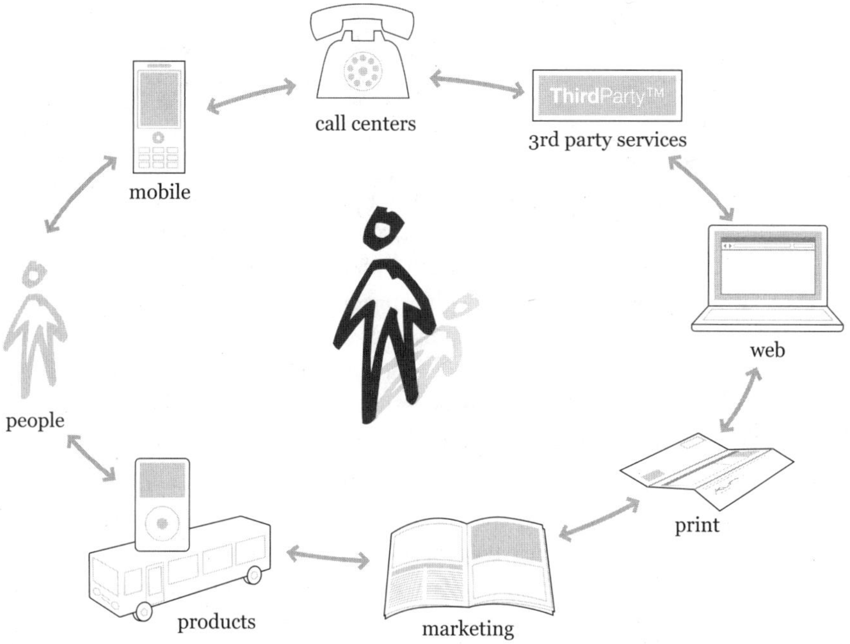

The key to the design of services is the attention to how an experience flows across touchpoints rather than the quality of an interface in isolation.

centric measure of success is how much people love the service and are happy to make it part of their lives. However, this is usually too subjective a measure for the people that commission projects from us.

RETURN ON INVESTMENT

Even though we as designers accept user satisfaction as proof of quality, this alone is rarely sufficient to justify the expense of design for our clients. They have other metrics that drive their activity, perhaps profit or value for money. They need tangible indicators to measure the performance of the service and to be able to demonstrate return on investment. They also need to know how to improve their service to keep ahead of competition.

Below, we present three approaches we have used in recent years to validate quality. In two instances, we have calculated the return on investment on the design work. In the last case, we show how we boil the measure of the service design down to a single number.

1. **Gross Value Added (GVA)**

   One-third of our projects at live|work are in the public sector. In public service design and innovation, success can't be measured by competitive advantage, but rather by the value it brings to society. This is hard to measure, particularly in the multifaceted network of a community.

One method the public sector uses to measure its achievements is gross value added (GVA). Like gross national product (GNP), this is an economic measure used to estimate the value of goods and services produced in an economy.

Our work with services for unemployed people in the northeast of England presented a challenge in demonstrating GVA. The work was for the regional development agency ONE North East and the Newcastle-based Design Innovation Education Centre (DIEC).[4] Over the past four years, in an ambitious drive to improve the economy of the region, they have engaged with a series of public agencies to stimulate growth through better design of their services. One of the projects, sponsored by a local authority, Sunderland City Council, aimed to improve services for people who have been on long-term incapacity benefits and to help them get back to work.

Over a three-month period, we undertook research and codesign work with twelve of these clients and a wide range of stakeholders engaged in providing services to help them back to work. This first discovery phase of work culminated in a project brief and an early iteration of service concepts. In addition, the project sponsors needed estimates that could prove that the results would justify the investment.

According to U.K. national statistics, GVA measures the contribution to the economy of each individual producer, industry, or sector in the United Kingdom. Beyond calculating that getting even a small percentage of people back to work would return massive savings, we found it virtually impossible to produce validated numbers for an initiative the size of a typical design project.

Our solution was to estimate numbers on the basis of the effects on a small prototype community. At live|work, we always try to involve potential users in the design and live prototyping of the service. Since the "manufacture" of a service is in the delivery, we create a live prototype where we actually deliver a "hand-made" version of the service to a limited number of people to find its weaknesses and opportunities and define the design detail.

There isn't a specific number for how much one workless person costs society, but we were able to find that the state spends between £10,000 and £40,000 per person out of work per year in benefits and other social costs. We know the rates of worklessness in Sunderland currently and are able to calculate the uplift created by our service design by prototyping it with a small prototype community. We now had a metric for calculating the value of our design intervention. When the uplift overtakes our investment, we will have a positive ROI for Sunderland.

By showing return on investment at a project level, we could also demonstrate that the project would add to GVA and that, if scaled up, the benefits would be massive—one hundred people in work creates a minimum £1 million savings per annum. In the public sector, where the networks of value exchange are too complex to accurately measure the full impact of a design initiative, we have found ROI on project level to be a practical and useful tool for making value tangible.

Sunderland City Council believed in the potential defined by this initial project and, on the back of it, we shared our insights and concepts in workshops with more than two hundred operational council employees to enable them to improve their services. The project is currently in the pilot phase, where existing services are being reworked to apply the new service design, and the effectiveness of the model is being measured in parallel. Our goal is that for every £1 invested, there will be a £2 saving to the public purse—a 200 percent ROI.

2. **Triple Bottom Line**

Another system for measuring the value of design is the triple bottom line. This concept came out of the sustainability movement during the '90s and captures the idea that organizational success should be measured as the sum of the economic, environmental, and social effects of an activity.[5] It reflects the idea that corporate social responsibility should be for anyone who is affected by what the organization does, not just customers, employees, and shareholders.

Sustainability is a key issue that live|work believes service design can address, and we try to apply the triple bottom line to all our projects. Our collaboration with London-based car-sharing company Streetcar gave us a chance to apply our skills to a service that represented our values and our ultimate design challenge—shifting desirability from ownership to use.

Streetcar offers members self-service cars for rent by the hour, day, week, or month. The vehicles are parked in a dense network of dedicated spaces in several U.K. cities and can be booked for as little as thirty minutes or as long as six months, and members receive monthly bills for their car usage.

Studies show car sharing significantly reduces the number of cars on the road. Every shared car resulted, on average, in six fewer private cars on the road.

When we contacted Streetcar in 2004, we found them the most promising of a series of similar services that catered to particular groups of people with narrowly defined needs. We shared an ambition with the company to move the concept of car sharing into the mass market and, together with them, came to the conclusion that we had to elevate the experience of car-sharing to a level where it would compete with the experience of car ownership. It was an obvious instance in which design could deliver economic, environmental, and social return on investment.

In order to achieve this, we analyzed the whole user journey, from joining Streetcar for the first time to paying the bills. The major barrier to growth for Streetcar was that the car was too difficult for new customers to use because they had to input a PIN code in an in-car computer in order to start it. We also discovered that people couldn't compare the Streetcar service to anything they had used before, which made it difficult to manage their expectations.

We blueprinted the entire service journey and redesigned the complete range of touchpoints involved, from the joining process to the printed information, including the manual, as well as the Web site and car booking interface. From this first iteration, our role has been to provide continual design input as the service grows.

In the years since it launched in 2004, Streetcar has achieved its ambitious goal of taking car sharing into the mass market. The company's commitment to delivering a consistent experience across its touchpoints has distinguished it from the competition, and it is now the largest club of its kind in the U.K., with more than 25,000 members and more than six hundred cars in six cities.

In order for us to measure the impact of Streetcar and to evaluate our contribution, we created a triple bottom line overview taking in both Streetcar's and the customer's perspective.

Although this way of reporting value is hard to use for comparison since it incorporates both soft and hard measurements, we believe it gives a good overall picture of the value of the service. It also allows us to incorporate aspects of design that can't be broken down into numbers—such as self-expression, status, and new patterns of behavior.

After Streetcar, we embarked on a transport project in which we tried to push the triple bottom line one step further, estimating economic benefits across all three areas—economic, environmental, and social. In collaboration with the Design Innovation Education Centre, we worked on making innovations to public transport in the rural county of Northumberland in the North East of England.

Local government is under obligation to provide transport to citizens ranging from schoolchildren to the elderly. This has resulted in a multi-

	Economic	Environmental	Social
Streetcar	Profitable within 18 months, the company plans to go public during 2008. Largest club of its kind in the UK.	Has taken more than 3,000 privately owned cars off the road. Users drive 69% less.	Expands mobility options for individuals and connectivity between transport modes. Reduces congestion and local pollution.
Member	Car owner spends on average £2,749 per year vs. Streetcar = £707 per year, (UK Automobile Association figures)	63.5% of car club members either give up their cars or don't buy a private vehicle. Streetcar will prevent 2,000,000 kg CO2 emissions over the next 2 years.	Rethinks a behavioral norm (hassle-free mobility). Creates a sense of community.

Streetcar is the U.K.'s largest car sharing club, with more than 25,000 members. live|work saw the Streetcar project as an instance in which design could deliver economic, environmental, and social ROI.

tude of transportation services, from taxis to ambulances to school buses, and they are poorly coordinated, if at all. At the same time, the people and organizations that need transport have few ways to coordinate their needs.

Our work focused on designing ways to integrate provision and needs better through easily accessible touchpoints. The key concept was a new organization that would enable better overview and a more dynamic marketplace for offering and requesting transport. This organization, called RAMP (Rural Access and Mobility Project), would aim to reduce costs for public bodies, create better revenue for providers, and improve quality of service for those who needed transport.

As with our unemployment project, we decided to legitimize the concept and inspire the client to take action by showing value at a project level. With the help of transport economists, we were able to demonstrate potential return on investment on the economic, as well as on the environmental and social, level.

Our calculation showed that for every £1 currently spent, the county could expect a future return from the proposed service worth £1.65, based on the following breakdown (based on approved metrics used by the U.K. Department of Transport).

Our calculations across the triple bottom line showed that the design project would pay itself back to society in four years, and that the new service would break even during operational year two.

£1.25 (76%) = Financial return	Money saved on reduced numbers of miles driven to fulfill transport needs, as well as reduced management costs
£0.12 (7%) = Environmental return	Costs saved on reduced number of vehicles, congestion, and emissions
£0.28 (17%) = Social return	Value created by providing people with the ability to travel to alternatives to day-care and other costly community services

Northumberland County Council is currently tendering for an operational supplier to deliver the new model based on the RAMP project, and the work has caught the attention of Oppland county managers in Norway, which faces similar challenges. They have now brought in live|work to help design new integrated transport propositions for their rural citizens.

3. **The Service Usability Index**

The value of design does not have to be measured in terms of money to be of use to our clients. What they really need from us is to understand design quality well enough to implement improvements that release value.

The third method for measuring the value of design in the service sector is one we have designed ourselves, called service usability (SU). This method was a direct response to the lack of a quality testing method appropriate to service experiences. Service usability isn't a way to qualify ROI, but rather a system that measures the quality of a service experience in concrete terms and enables organizations to take action to improve their designs.

Whereas there are a multitude of methods for testing particular touchpoints such as Web sites, printed material, and products, we couldn't find one single system for addressing service experiences that are made up of multiple touchpoints and that take time into account. For example, when we think about health services we need to take into consideration how the relationship between the person and the service changes over an entire lifetime.

Customer satisfaction ratings go part of the way in terms of validating complete service experiences, but fall down on providing actionable results. It is good to know whether customers like a service or not, but what an organization really needs to know is what is wrong, why, and how it affects the experience. We built SU to address these questions, focusing on finding a way to create actionable insights into service quality that could be applied from boardroom to the front desk. Our starting point was a combination of classic service marketing theory and recent developments in Web usability testing.

At the most abstract level of measurement, we created the SU index, which rates the quality of the service with a number between 0 and 10. We define the number by four key parameters:

- **Proposition.** Do people understand the value proposition of the service?
- **Experience.** Do people feel good about the service?
- **Usability.** Can people easily use the service?
- **Accessibility.** Is the service universally usable for everyone?

We arrive at the final number through in-depth interviews and by shadowing users as they use the service in their own environment and time.

An SU report is a detailed document that describes all major issues that affect the experience and recommendations about how to fix them. For boardrooms, we synthesize reports into one page that lists the top three issues that affect the service, as well as how many issues affect the four key parameters and, finally, how well each service touchpoint performs.

Another feature of SU that our clients appreciate is our two top-ten lists: "Issues that prevent you from making money" and "Quick fixes," things that are easy to fix to improve the quality of the service.

We SU-tested Streetcar after our first design iteration to reveal how it could make its service experience even better and found that the joining fee was a

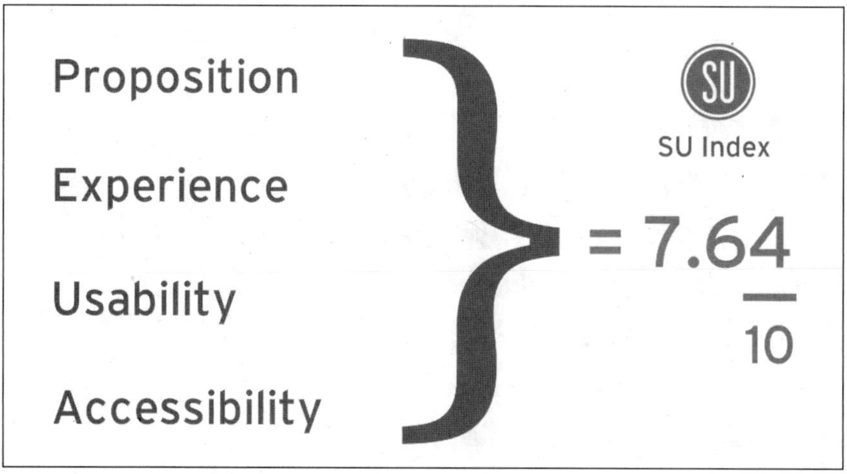

The service usability (SU) index rates the quality of a service through in-depth interviews with users and gives it a number between zero and ten. The Streetcar project, for instance, achieved 7.64, which is a fairly average rating.

The boardroom version of the SU report provides a quick overview of how well the service performs and what can be done to improve it.

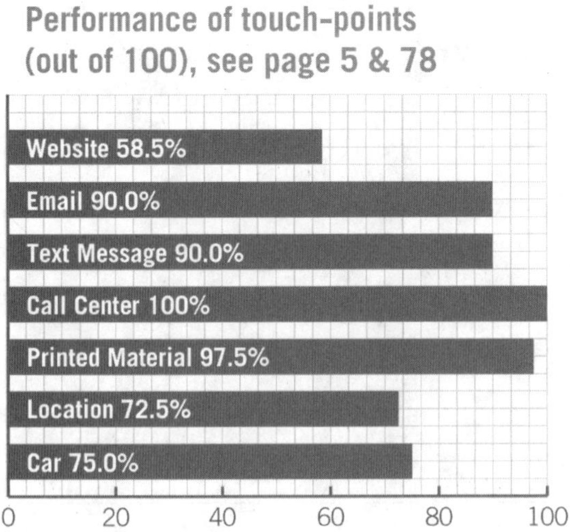

People who called Streetcar had a great experience, but the Web site and in-car computer presented usability problems. Surprisingly, many people also had difficulties finding the cars.

major barrier to use. People felt a need to try this new type of service before they could fully commit to it. We also found that people didn't have a clear mental model of the process of using Streetcar, and this made it difficult to meet their expectations.

Our ten recommendations therefore included dropping the joining fee and providing a simple explanation of the Streetcar experience.

Typical of Streetcar's commitment to creating a great service experience, the company implemented all SU top-ten recommendations. The results have been impressive. For example, Streetcar embraced the fact that people need to try before they buy and dropped the joining fee as we had suggested. This resulted in a rapid increase in new members. To clarify and explain the way in which the service worked, Streetcar added simple step-by-step explanations that immediately reduced the number of questions typically asked about how the service works, creating efficiencies for Streetcar and making users more confident.

We have now used SU to test the services of a number of organizations, from mobile operator Vodafone to Danish train operator DSB—even the English Parliament.

CONCLUSIONS

Meaningful measurement of design depends on the context of the service and the provider.

In the public sector, we have found it useful to estimate ROI on a project level, and we use this to argue contribution to the economy in general (GVA). We have also found this to be a productive tool in the concept phase of the design process to motivate further investment.

Since the operation of services involves more people and touchpoints than products, we find the triple bottom line system particularly relevant to the service sector because it addresses a broad range of issues affected by the activity. We also believe the method is useful in the context of measuring design, because it allows a mix of hard and soft measures that is appropriate to understanding what an experience is.

The third measure we use, service usability, shows that it is possible to assess the quality of design in the service sector and that the detailed investigation of a customer's journey through the service provides actionable results that lead to a better user experience.

Endnotes

1. Design Council, "Design in Britain 2005–06," *www.designcouncil.org.uk.*

2. *www.servicedesign.org.*

3. Gillian Hollins, Bill Hollins, *Total Design: Managing the Design Process in the Service Sector* (London, U.K.: Trans-Atlantic Publications, 1991).

4. *www.diec.co.uk*

5. John Elkington, *Cannibals with Forks: The Triple Bottom Line of 21st Century Business* (British Columbia: New Society Publishers, 1998).

Chapter 16

From Small Ideas to Radical Service Innovation

by Mark Jones, Lead for Service Design and Innovation, IDEO
and Fran Samalionis, Head of Service Design and Innovation, IDEO

The quest to discover and implement strategies on the frontiers of service design demands a measured blending of creativity and discipline. Mark Jones and Fran Samalionis probe challenges and pitfalls in the process and outline five steps that leverage positive results. Their commentary addresses the nuances of such an effort, as well as the big picture—insights they illustrate with a case study on 1st Source Bank in South Bend, Indiana.

TO COMPETE IN the marketplace and maintain relevancy, service companies need to innovate constantly. Most top service company executives will tell you that the introduction of innovative new services is a priority. In fact, a global survey by McKinsey in October 2007 of a broad range of companies (including service companies) found that more than 70 percent of corporate leaders named innovation as one of their top three priorities for driving growth. But while there is a desire to innovate, actually getting innovative new services to market is rare, and what we call radical innovation—new services that dramatically change the marketplace—is even rarer.

When asked about the pathway to radical innovation, service company executives will also tell you that ideas are a dime a dozen. What's more important is the execution: the alignment of the right idea, the right team, the right development process, the right leadership, the right level of risk management, the right target, the right time to market, and so on. In this article, we talk about this pathway to innovation. It is not just a matter of "Aha" ideas; it is rather a process that requires a disciplined approach to rigorously identify and execute the most promising ideas.

IDEO has developed a staged innovation process that allows good ideas to be pushed and refined and turned into great ideas that can change markets—before those ideas are killed.

STRUCTURAL BARRIERS TO INNOVATION

There are several well-documented structural barriers to innovation in service companies, some of which are:

- Service organization silos that are designed to support operational efficiency rather than rapid change; particularly true in service companies
- Many competing agendas within the organization, all vying for the same resources
- Lack of a consistent team or champion for the long time period between idea generation and bringing those ideas to market
- Measures of success (and accountability) that are ill defined
- The large scale of some service organizations, which makes it hard for them to match the nimbleness of the marketplace
- Last but not least: the fact that change is expensive

COMMON MISTAKES

It's not that service organizations don't try to introduce innovative new services. On the contrary, companies are aware of these structural challenges and proceed with a concerted innovation effort nonetheless. But they are rarely successful. Following are some common mistakes they make on their path to innovation.

- Even when companies talk about radical change, they tend to mean incremental service improvements that do not affect the marketplace in the same way truly radical change would.
- Ideas get killed too soon for the wrong reasons. They might not fit within the current operating paradigm; there is no clear filtering and prioritization process; people might not be able to dissociate the rough sketch of the idea from the real value proposition . . . the reasons are infinite.
- The ideas that make the cut are sometimes chosen based on operational viability or existing technologies, rather than on real customer need. The result is a repackaging of existing services that don't offer any new value.
- The team developing the new service concept does not have a strong enough champion within the organization to get the resources required to develop the new service and get it to market.

- The design development process is not carried out with due diligence, and companies fail to reduce the risks of innovation through experimentation and prototyping before bringing new services to market.
- The absence of an overarching goal might lead to a lack of focus or too narrow a focus; both are detrimental to innovation.

How can we avoid these mistakes? IDEO has developed strategies that service organizations can employ to raise their chances of developing a truly innovative service and get it to market with perfect alignment.

THE PATHWAY TO RADICAL INNOVATION

Radical innovation implies radical change for a service organization and the marketplace. Think about new services that have turned the world upside down—JetBlue, Netflix, Progressive insurance. The companies that introduced them had to be truly open to changing the nature of the marketplace. They had to consider new touchpoints, new revenue models, new technologies, and new relationships with customers. Focusing too much on the current reality makes it hard to envision a world that is different.

Once teams have developed some real ideas for new services, it is natural to start looking ahead to see the implications for business and operations (viability and feasibility). But it is the degree of weight that is put on viability and feasibility that is important. It is too easy to kill an idea early in its development because it does not fit easily into the current operational model or does not meet the typical threshold for a business case. Indeed, good ideas often overcome challenges inherent in the current operating processes, and radical innovation may require a new way to develop a robust business case.

We advocate looking ahead to inform and improve new service concepts rather than kill them. A theme that runs through the discussion at each of the stages is how to maintain the discipline to focus the development team's efforts on the stage at hand. This allows a rigorous exploration at each stage to uncover truly valuable new services without letting conventional business and operational assumptions derail the process. It takes a little leap of faith and deep trust in the process to protect a fledgling innovation from the encroachment of convention.

THE FIVE-STAGE FRAMEWORK

We will now detail the framework for a process that has allowed IDEO to successfully collaborate with a broad range of service companies in designing and piloting radically innovative services. Our basic philosophy is that, during the early stages, it's necessary to let go of reality—to be expansive and inspirational and root your efforts in market insights. And when you've developed a rich portfolio of promising ideas, the next step is to put those ideas under the lens of maximizing consumer desirability, technical feasibility, and business viability. But all the while, you must maintain your focus and rigor so as not to derail the innovation process.

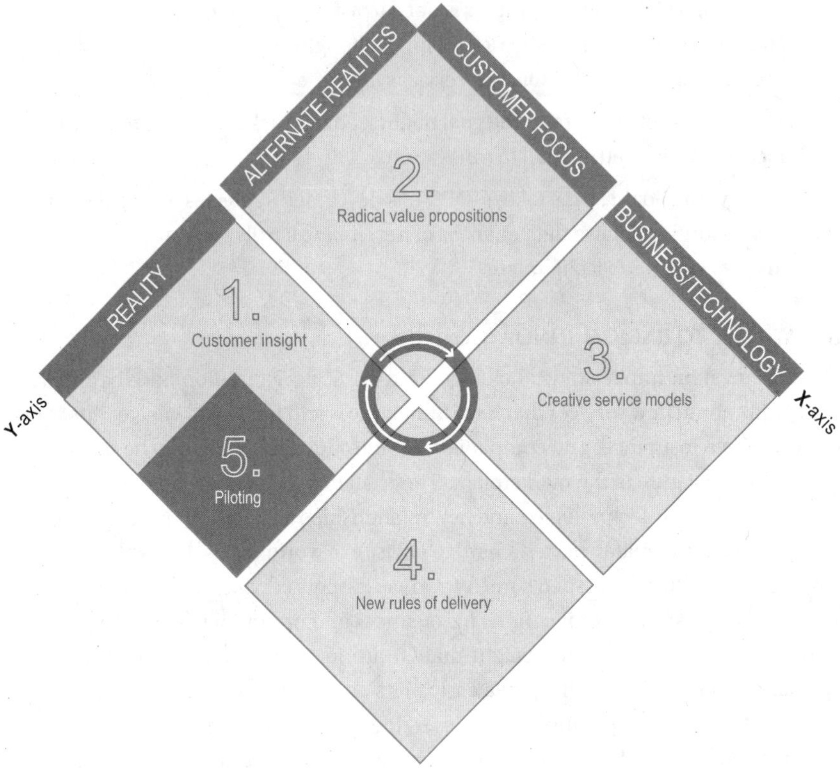

The x-axis shows the continuum from "focus on customer desirability" to "focus on business viability and technical feasibility." The y-axis shows the continuum from "looking at existing realities for inspiration" to "letting go of the existing realities to envision an alternative world."

This process can be broken down into five stages:

- Develop insight about the market.
- Create radical value propositions.
- Explore creative service models.
- Bend the rules of delivery.
- Iteratively pilot and refine the new service.

1. Develop Insight About the Market

Innovation is based on a deep insight about the marketplace that inspires great ideas. Much has been written about this of late, and many companies we work with routinely conduct customer insight research. In addition, many have begun to integrate observational and ethnographic methods into their toolkits. This is great news for services, and we expect the trend to continue.

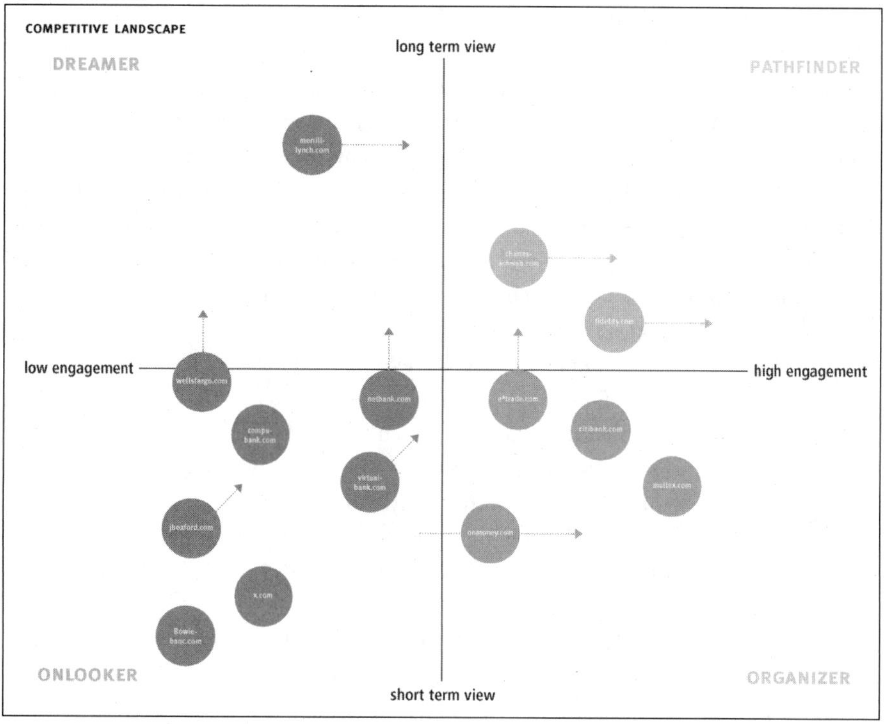

For a financial services company, our framework represented a deep understanding of how customers thought about their money. It also provided insight to the team and helped them design solutions for an underserved area in the market landscape.

Develop insights about customers, the business, and technology in parallel. Simply observing customers may not be enough to drive the kind of innovation that changes markets. Inspiration can come from many areas, so don't stop at getting insight about your customers. Be as insightful as you can about alternative business models, market landscapes, and operational and technology infrastructure. Innovations will come from the union of these perspectives and will be successful when aligned with customer needs.

Develop frameworks that clearly describe the "pain point" and the opportunity space. What you do with market insights is more important than the insights themselves; too often, companies don't take advantage of their full potential. The excitement over customer insights alone can lead teams to jump the gun and start brainstorming service solutions that solve only specific issues. This tends to result in incremental service improvements rather than the more substantial leaps the team is looking for.

It takes time for a team to immerse itself in the nuances and develop meaningful frameworks that can structure ideation. A team knows it is ready to move on to ideation and prototyping when it sees an opportunity for a radically different way to serve customer needs.

2. Create Radical Value Propositions

Radical innovation is about acquiring new customers and tapping underserved markets, as well as retaining those people once they become customers. Giving people a reason to try your service in a crowded marketplace requires going a step above what they experience with their current service. And if what you are offering is a new class of services—think of Zipcar, for example—then you'll have to help your customers recognize the value of trying something new. Sometimes, radical services fill an obvious gap in the marketplace—think Google 411 and SMS information services. At other times, they help steer markets in new directions capitalizing on existing but fragmented behaviors—think Apple's iPod and iTunes.

Involve front-line personnel and executives simultaneously. Many executives are experts at tracking the profitability of their services, as well as how they rate against the competition. So you would think that these executives are familiar with the challenges faced by their front-line personnel in delivering a high-quality service. But that is not the case. We have found that few executives truly know what their front-line employees think and are often in the dark about how they might leverage them to support a new service. This is a big gap, because those personnel are a very important part of the service ecology.

How do you mind this gap? Deep collaboration is key. Just telling executives about what front-line personnel think and can do is not enough. We have found that execu-

Stickpix was a service concept that allowed users to send images taken with their mobile phone in order to receive those pictures back as stickers they could stick anywhere. This image is one of a series of images that were mocked up to visualize how the service might come to life at various touchpoints of a consumer's journey.

tives need to hear ideas about new services directly from their employees. Many executives are surprised and inspired at how nimble and flexible their customer-facing employees can be.

Prototype extreme service propositions early to stretch the organizational mindset. Quick, low-cost mock-ups allow emerging ideas to be expressed, explored, modified, and shared with customers, experts, and stakeholders in a very tangible and emotive way. They encourage informed decision-making more than a paper description could ever do, and they encourage the idea to continually evolve. Since they often deal with the intangible, service ideas may also require simulation or even the acting out of a scenario. For example, simulating a customer's experience of interacting with a service can be an invaluable tool.

Experience prototypes that look like and behave like—but are not built like—the innovative new service allow a diverse range of customers, as well as stakeholders (those involved with brand, marketing, technology, customer care, delivery, and so on), to engage with and build on the new service from their specific perspectives. A good prototype will prompt questions around consumer desirability, business viability, and technical feasibility.

Conduct formative research to tease out desirability, viability, and feasibility. Formative research employs prototypes to get feedback from potential users to refine and improve a new concept. Many service companies are used to some form of concept testing. However, in most organizations concept testing is done to either kill ideas or to validate them, rather than to build on them and make them stronger. In contrast, formative research involves bringing ideas to life as prototypes and exposing them to customers, experts, and stakeholders for feedback. The goal is to understand how well the customer and business needs are addressed, and the tone of the research is exploratory and positive rather than judgmental and negative.

It is critical that this form of research is done at the right time and at the right level of fidelity during the innovation process. The prototypes need to be strong enough that they can be visualized to elicit feedback. However, the visualization should not be too polished because that can hinder the feedback process in two ways: one, the customers and stakeholders will get judgmental or will hold back; and second, the design team gets too invested in their own ideas and are unable to use the feedback constructively.

3. Explore Creative Service Models

Established business and operational constructs are not always useful in supporting radical innovations, since they are tailored for existing services. Innovations that have the ability to change the marketplace usually require radical or fundamental changes inside the organization, as well as creative solutions to make these new service offerings viable from a business perspective and feasible from a technology perspective.

Challenge the existing operational realities. Successful innovation requires business and technology team members to be as creative as their design counterparts—think of YouTube's or Google's service model, which allows them to monetize their offerings through ad revenue without compromising the value provided by the service. It is critical to remember that the success of their offerings rejuvenated the advertisement industry, which was not showing too much promise at the time.

Champion customer desirability as viability and feasibility are modeled. It's easy to revert to traditional benchmarks and models of viability and feasibility, but doing so dramatically reduces the innovation from radical to incremental. Championing the desirability of an innovation forces the organization to build new constructs that will nurture radical innovations. And this is not an easy task.

4. Bend the Rules of Delivery

Service companies are, at their heart, operationally focused organizations. Delivering consistently high levels of service requires an operations mentality that enforces rigorous processes, standards, and training. Introducing new services almost always requires changing the rules, sometimes significantly. Because the production and the consumption of a service happen simultaneously, changing the way a service operates is even harder.

Get permission to fail. Radical innovation is risky in the sense that getting it right the first time, every time, is highly unlikely. Companies should expect failure as a part of the innovation process. Teams need to have buy-in from leaders so that they feel confident trying new service concepts that have many unresolved questions. Teams that are afraid to fail make radical innovation, by definition, impossible. Set up for successful experimentation by getting buy-in from leadership, and then use that buy-in to get permission to fail.

Design new metrics for measuring success. Rules about metrics can be a huge barrier to innovation. This is especially true within service organizations that have adopted Six Sigma methodology. Funding guidelines that work well for the evolution of incremental improvements to services are often at odds with the scale and ambiguity of radical innovation. Radical service concepts may not have a business case that meets Six Sigma guidelines; waiving off those criteria can open up opportunities that would normally be squelched. Innovation efforts are likelier to be successful if they are funded and measured separately from the rest of the organization.

5. Iteratively Pilot and Refine the New Service

Radical innovation is inherently risky as it involves new-to-the-world offerings. Piloting a service is the best way to manage this risk—before it is scaled. But most service organizations are paranoid about exposing their intent to the market. Therefore, they are reluctant to pilot in order to protect their first-mover advantage. That reluctance needs to be balanced against the advantages that pilots offer in informing investment decisions.

Don't wait for the service to be perfect; get comfortable with beta. Radical innovation is fundamentally based on evolving customer behaviors and market trends. These changes are hard to predict accurately, and the success of a service can hinge upon a small nuance that is hard to pinpoint unless it is highlighted in a pilot. A works-like prototype can be easily piloted on a small scale to drastically reduce development cost, and it allows for iterative refinement that is critical to risk management.

When we worked with a health-insurance service center, the team developed service concepts that would actually significantly lengthen the average call time—exactly the opposite of most call center initiatives. The top team had to reframe the call center's metrics, which had been primarily customer satisfaction and handling time. The new metrics were centered on the call center's role in changing health outcomes and how it functioned in getting members to make choices leading to healthier outcomes and more cost-effective care. This affected the entire funding structure of the service center.

While developing a group communication service for a wireless carrier, we piloted a works-like prototype with a small number of customers for a limited time. The goal was to understand how they used the service and how their behavior changed as the result of being part of a group. In order to get the pilot out sooner, the prototype was developed on stand-alone technology instead of the company's core systems. Through customers' use of the prototype, we were able to determine that customers would indeed behave differently in groups; in addition, we learned that the new service would not necessarily cannibalize other revenue streams such as text messaging.

The organization not only tested desirability and viability with a works-like prototype but also developed, in parallel, the software required to enable group communication services across multiple technology platforms. As the design of the group communication service was refined to better meet customers' needs, the insights from the pilot informed the development of the technology platform.

Use the time during piloting to prepare for large-scale rollout. Any new service will remain radical only for a short period of time. Design teams need to be cognizant of this and act accordingly. To maintain first-mover advantage, organizations should use the time spent on the pilot phase to invest in the infrastructure required to roll out the service on a larger scale. This will ensure that the infrastructure will be ready when the service is fully worked out at the end of the pilot.

SUMMARY

Today, the market landscape for services is evolving constantly and rapidly. Frequent and radical innovations are key to being relevant in such a landscape. Both the market and customers expect nimbleness when it comes to innovative services, and service companies are interested in delivering it. The process we have described here is a pathway to delivering this kind of innovation. It will allow companies to introduce radical services to the marketplace predictably and at lower risk. The result will be a dynamic and a more customer-centric service landscape.

CASE STUDY: 1ST SOURCE BANK

In 2004, 1st Source Bank, a regional bank based in South Bend, Indiana, hoped to increase the number of branches in its system by 50 percent in a short period of time. The potential expansion prompted the bank to examine how it might change the customer experience in its branches before it invested in building new branches. At that time, the 1st Source branch experience was driven by industry-standard operations rather than by customer needs. The processes and facilities upon which they were based were complicated and tended to be impersonal.

1st Source's CEO championed the idea of collaborating with IDEO on the challenge of designing a paradigm for a new branch banking facility. This was immensely helpful, since it gave the development team the permission to explore radically new service concepts. The CEO successfully communicated to the rest of the organization how important it was to commit the time and resources needed to ensure success, and key personnel were drawn from various parts of the bank to be part of the team.

A key insight that emerged from the initial research was that 1st Source could leverage its brand as a local bank in ways that national banks could not. We also found that tellers felt constrained by their role and were frustrated by not being able to act more broadly and effectively on conversations they were having with customers. We found that customers connect to people that work in banks, not to banks as institutions, and that customers want to be treated with respect and concern. While bankers intuitively understand this need, the bank's service model and facilities did not support it. The team agreed that a solution should support bankers in building relationships with their customers and bridge the gap between routine banking and episodic activities, such as getting a loan.

We brought a wide range of bank stakeholders, including the management team, as well as front-line personnel, into a workshop setting for joint ideation. Tellers were the first to see the difference that getting out from behind the teller wall would present, and they quickly role-played how they might use technology to interact with customers in an open space. The top executive team was surprised at how the tellers could envision themselves working in such a different way. Side-by-side banking emerged as a key component of the new service model.

CASE STUDY: 1ST SOURCE BANK

This foam core mock-up of a new banking concept for 1st Source Bank allowed the development team to quickly simulate routine banking activities with the side-by-side banking configuration The feedback from customers and tellers helped resolve issues around privacy, cash management, and orientation.

This shows the first branch that employed the side-by-side banking configuration. The final realization of the concept is a substantial departure from conventional banking.

CASE STUDY: 1ST SOURCE BANK

Removing the teller walls presented a number of challenges. To further understand and tease these out, we built a full-scale foam-core mock-up of core elements of the entire proposed configuration to explore what the new service offer might be like. We brought in bankers, as well as customers, in a simulation of the new process. This confirmed that side-by-side banking could work, but it also highlighted issues such as security and privacy that would need to be addressed in further iterations.

The concept was ready to go live. Instead of building the entire infrastructure to pilot the new banking process, 1st Source introduced the new service model in a part of one branch, using an adaptation of existing software and fixtures. That experiment was followed by a new branch design that fully employed the new service model.

The branches that have been converted to the new concept have performed significantly better on key metrics than the older 1st Source branches. New accounts, deposit growth, and loan sales are all more than 30 percent higher than for similar branches lacking the new service model and facility elements.

Chapter 17

Would You Like Service with That?

by Chris Bedford, President, Karo Group (Calgary)
and Anson Lee, Director, Customer Experience Strategy, Karo Group (Vancouver)

Service design is a system of thoughtfully executed customer interactions. Chris Bedford and Anson Lee explain that it is a discipline that has been around for some time and that has become a critical element in what is now referred to as the experience economy. In this context, they analyze a spectrum of design strategies they developed for an auto dealership in Vancouver that, within a year of execution, contributed to a 28 percent increase in sales.

THE INCREASED COMPETITION for customers and customer loyalty drives organizations and brand managers to constantly revisit the question of what customer service means and how to best deliver "good service" in the variety of venues and contexts in which customers seek product, advice, or interact. Perhaps the strongest evidence that service design is worthy of our renewed attention was Howard Schultz's letter to customers earlier this year as he announced his return to Starbucks as CEO and his promise to make "the Starbucks experience as good as it has ever been and even better . . . in the way stores look, in the way people serve you, in the new beverages and products we will offer."

While service design is obviously not a new concept, it has become increasingly relevant over the past decade. The economy has shifted dramatically toward growing customer demand for a level of personalized service that has been lost to big-box retailers, discounters, and volume merchandisers who sacrificed most, if not all, aspects of customer service in the pursuit of greater profits from low-margin products.

Yet, as history has taught us, price is both the lowest common denominator and the worst differentiator, driving companies to move back toward a service model and a more human connection. Thus the need for designing better service and services.

But what exactly is service design? And how is it different from what we currently term experience design? The truth is that one is an extension of the other, as has been described so well in Joseph Pine's and James Gilmore's popular book, *The Experience Economy*. Pine and Gilmore argue that everything can be commoditized, and therefore to keep customers loyal there needs to be an emotional connection between the goods and the services companies provide. It's precisely this connection that we call the experience.

The Danish Design Center offers a particularly useful definition of service design:

Service design as a term generally refers to design of systems and process around the idea of rendering a service to the user. The typical medium for presenting the service is through the business of commercial or noncommercial entities (for example, pizza delivery, public healthcare, airlines). Very often, the service element is attached to a physical product or offering, but at times it can be purely an intangible offering: for example, legal consultation.

Most service is deployed through what are commonly referred to as touchpoints. These could be in the form of virtual interfaces, physical interfaces, and people. For example, in a bank, the touchpoints are the ATM, credit card, printed statement, call center representative, branch office, online bank, and so on.

SERVICE AS A SYSTEM OF CUSTOMER EXPERIENCES

If we think of service design as a complete system of considered customer interactions, then all of the sudden the role of design and the need for design thinking and design strategy become increasingly important for the market success of service brands. Unlike many products and most packaged goods, services are often intangibles, and the characteristics of good service can be defined quantitatively and qualitatively, tangibly and intangibly.

Consider an airline that lets you book your tickets and print your boarding passes online, provides a flight that leaves and arrives on time, gives you a seat that is comfortable, serves food that is palatable, and provides an experience that feels safe, delivered by helpful and understanding attendants. These are all goals that need to be considered within an overall system that we refer to as service design.

At the same time, companies all too often use specific initiatives to bolster a brand that are tied to only one facet of a customer's experience. The problem with this approach is that a single element in and of itself will not change the customer's overall perception of the organization. For example, airport check-in kiosks and Web check-in systems are efficient and make good use of the latest information technologies. However, they are probably the least powerful in changing a passenger's feelings toward an airline, as the brand equity they build is easily lost when baggage drop lines are excessively long, security is backed up, and your luggage lands in a different city than you do. When you consider the many factors involved, especially in qualitative situations, it becomes harder to control quality and for organizations to manage outcomes.

Service design is therefore a highly relevant concept when thinking about improving an organization's brand. To think about service design is to think on a higher plane and not at the level of the design of a specific product, environment, or interaction. Instead, think of a customer existing within a system of experiences—and ask how all these things work together and in support of one another.

Staples is a company that has used service design to differentiate itself in the market through its "easy button" program. The easy button started out as an advertising and brand-building campaign centered around the small to medium-size business owner and the "customer pain" involved in the time-consuming task of procuring office supplies and equipment. The advertising campaign, which features a physical red button that, when pushed, says, "That was easy" (the Staples brand promise), signifies the exceedingly well implemented and executed service design initiative that has enabled the company to deliver on the "easy" promise. Doing so was no simple task, as it required a strong focus on staff training to design the desired human interactions, as well as the technical ones.

As an example, instead of sales associates asking the proverbial "Can I help you?" when customers enter the store, Staples staff associates are trained to ask "What can I help you find today?" The focus is on solving specific customer needs in a personal way. The program has not only symbolized customer needs but also led to innovative new products and outstanding market success. The philosophy of maximizing buying convenience extends into the physical and online shopping experience, as well. Staples redesigned its stores to be smaller and less cluttered. Shelving systems were made lower in the front of the store, affording better visibility to the spaces in the rear and periphery. It developed specialized Web sites to target specific types of corporate buyers. The tedious task of collecting receipts, barcodes, and forms to apply for manufacturer rebates is handled through a service called EasyRebates, which electronically submits all product and purchase information to the manufacturer for processing. The easy button eventually evolved into a mini-desktop application that allows customers to make orders and query Staples.com without having to visit the Web site. The only customer complaint was that pushing the easy button on the Web site didn't respond with the audio payoff! After more than fifteen years in business, Staples realized that low prices weren't good enough—the key to really differentiating itself was to design an easy shopping experience. But perhaps the real proof that this service is well-designed is the fact that the company now gets twice as many compliments as it does complaints.

While Pine and Gilmore suggest that the experience economy actually evolved from the service economy, the service or means by which value is rendered for a customer is still a valid driver of an overall experience and deserves consideration. This raises questions: How does one engage in service design? And why is it so challenging? Choosing to look at the subject of service design from the perspective of business processes enables the entire organization to revisit the way it is structured to deliver services to its customers and to explore which tools, training, and metrics are required to ensure continuous management of the customer experience.

BEGINNING TO SOLVE THE PROBLEM

The larger the organization or number of products or venues involved in rendering a service, the more complex this system becomes. However, without the broader view of the continuum of customer experiences, your efforts may be patchy and have little effect on your organization and its overall brand success in the market. To begin to develop a picture of your service offering and system, it is useful to explore a variety of interconnected design disciplines.

The key is to start with a solid definition and a clear understanding of the problem you're trying to solve. Customer experience mapping, or the process of storyboarding and documenting a variety of possible scenarios with detailed interactions and outcomes, is a useful means of probing and uncovering opportunities to design a better service. This technique requires that all aspects of the customer experience be connected by a set of specific services and include all the customer touchpoints. Visual identity and brand language indicate relationships throughout the organization, reminding employees, as well as customers, of the presence of a larger system.

The experiences customers have are the direct result of their personal interactions with staff, products, services, and technology-based delivery systems, such as Web sites, kiosks, and voice automation. New research in behavioral science suggests that what matters most in the service equation is customer perception. This reminds us that service design is about attention to detail, as even a staff member's failure to say "thank you" can leave the customer with a perception of inferior service. Looking for opportunities to influence positive perceptions should be part of the service design process.

CASE STUDY: OPENROAD AUTO GROUP

Service design in many ways also involves meeting previously unmet customer needs. Consider the case of OpenRoad Auto Group, in Vancouver, Canada. This is a dealership brand Karo Group helped to create. The real work began with the recognition that the problem OpenRoad was trying to solve lay not in selling more cars but rather in providing better service. Most dealerships fail to recognize that their job is not to create the car brand and the car experience; that's the job of the car manufacturer. (In fact, in many cases the customer has already decided which vehicle he or she wants to buy before setting foot in the dealership.) Thus the greatest opportunity for differentiation comes from designing and delivering a better dealership experience, not from leveraging the automotive brand.

This required a huge shift in thinking that necessitated a total organizational change in the company (figure 1). What we set out to design was a new kind of dealership, one with strong street appeal that would increase foot traffic. We also needed to integrate the sales and service areas and to take customer service strategy to a new, higher level. To do all this, we had to address a variety of strategic business issues.

First, the dealership wanted to maximize the available floor space in order to generate the highest sales per square foot possible—without sacrificing the customer experience. This meant rethinking all aspects of merchandising, as well as formulating a variety of customer experience scenarios. Second, the design had to support the dealership's new sales vision, which intended to shift the power and control from the sales associates to the customer—something that was almost unheard of in the automotive retailing world. Third, and most important, was to create a comfortable experience that encouraged customers to spend more time in the dealership and discover more about OpenRoad.

Figure 1. Karo considered how the service design for OpenRoad, a car dealership, could encourage behaviors and cultural changes that would lead to the creation of excellent customer experiences and drive growth, as well.

Figure 2. Visually interesting displays, including a system of stacking cars outside the showroom, welcome and engage new customers, as well as maximize floor space.

What we developed was an innovative retail environment never before seen in the market, one that supported informed product decisions at all levels of sales and service. The curb appeal came from a system of stacking cars on the outside of the showroom that served both as innovative merchandising and fulfilling our goal of maximizing available floor space (figure 2). Long, curved windows created an expansive view of products and options. We posted the OpenRoad Auto Group "experience promise" at the door so that when customers entered, they immediately knew they, not the sales associates, were in control of the buying decision.

We introduced the idea of Internet kiosks that allowed customers access to information that would assist them in their buying decisions (figure 3). We designed the retail displays to be informative and educational in much the same way one would find information in a museum or interpretive center.

As we've already stated, service design requires a full consideration of the customer's needs in a variety of scenarios. In keeping with this idea, we designed a coffee lounge, complete with automotive reading, resource materials, and a 300-gallon aquarium and kids' play area that ensured children's entertainment while their parents spent unpressured time considering a purchase decision. (Consider that from a consumer's viewpoint, the purchase expense of a car is second only to that of buying a new home.). The showroom floor features three vehicle displays with moving-image screens and reflective floor tiles that create a sense of color and motion (figure 4). In addition to other vehicles on the floor, these displays create a focal point for customers, generate a desire for discovery, and bring the OpenRoad brand experience to life.

It is after the car is bought and paid for that most customers really get to know their dealership—and, ironically, this is when customers frequently have their worst experiences. The service design strategy for OpenRoad was quick to take this into consideration, relocating the customer from the greasy service bays to the showroom café. Instead of forcing customers to wait in the back of the shop and to drive their vehicles out of the service bay, OpenRoad now encourages customers to settle their accounts in the comfort of the showroom while an attendant brings their cars around for them.

Figure 3. Internet kiosks give customers access to pertinent information and support the buying habits to which customers are already accustomed.

Figure 4. Vehicle displays on the showroom floor offer moving-image screens and reflective floor tiles that bring content and context together to encourage exploration and engagement.

The results of this service design strategy have been nothing short of remarkable. They contributed to a 28 percent retail sales increase in their the very first year, leading to OpenRoad being named the top-selling Toyota dealership in all of Canada in 2006, and to its validation as the only Toyota dealership in western Canada to receive the President's Recognition Award from Toyota.

INNOVATION AND SERVICE DESIGN

Clearly, service design offers many opportunities for innovation. When you look at an entire service system with a mind open to making adjustments in multiple dimensions, it helps you make better decisions when integrating new technologies and new approaches. The role of design is therefore unique because it brings forward creative opportunities and divergent approaches to business problem-solving that rarely come into play. Unlike management consultants, who are often hired to help companies formulate new service strategies by analyzing and optimizing what already exists, design can help organizations visualize future possibilities from the customer's point of view. In the process, they can invent entirely new market spaces and opportunities.

As noted earlier, the concept and practice of service design is not new. However, it is possibly a more universal way of bringing together the many facets of design and business under a common framework of thinking. Designers, by their nature, are generally less willing to accept that technological and operational constraints are acceptable reasons for not changing or adapting service delivery to meet customer needs. Design thinking can and does create a healthy tension in the search for better and more innovative ways to create new systems, design new services, and deliver an enhanced customer experience, capable of truly helping service brands succeed in the market.

Chapter 18

Service Design via the Global Web: Global Companies Serving Local Markets

by Brian Gillespie, Director of Strategic Design, Molecular

For international companies, the Internet is an essential but inherently complex interface. In the framework presented here, Brian Gillespie critiques a range of options related to gateways, scope, user research, uniform versus local presence, language, content development, design, site implementation, domains, and URLs. It is an enlightening overview for both executives and managers.

A FEW YEARS back, a colleague of mine was doing research on global brands. In the course of interviewing a senior marketing manager at Microsoft, he raised the topic of the company's global Web presence. The manager mentioned that Microsoft had 180 Web sites worldwide, of which he absolutely knew around two-thirds to be "on-brand." He was relatively satisfied with this state of affairs. After all, it had been and could still be a lot worse. Today, I expect that manager has made sure that all Microsoft sites are on-brand, but the issue at the core of his observation—the difficulty of maintaining a consistently on-brand Web presence—is something that many global businesses struggle with.

The challenge is not simply a global Web site design and branding issue; it's much larger than that. It's about how companies approach the globalization of their businesses and brands, and the tangible manifestations of their business and brand as experienced by different markets throughout the world. Often, the crux of the matter has to do with how global a company actually wants to be. How a company positions itself—as

McDonald's global Web presence is a good example of the global, diverse, international type of Web presence. All local markets are responsible for their own marketing. Above are the home pages for McDonald's in Brazil, the Czech Republic, and China.

a national company operating in foreign markets or a global company operating in local markets—will have a big impact on its globalization strategy. There is a spectrum to globalization, the range of which can be seen in how the balance tips between the desire for uniformity and the desire for diversity, between international and national, between strict standards and looser guidelines that companies may choose to adopt. Where a company fits within this spectrum is often determined by the very nature of the business itself.

Before launching a global Web presence, a senior manager has to answer the basic question of what globalization means for his or her company. Does the company possess a uniform global persona, or a diverse persona that means different things to different people? How can the company balance catering to the diversity of markets with desires for consistent application of the brand and corporate persona? What shape of Web architecture best reflects not just the brand architecture, but also the expectations of Web audiences worldwide? All these decisions have ramifications for marketing and design teams tasked with implementing a globalization strategy.

As the role of the Web in servicing the needs of customers throughout the customer life cycle grows with each passing year, managing the design of online services becomes a critical task. This paper provides a broad overview of the challenges that companies face when launching a global Web presence aimed at servicing current and future customers, including issues that affect the design and branding decisions that must be made along the way. It also offers practical suggestions and strategies for overcoming these challenges.

THE SCOPE OF GLOBALIZATION

One of the many problems companies encounter when launching a global Web presence is the issue of scope. How extensive should Web-based services be? Many Web sites are designed with a closed-loop marketing approach; they are meant to attract, convert, and retain prospects and customers. Attracting prospects can be accomplished through a basic, information-based site that is optimized for search and contains content clearly written for target audiences. Adding transactional capabilities, such as product/service selectors, contact forms, and e-commerce, provides opportunities to convert those prospects into paying customers. The implementation of added-value services that help customers manage their businesses and their relationship with you in an efficient and easy-to-use manner (such as a client extranet) builds a loyalty that often lasts longer than similar analog-based services.

The extent to which you require your global Web presence to serve all stages of the customer life cycle—from initial customer attraction through to retention—will determine the size and scope of your globalization effort, and indeed account for the resources it will take to establish such a total infrastructure and to roll out the functionality worldwide. To effectively manage scope, most companies start with information-based sites

HEED THE WARNINGS

What are the signs that your company needs to address weaknesses in your global Web presence?

- Most of your global content is in one language, with little in-language local content.
- You look around your company and cannot identify clear ownership for the Web.
- Your IT structure is fragmented with multiple systems for managing the Web.
- You look at a handful of Web sites and see a fragmented user experience.
- You recognize that your one-size-fits-all globalization strategy does not fit all markets.

with basic information transactions before rolling out the more technologically robust platforms required for customer relationship management (CRM) and e-commerce. Keep in mind that big-bang total solutions take time, money, and massive commitment. Don't be afraid to start small, as long as your efforts are the first steps in carrying out a larger, longer-term service strategy.

HOW GLOBAL? HOW LOCAL? LOOK TO YOUR BRAND.

Going global compounds the number and types of interactions the market has with your business and brand. The Web experience is just one of many analog and digital interactions, and beyond experiencing an actual product or personal service, it can be one of the most accessible and defining experiences your customers have with you. As such, the site design and online experience should be built upon the solid foundation of the global business and brand strategy and should reflect the values, attributes, and other aspects of the overall brand personality. In addition, it requires a clear understanding of the customer, the markets in which they transact, the differences between markets, and the competitive landscape in each.

To demonstrate a brand's impact on globalization, consider two giants of American motoring: Harley-Davidson and Ford Motor Company. Whereas Ford produces differ-

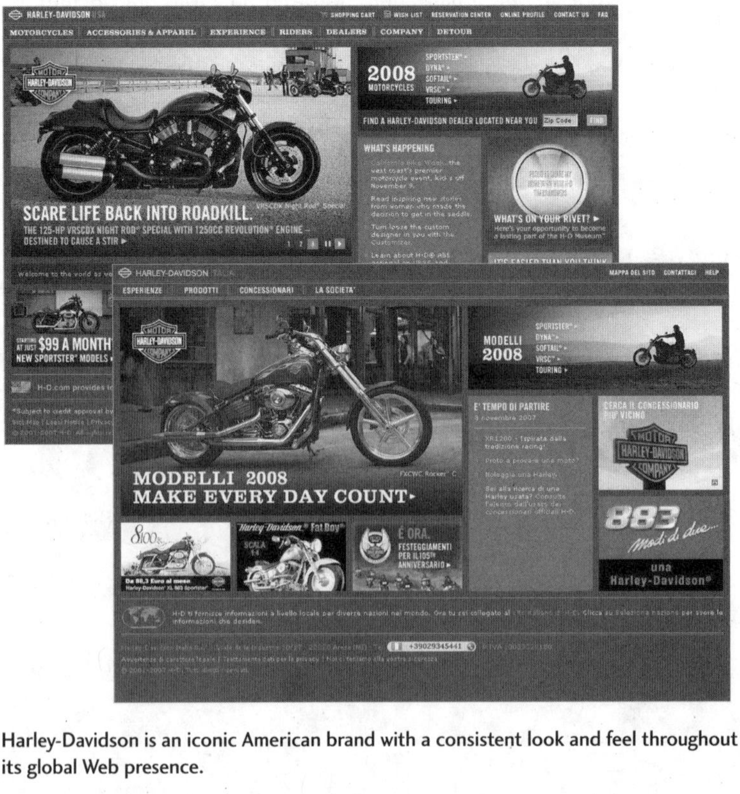

Harley-Davidson is an iconic American brand with a consistent look and feel throughout its global Web presence.

ent models for different markets, Harley-Davidson is an iconic American brand with a consistent look and feel throughout its global Web presence. These two very different approaches require different forms of design, market research, and validation—and ultimately a different Web architecture and experience. Companies like Harley-Davidson that reflect the uniform side of the globalization spectrum can take a broader approach to managing their global brand presence. Companies on the diversity side, like Ford Motor Company, must focus on the finer details and give greater consideration to the localization aspect of going global. This latter approach requires that greater care be given to selecting the resources that are applied and the outcomes that are desired. Despite this, each type of global company will have the same challenges when it comes to deciding what online services to provide—services that support the differences in their local markets. The selection and application of design research tools and methodologies employed to understand consumer needs, goals, habits, and motivations can greatly contribute to a positive end result, no matter what your ultimate goal may be.

CREATING A GLOBAL GATEWAY

Global gateways are central to establishing a simple, easy-to-use global Web architecture. A global gateway that effectively directs visitors to locally relevant content can have an immediate impact on a company's bottom line.

Gateways can take a variety of shapes and sizes. They reflect the scope of global operations and the extent to which a company has applied resources to its global business operations. They range from simple, single-page sites, where visitors select a language or a country before accessing content, to multilayered sites with extensive content and functionality.

The best gateway is the gateway that works best with your visitors and your site. For example, the gateway you build will be different if you have thirty localized sites, as opposed to just two or three. Let's take a closer look at the different types of gateways. We'll use a hotel metaphor, where some sites can be regarded as lobbies, some as hotels, and others as hotel chains.

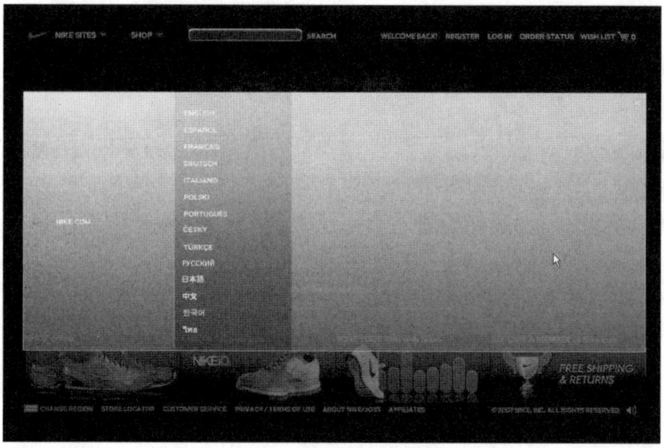

Before accessing any local content, visitors must first select a language and then a country.

The Entrance

The basic gateway rarely contains any content. It is simply a traffic direction that takes users to local Web sites where content is generally localized to target that market. A good example is Nike's site (*www.nike.com*). Before accessing any local content, visitors must first select a language and then a country. The goal of these sites is to drive traffic to a local solution as quickly as possible. Ikea's site (*www.ikea.com*) is similar to Nike's; however, the Ikea gateway allows visitors to explore content on the company's global brand proposition, a factor that brings it closer to our next type: the lobby.

The Lobby

Lobby sites tend to orient visitors to the type of content they can expect to find on the local site, but encourage them to visit the local site to get further information. Shell's global gateway (*www.shell.com*) is a good example. In addition to providing access to Shell's global Web pages, the site hosts investor and corporate information, as well as basic information about Shell's products and services for its two principal customer groups, consumers and businesses. To access deeper and locally pertinent information, visitors must select their country of origin. Although the site provides some introduction to the business and brand, visitors must navigate locally for product details. From a service perspective, lobby gateways set an expectation with customers about the kind of service experience they can expect at their local sites.

The Hotel

Hotel sites are essentially the master version of local content. Local sites are variations on the master. A good example of the hotel is Unilever's site (*www.unilever.com*), where the global gateway provides all possible information on the company, its values, and its brands. From this gateway, visitors can also access country sites where the content is a collection of master brand content localized for the market, as well as some local-specific content, such as news, events, and community involvement. In many regards,

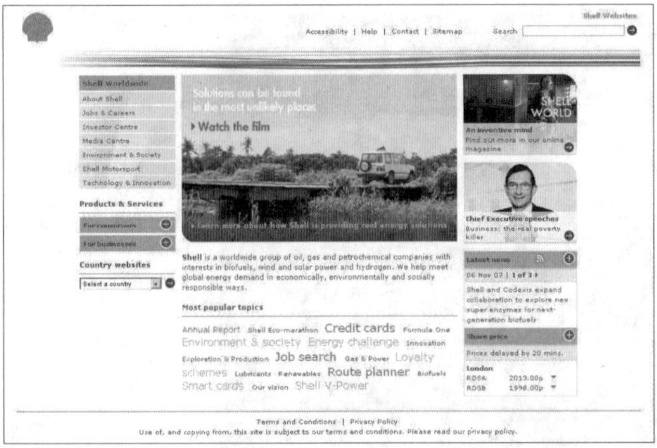

Lobby sites tend to orient visitors to the type of content they can expect to find on the local site, but the visitors must visit the local site to get further information.

Unilever's site is a good example of the hotel type, in which the global gateway provides all possible information on the company, its values, and its brands.

these sites follow the hotel chain model in that there is a global brand consistency to all the properties, yet each has a strong local focus. Though sites may follow a similar template from country to country and not appear to be distinctive, sites like Unilever's do a good job of servicing local and global information transaction needs.

DESIGNING YOUR GLOBAL BUSINESS

How a company is structured and managed also has a bearing on which of the above variations becomes the model for your Web architecture's design. Whether you are embarking on your first major effort to create a global Web presence or simply revisiting your current structures, a solid and logical organizational structure contributes greatly to the speed and effectiveness with which a global Web presence can be rolled out. The considerations are different for a single-brand company operating in the United States and Europe, and a multibrand, multiproduct, multiservice, multinational company operating in sixty countries throughout the world.

Regardless of the size of your globalization effort, a key principle for success is communication and inclusion. As you embark on your globalization efforts, it is important to build a global design and development team that is fully engaged in the process. At a minimum, begin to include regional stakeholders and develop an understanding of market variations. This knowledge and support will be critical to a successful launch and ongoing maintenance. You may also consider creating a central team to provide governance for the entire project and supply specialty knowledge and expertise to local teams to aid in design localization. A multifunctional steering committee consisting of senior managers from all divisions should drive the globalization strategy and provide review and approval input to the design and development teams for all major milestones. A central Web team can also be responsible for day-to-day Web operations, providing tactical support and implementing design and development decisions. Finally, a Web globalization initiative is often an element of broader corporate strategic goals. The involvement of board-level management can be important to keeping a project on track.

LOCALIZING YOUR DESIGN

There are many ways to service customers and prospects online. There are limitless opportunities for businesses in just about any industry to build Web applications that delight customers. How do you decide what to build (since what is likely not limitless are your resources)? In a word, before you localize, internationalize. Craft a scalable master design that represents the major aspects of your business worldwide and anticipates the degree of localization that will be required in each market. The degree of localization can have a real impact on budgets and timelines.

Customer research is fundamental to all user-centered design, and therefore is a critical aspect of localization. When your design goal is a single Web site within a single market, the extent of your research is certainly manageable. Field studies, interviews, surveys, and other tools can be channeled into customer segments and a set of user and customer personas developed to drive design decisions. Because there are likely to be many service options at your disposal, knowing whether your largest segment is likely to adopt a new innovative tool is critical to managing your investments and achieving the return on your design investment.

However, when venturing into new markets, how do you manage user involvement for a site launch that covers upward of forty countries? How do you incorporate the obvious differences reflected in each market? While you may be tempted to simply avoid attempts at extensive differentiation from market to market, there are options for including design best practices that won't break the bank. In many cases, it's a matter of tradeoffs. Creating an internationalized and template-based master design, which incorporates high-level input from regional business stakeholders and users, is a good starting point. This master design may be built upon considerations of a small number of markets that represent your largest markets, or those that are most profitable or fastest-growing—whatever is important to your business. As models for other countries, the exercise required to localize sites can be termed a design gap analysis, which identifies the key areas of difference from market to market and suggests how the design may be adjusted to reflect those differences. Again, the effort could be regarded as a matter of scale. After an initial assessment, which outlines the approaches that can be taken, the range of effort may look as follows:

- **Basic:** A basic approach might involve content gap analysis, resulting in localized information architecture documents and content catalogs, and basic translation.
- **Intermediate:** An intermediate approach would include the basic activities described above, plus content customization and translation, image research and graphics localization, and simple layout changes to accommodate unique local features.
- **Advanced:** A typical advanced approach involves revisiting the design process and may include research around culture, lifestyle, and aesthetic preferences. The outcome may be a revamp of the information architecture with new

Initial Global Gateway (*www.initial.com*) and Initial Washroom Services (U.K.).

navigation models, new forms of interaction, and a creative brief for localizers (designers, writers, translators). It will also provide a technology road map upon which you can establish your future online service strategy. Ideally, the master design is flexible enough to facilitate the required changes, and the local design maintains a design language that clearly establishes it as part of the global family of sites. Finally, local usability testing, particularly in strategic markets, will play an important role in validating your design decisions.

The current emerging global Web architecture for Initial, a leading global service brand for Rentokil Initial, is a good example of how this model can successfully unfold (see illustrations above).

DOMAIN AND URL STRATEGY

A company's domain and URL strategy is another critical consideration when launching a global Web presence. For example, the dot-com domain has emerged as almost entirely U.S.-centric. Companies relying on the dot-com domain as their leading centralized gateway to the world present a U.S.-centric image that may or may not resonate with local markets. While this approach may be fine for brands that have "American" as part of their brand DNA, it may not work, for instance, for a service company that is staffed entirely by locals and where the local value proposition changes from market to market.

A more global approach is to secure all national domains for your global company, brand, product, and service names. Local domains build positive perceptions about your commitment to the local market. In addition, local search engine spiders give points to local searches producing links to local URLs, which helps your positioning on that all-important first page of search results.

In many cases, you may not be able to acquire all the necessary local country domains. An early assignment should be to audit all currently owned domains for all the company's principal brand names (including obvious misspellings), followed by the development of a domain name acquisition strategy that ensures you have local URLs upon which to erect your new sites. This audit may in turn lead to a rationalization of sites that helps avoid the issue of sites competing for search results in local markets.

The relationship of your overall organizational structure to your customer-facing service and brand architecture affects how logical your domain names are, and in turn, your URL strategy. Simple matters such as how you name your businesses and services will affect the domains you establish. Without a sensible brand architecture, it is nearly impossible to build a logical and scalable Web architecture and URL strategy. And without a sensible URL strategy, potential customers will encounter usability issues, and internal marketing departments will find it difficult to take full advantage of all the benefits of optimized organic search. Take, for example, Initial, part of Rentokil Initial and one of the U.K.'s largest providers of property and facilities services. Initial has begun the process of aligning a diverse group of service brands under a consistent URL naming structure. Though the global gateway (or lobby) is hosted at *www.initial.com*, each local URL begins with the service brand delineator followed by the local domain. Examples are found at *www.facilities.initial.co.uk* and *http://medical.initial.co.uk*.

THE IMPORTANCE OF SEARCH ENGINE OPTIMIZATION

A logical URL strategy has other important benefits for globalization beyond usability. It is also a major contributing factor to a successful search engine optimization (SEO) strategy, which in turn is of great importance to prospects seeking products and services. Search engine algorithms rely on URLs and information contained within them to determine what a Web page is about. Furthermore, they rely heavily on the country-specific domain extension to help determine the relevance of content to a local searcher.

Search marketing firm iProspect has this to say:

> Our clients typically see an increase in visibility and resulting traffic when URLs and sub-domains that include high-frequency, in-language keyword phrases are used. By using keyword phrase-dense URLs and implementing service-focused sub-domains, iProspect believes companies will see an increase in rankings and, consequently, an increase in traffic to their Web sites from the target market audiences.
>
> The recipe for a successful SEO strategy is often complex, involving a finely tuned mix of URL, site structure, content with keywords, meta data, prioritization and indexing, page design, and development. However, a simple guideline is to select a domain structure that is as clean, concise, in-language, and key-

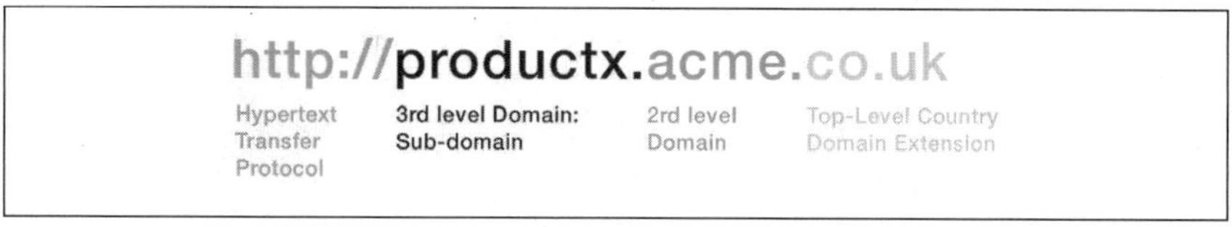
http://productx.acme.co.uk
Hypertext Transfer Protocol
3rd level Domain: Sub-domain
2rd level Domain
Top-Level Country Domain Extension

Anatomy of a URL.

word phrase-dense as possible. For example, a company operating in multiple markets with multiple sub-branded products and services might use the following structure, where "Acme" is the company name, "ServiceX" is the principal keyword associated with one of Acme's products, and the United Kingdom and Germany are target markets.

United Kingdom: *http://servicex.acme.co.uk*
Germany: *http://servicex.acme.de*

MANAGING CONTENT

The efficient and effective management of global and local content is critical to a successful Web globalization strategy. One of the benefits of a content management system (CMS)-based global site strategy is the ability to present the same consistent on-brand content in all markets. However, to enjoy the benefits of consistency, companies must first choose a content management system that is right for them. In order to properly select a CMS, supplier companies must have clear requirements and a plan for ensuring the successful deployment and acceptance of the CMS among geographically dispersed teams. The number of brands, channels, countries, content stakeholders, and degree of decentralization of marketing responsibilities are all factors that affect choices. Companies quickly realize that content management is not just about content, but also about people, organizational structure, process, and change.

One of the most important points is that the system should be easy to use for non-technical people—in other words, the people who will be servicing your customers and prospects with fresh content on a regular basis. A browser-based interface is best for geographically dispersed teams and should include a secure administration that can be managed globally to ensure that all who need access rights have them. From a translated content perspective, the more easily the CMS integrates with your translation vendors, the easier it will be for content managers. The efficiencies of time (and indeed budget) gained here can be critical when deployment dates are rapidly approaching and there are still pages of content to be translated and published.

LANGUAGE AND TRANSLATION

A fundamental aspect of Web site and service localization is the translation of content. For many global companies, the master brand content is often first written in English and then translated for local markets. However, great care must be taken to ensure that translations are not just literal translations, as many English words and phrases simply do not translate. Companies should also be wary of automated translation programs. Though they may appear to have cost-saving benefits, the impact of a poorly expressed local value proposition can hurt the overall perception of the company. In fact, the problem can still exist even with human translation.

To address the challenge of generic translations, companies need to take steps to ensure translations make sense in local markets and that content has been translated with the correct tone of voice to truly reflect both the brand and its local proposition. Involve your translation partner early in the planning and budgeting process and provide guidance to translators on desired nuances. Techniques such as creating a language glossary of key terms and translating sample batches will help guide the translation company to the style of your desired result. Involving local business stakeholders in reviews is absolutely essential.

Initial Medical Services (U.K.), Initial Facilities (U.K.), and Initial Washroom Services (Germany) have a shared look and feel, structure, and content management system.

Translation can also be expensive and time-consuming, so be sure to set a budget early in the globalization project and incorporate a realistic timeline into your project plans. Companies that take the time to incorporate an understanding of local factors into their brand-related communications have a better chance of succeeding in local markets. There are ways to reduce the cost and time of translation, including establishing a plan for a hierarchy of content and selecting a CMS that easily allows for translation to occur within the system. Translation memory software will also help to reduce the amount of content that needs to be translated and reviewed. In case you need to replace your translation vendor, make sure you own the memory so that future translators can take advantage of the invaluable knowledge you have established over years of translation.

GUIDELINES FOR ACTION

Recommended considerations when addressing your global Web presence:

- Ensure that all your goals are solidly driven by greater business objectives.
- Establish clear strategic ownership of the Web.
- Establish an organization model to drive and implement strategy that ensures cross-discipline participation.
- Establish a solid understanding of the current situation and the competitive landscape within which you operate.
- Establish a clear understanding of the markets you are aiming to serve and satisfy, both from the perspective of local business stakeholders and local customers.
- Start content planning early and establish a content strategy and management system that accounts for easy, agile, and efficient post-launch maintenance.
- Encourage communication planning and execution that engages local stakeholders in new changes.
- Use effective change management to allow for adoption of new processes and responsibilities.
- To manage costs and effort involved in developing and translating content, consider a tiered approach that scales according to strategic importance of markets.
- It's about people first and technology second.
- There is no big-bang total solution. Don't be afraid to start small and build from a solid foundation.

STANDARDS AND GUIDELINES: POLICY OR PROTOCOL

No matter what type of company you are, there are great benefits to forming a unified global design and branding protocol. Whether you plan to centralize your design and marketing efforts or devolve extensive freedom to local marketers and service providers, a policy or protocol that outlines the roles and responsibilities of all principal stakeholders is essential to speedy deployment and cohesive ongoing maintenance.

The degree to which control is passed on to local stakeholders will determine the balance between the application of strict must-adhere-to standards and directional guidelines that provide a looser framework so that local businesses can adapt more quickly to local circumstances. A global Web presence allows companies to take advantage of economies of scale that can positively affect the costs of global marketing communications. A content management system, customized for global and local administrative rights, is inevitably a key factor in the implementation of your standards and guidelines that allows you to take advantage of this economy of scale.

CONCLUSION

Digital channels to customers provide companies with opportunities for great innovation in how they provide services to their customers throughout the customer life cycle. Whether directly through the Web or through a range of information appliances, the ways in which companies in diverse industries can build useful service experiences that produce satisfied, loyal customers continue to expand.

Building a cohesive, consistent, integrated, and on-brand global Web presence, critical to successfully realizing this opportunity, requires a steady global commitment over time. There is no one-size-fits-all solution—global Web architectures must naturally adapt to the particular circumstances of each company in terms of strategy, structure, and available resources. While the tools and technologies that support Web globalization strategies have improved considerably, the challenge is pulling together the right suite of tools for your company's unique circumstances and having the human resources in place, globally and locally, to see it through. The fundamental question to answer then is, "How local do I want to be?"

SECTION 4

CREATE EXPERIENCES THAT MATTER

MEANING

LOYALTY

STRATEGY

SCENARIOS

CO-DESIGN

TELL STORIES

EXPERIENCE

ETHNOGRAPHY

Chapter 19

The Mathematics of Brand Satisfaction

by Chris Rockwell, President, Lextant

Great design does not, in and of itself, ensure the effectiveness of a brand. What matters, as Chris Rockwell points out, is the interplay between expectations and experience. In this context, he enumerates research methodologies that can be used to distill expectations and recommends that designers give special attention to those touchpoints where there is the most at stake, noting that brands fail when these key experiences are disappointing.

BRAND ESTABLISHMENT HAS served as the bull's-eye of product and service strategy in recent years. Define a brand's meaning and value clearly, and you promote consumer affinity, acquisition, retention, and loyalty. Establish and consistently reinforce these core values at each of the brand's customer touchpoints, and the brand will earn the love and respect of consumers. If we build it, they will come.

Nice, but no.

The hard reality of an increasingly consumer-driven marketplace is that the customers themselves define the brand in the marketplace. Satisfaction and meaning are established only by the experiences that customers have, across each of the brand's touchpoints, over the course of time. Like it or not, these customer experiences—more than our design and marketing—define what the brand is all about.

Successful companies are recognizing the cumulative effect these customer experiences have on the brand. They are incorporating experiential research and design thinking to anticipate customer needs, identify areas of emotional resonance, and discover desired experiences. The resulting clarity and frame of reference informs and inspires team innovation and creates an ecosystem in which a great brand can prosper.

THE ACCUMULATION OF EXPERIENCES

Brand desire and meaning emerge in the consumer's mind through the accumulation of experiences across all the brand's touchpoints, from advertising to packaging to the out-of-box experience, from the product or service itself to customer service and informational channels. Each experience on this journey moves the "satisfaction dial" and cements in the consumer's mind what the brand stands for, its relevance and ultimate desirability. This accumulation of experience has a direct bearing on whether—and how far—the customer will move through the adoption process from awareness and consideration on to acquisition, adoption, retention, and referral, and it eventually drives the offer's success and the bottom line for the brand.

THE COLOR OF EXPECTATION

Add to these experiences the expectations consumers bring to each touchpoint encounter. The resulting satisfaction with the brand is, in a large way, shaped by these expectations. They are formed in many ways—through media and social networks, through experiences, and through the value promises conveyed via design elements, such as packaging, product aesthetics, and functionality. Emotional factors, such as anticipation, apprehension, urgency, and apathy, are determining factors in how we assess an experience. The accumulation of experience further shapes expectations and colors customers' attitudes toward the brand, for better or worse. In short, experiences and expectations are dynamically related, and understanding this relationship is central to achieving and sustaining brand success through design.

Examples of this dynamic relationship surround us. Just recently, the Sony PlayStation III was hyped in the media and user forums as the next great gaming console, fueling expectations for the product. The ground was fertile, given Sony's reputation for innovation and excellence in consumer electronics. Relying on past strategies—fast hardware, beautiful graphics, and slow gaming release schedules—Sony hoped that consumers would buy into the expensive technology. Its investment in the design and marketing of the product were considerable. But experiences with the new product were neutral at best, resulting in a general letdown for consumers across the market.

Along comes Nintendo's Wii. Plenty of hype here, too, but that brand had struggled over the past few years. The expectation was for a boring, "me, too" product. What a shock it was that the more physical Wii interaction design completely changed the gaming experience—opening the gaming market to new players, from families to seniors delighted by the fun and approachable system. A happy accident of this success was that the resulting product scarcity further boosted the anticipation of owning a Wii—driving consumers to seek out and adopt the product.

In the end, the "revolutionary" gaming experience delighted consumers to a degree that resulted in unprecedented market success. Consumers bought into the experience of the Wii, sending Nintendo's stock up more than 300 percent since 2005.

THE MATH OF TRUE BRAND MEANING

What's happening here? The answer lies in the dynamic interplay between expectation and experience. Consumer satisfaction with a product or service interaction is a function of the experiential outcome in the context of the customer's expectations across brand touchpoints. Thus, the outcome of each interaction eventually defines the brand. Cumulative brand satisfaction, then, can be expressed in an equation as the sum of interaction experiences across all brand touchpoints (see figure 1).

For example:

- ▲ If a customer has a poor (low) experience with a highly touted product or brand (high expectation), the net effect is doubly low satisfaction—a failure to deliver on the brand promise. A customer is lost.
- ▲ Alternately, if a customer has a great experience (high) with little or no expectation going into that experience, the net effect is very high satisfaction, consumer delight, and a positive entrenchment of the brand in the consumer's mind. A customer is won.
- ▲ If the experience is positive (medium), as would be expected from a known brand or an established product, then you have status parity—effectively a solidification of the brand though a promise kept in the consumer's mind. A customer is retained.

To take the mathematical analogy further, the derivative of this brand satisfaction equation (the slope of the satisfaction curve across time) dictates what the brand stands for to consumers, ultimately defining the brand's meaning (figure 2). Increasing customer satisfaction over time defines and reinforces positive, resonant, and differenti-

$$\text{BRAND SATISFACTION} = \sum_{\textit{Brand Touchpoints Over Time}} (\text{Brand Experiences} - \text{Brand Expectations})$$

Figure 1. Brand satisfaction is ultimately the accumulation of customer experiences and expectations with the brand across time and brand touchpoints.

$$\frac{\delta \text{ Brand Satisfaction}}{\delta \text{ Time}} = \text{BRAND MEANING}$$

Figure 2. How brand satisfaction changes over time ultimately determines what the brand stands for and its relevance to a consumer—its brand meaning.

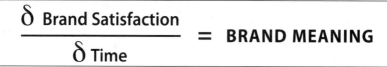

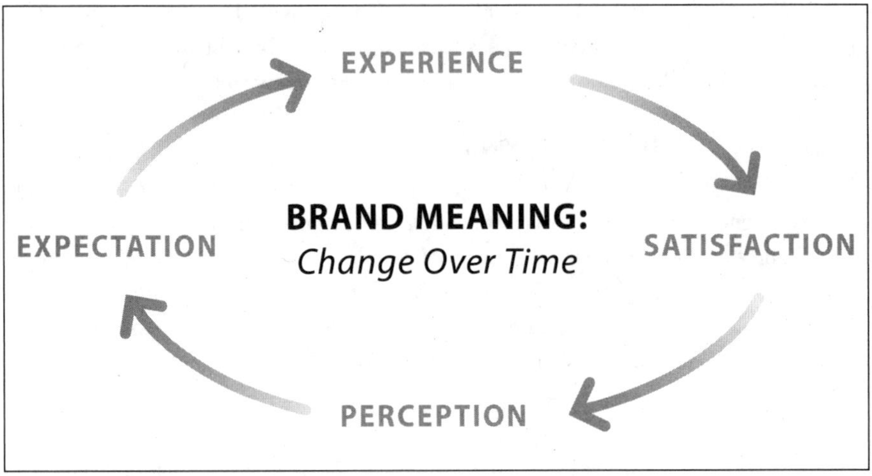

Figure 3. Each brand experience changes the brand's meaning for customers and influences expectations for future experiences–for better or worse.

ated core values for the brand. Decreasing customer satisfaction over time characterizes negative or irrelevant values for the brand.

So, these consumer experiences result in a constant circular process to define brand meaning. Expectations derived through experiences or product signals (advertising, design affordance) are assessed against experiences with the product. The resulting satisfaction is used to reinterpret the brand's meaning, which in turn influences expectations for future brand experiences (figure 3).

IMPLICATIONS FOR THE MODEL

The Disintegration Curve

This model underscores the importance of the motto, underpromise and overdeliver. Promises set expectations. As a company establishes a great brand, the expectation increases for the brand to continue to deliver with equal or better quality. It is true that a brand can build an "emotional bank account" through positive experiences, and consumers will forgive certain less-than-ideal experiences. However, each of these poor or even average experiences erodes the brand quickly because of residual high expectations.

The result is a fast-sloping disintegration curve for the company with an established and reputable brand. This is the price of success for big brands—the constant pressure to innovate and consistently over-deliver to maintain reputation and mind-share in the market (figure 4).

HOLISTIC VIEW OF EXPERIENCE ACROSS CUSTOMER TOUCHPOINTS

The disintegration curve model also underscores the importance of understanding and designing for all brand touchpoints. While each experience with the brand's

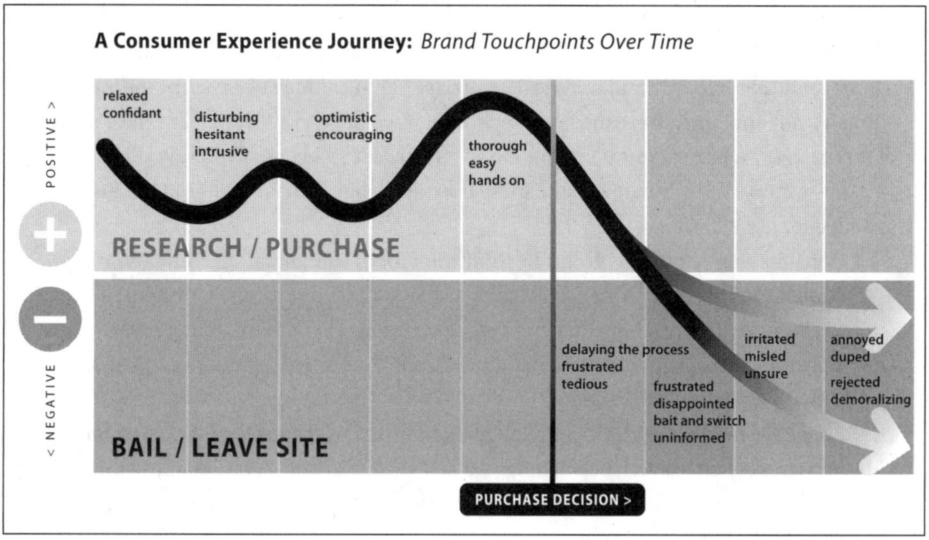

Figure 4. This experience profile shows the let-down (deflation) of brand satisfaction at the critical conversion touchpoints in the purchase process. Note how characterizations of the experience and brand change. Customer journey research can help understand and model a customer's experience and satisfaction profile over time.

products and services influences how customers ultimately define the brand, many of these touchpoints are designed by accident, with little or no effort to understand the customer needs and desires at that point in the customer's journey. It's also important to recognize how each touchpoint interacts with the others to create a cohesive brand experience.

For example, note the value of customer service underscored by this model. Often stigmatized as an overhead expense, customer service defines one of the most critically designed (by default or intent) touchpoints in the consumer's mind for the brand. When a customer calls a support or help line, he or she strongly anticipates and expects the company to stand behind its product. A poor experience—endless transfers, uninformed or unempowered customer service representatives—results in a highly negative impact to the brand. It's a hinge point of experience. Lose a customer through bad service and you may never win that customer back. Become an advocate for the customer at this touchpoint and you make great gains in keeping the customer for life. These high-expectation touchpoints should be the focus of brand establishment and design efforts—not an afterthought, outsourced and understaffed as a loss bucket.

The Research Key to Unlock Satisfaction and Meaning

The key to maximizing customer satisfaction and brand meaning, then, is to first determine what customers expect—how they define excellence—and then deliver on that expectation through great experiences wherever the brand is found.

Understanding Expectations, Finding Desired Experiences

The first question we have to answer is, "What do customers expect, and how can we go beyond that in our brand and design efforts?" That is today's challenge for innovation. It's not enough to have the latest technology; we have to deliver great experiences. Fortunately, we have at our disposal one of the biggest assets in any design program—our customers. They are the experts in their experiential domain and hold the insights needed for great design.

Our first step should be to go beyond traditional marketing or ethnographic research techniques, which often only scratch the surface of customer insights. Today, new techniques are emerging that can help us to understand the customer's true ideals and how they make emotional connections through designed experiences. With these techniques, we can see into their desires.

Projective research techniques allow customers to recall and express emotional and ideal experience characteristics—things we can't see using observational research and that are difficult for consumers to discuss using traditional interview methods.

Participatory design interviews allow us to design with customers rather than for customers—tapping into their inherent creativity to learn more about their experiences and desires.

Multisensory methods tap into the sensual aspect of experiences. Since experiences are multifaceted, we've advanced these anthropological tools by combining words and images with textures, smells, and sounds to complete the expression palette.

The power of these participatory techniques is that they give customers the ability to:

- ▲ Recall definitive moments in a desired experience
- ▲ Express the desire in a unique way that makes sense to them
- ▲ Embody their ideals in a story of a great product or service experience
- ▲ Translate that story into specific, operational design criteria and product attributes

These methods have been developed to ensure that the resulting insights are meaningful, actionable, descriptive, and aspirational—a highly effective way to understand customer expectations and specific desired experiences.

Samsung is one company that is combining these leading techniques to understand expectations with great design innovation. In a recent design research program, Lextant was asked to help Samsung understand the brand core value of rugged for the North American mobile phone market. How do consumers expect a rugged phone to look, feel, speak, and act? How do you reinforce the belief in rugged with every Samsung phone experience?

We developed a participatory research program using a prime/dream/create approach. We first used a priming assignment that allowed consumers to think about rugged experiences, asking such questions as: When do phones need to be rugged? What

Figure 5. Stimulus tools used in projective research can help brands understand expectations, ideals, and desired experiences for the design of processes, products, packages, environments, and services.

does rugged mean to you? What communicates ruggedness? Following that, we asked our consumer respondents to use words and images to dream an ideal rugged phone experience. Finally, we used multisensory tools to create characteristics of an ideal rugged phone (see figure 5).

The initial premise had been that there was a single definition of rugged; the research, however, showed that there were four consumer characterizations: industrial, high-tech, athletic, and feminine. Each definition resulted in differing expectations and ideals for the desired phone experience. When combined with channel research to understand ideal point-of-sale experiences, Samsung could develop a highly targeted, go-to-market design strategy.

Assessing Experience with Evaluative Tools

Whereas generative techniques, such as the participatory research used for Samsung, can be effective to understand expectations and ideal experience definitions, evaluative research techniques (including usability testing, customer journey mapping research, and out-of-box adoption studies) can help brands understand design effectiveness and identify areas for improvement. One example of this process, which also demonstrates the brand satisfaction equation, is a consumer study Lextant conducted in early 2000. In this instance, Lextant applied evaluative research methods to understand new member experiences for a major online service provider.

The research program used contextual techniques to understand in-store purchase experiences and lab-based evaluative methods to observe and capture the in-home set-up process. Respondents were asked to capture and photo-journal their experiences in the store. Store artifacts—receipts, installation CDs, and related items—were brought to the lab, where a home environment simulated the out-of-box experience. Using a think-aloud protocol, consumers verbalized their experiences setting up the service. Key metrics were gathered to map the user experience of the process over time and to assess satisfaction and success. In the end, we identified nine critical failure points during the initial out-of-box experience.

Fundamentally, consumers were unable to set up a new service they had just paid for. Three of the failure points were latent: Users didn't know they had made a mistake until later, when they were billed for a second account. The latent failures were particularly frustrating to consumers because the consequences of mistakes were removed from the moment the actual error occurred. New consumers had a very high expectation that they had correctly set up the new service when, in reality, they had already failed.

The resulting dissatisfaction with the out-of-box experience was compounded by the fact that this was an incentive rebate program promoted for its ease, convenience, and cost savings (setting high expectations). Further, it was the first substantial and highly anticipated experience consumers had with the company. This perfect storm of factors made it imperative that adoption be pure simplicity and joy. Instead, dissatisfac-

TIPS FOR MAXIMIZING BRAND SATISFACTION AND MEANING

- Treat each consumer touchpoint as its own experiential design program.
- Focus design activities on high-expectation touchpoints, such as out-of-box experiences and customer support experiences.
- Don't assume that a great offer in any single area will make up for weaknesses in other areas in establishing overall brand satisfaction and meaning.
- Use experiential research methods to identify high emotive drivers for consumers.
- Use design research to understand current experiences and customer aspirations.
- Develop consumer-driven brand values and associated design criteria for an ideal experience to establish and deliver brand meaning through design.

tion with the process drove up customer support costs and created a hole the brand would have to dig out of to gain further consumer adoption or referral. The experience also resulted in high costs associated with new-customer lawsuits. The brand took a significant hit.

Upon analysis, it was clear that these issues could have been identified by simple evaluative research techniques prior to the rebate program launch. Almost all the critical failure points could have been remedied with two simple design changes: one, modifications to the receipt information to clearly communicate the account established at the time of purchase, and two, simple interactive design modifications to one screen in the service set-up wizard clarifying the state of the customer's account. Once these changes were made, first-time customer satisfaction greatly improved, and the number of lawsuits filed by new members dropped by 70 percent.

CREATING ALIGNMENT WITH AND FOR THE CUSTOMER

In the end, then, customers determine a brand's meaning and value—for good or ill. The power in the brand satisfaction formula in figure 1 shows how understanding both expectations and ideal experience can provide brands with the tools to innovate for satisfaction and meaning for the market across all consumer touchpoints. Effective design research, using such methods as multisensory, projective, participatory, evaluative, out-of-box adoption, and customer journey studies, reveal the insights to make the formula work in the brand's favor. It creates competitive differentiation and customer loyalty in the marketplace. Moreover, it strategically aligns the brand with the desired outcome in the market.

Effective experiential design research is the key to successfully understanding and designing for the underlying mathematics of satisfaction.

Chapter 20

Will Meaningful Brand Experiences Disrupt Your Market?

by David W. Norton, Principal, Stone Mantel

Industries as diverse as household products and travel destinations are undergoing dramatic change. Referencing fascinating examples, Dave Norton demonstrates how this shift is caused by "disruptive innovation" and driven by the market's quest for meaningful experiential encounters. The impact is to transform businesses, as well as the design of the goods, services, and experiences associated with them.

ABOUT THREE YEARS ago, I wrote an article for the *Design Management Journal* in which I argued that because of shifts in consumer demand, we were seeing an evolution in product design.[1] In the 1980s, consumers were satisfied with products and services that combined a compelling brand image with unique design features that created product personality. For example, the hottest IPO in the '80s was offered by The Sharper Image.

In the '90s, consumer demand shifted to experiences. We bought lots of goods, but we spent more money in themed restaurants, on cruise ships, and buying T-shirts that told everyone we had had a really good time somewhere else. Soon, all kinds of companies began making the shift to more experiential customer encounters. The next step was demand for meaningful brand experiences, brought on by a dearth of cultural capital—that intangible benefit derived from our relationships with people, ideas, and things that matter to us. Consumers began to talk about simpler lifestyles, authentic living, and experiences like American Girl Place in Chicago, where values and commercial offerings combine.

You might remember that three years ago, the events of September 11 were still fresh in our minds and so many people were talking about companies having a higher purpose than shareholder value and about doing the right thing. By the start of 2005, some of what we felt about the first part of this decade had dissipated. Many companies had begun to regress back to business as usual. It's too early to tell how Hurricanes Katrina and Rita will affect consumer behavior. Will people see the events as examples of how fragile the institutions (that is, government, church, family, and enterprise) that create cultural capital are? Will they respond with a redoubling of efforts to find the experiences that matter most in their lives? Who knows?

I argued that a shift was underway and that was well before Katrina or even September 11. You should ask, "So, Dave, did it happen? Did consumer demand and market forces combine to produce a new era of meaningful brand experiences?"

DISRUPTIVE INNOVATIONS

The shift is real. It is happening. And it's really not being driven by cataclysmic events. Just look a little closer at what is going on around you. People are, in fact, getting goods, services, and experiences that are more meaningful, that produce cultural capital. All kinds of industries are going through changes driven by innovations that are clearly tied to the creation of cultural capital.

Perhaps you, like so many marketers and designers, have read some of Clayton M. Christensen's books, which include *The Innovator's Dilemma, Seeing What's Next,* and *The Innovator's Solution.* They are standard reads for anyone interested in innovation as a business strategy. You can hardly walk into a company today without someone bringing up disruptive technologies.

First, a little about these technologies. In *The Innovator's Dilemma,* Christensen demonstrates why mature companies with large customer bases often get their socks knocked off by upstarts that have an idea customers say they won't adopt—and then customers do. Darn those customers. In fact, in most cases, the losing companies were doing everything they were supposed to do—and the people who worked for them were really, really smart. That's what makes disruptive technologies so scary. You do everything according to plan and the market still ends up dropping you and moving on to the new guy.

By technology, Christensen means "the processes by which an organization transforms labor, capital, materials, and information into products and services of greater value"[2]—a nice, wide-open definition that pretty much encompasses everything from marketing to shipping. So what we are really talking about is the whole innovation strategy of a company. Christensen shows how companies, listening to their customers, develop a product and continue to add on new things to the product. These add-ons are called sustaining technologies and improve product performance over time. As products improve over time, the performance demanded by customers goes up incrementally at both the high end and the low end of the market (figure 1). Pretty soon, the add-ons outperform the demands of the market. For example, pick any software program and think about all the features you don't use or need.

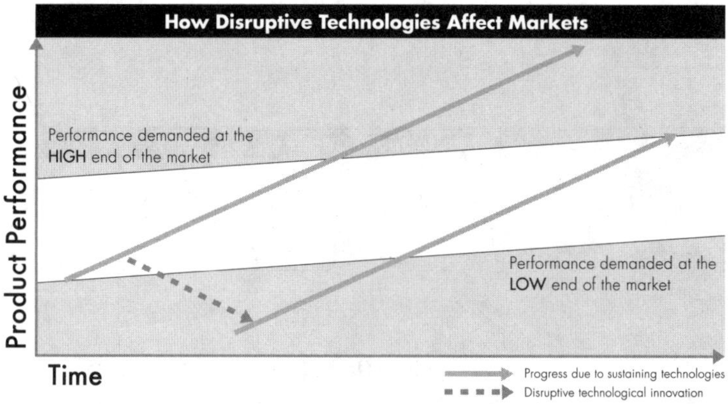

Figure 1. The problem for brands is that most of their innovations are value-sustaining innovations that eventually outpace what the market demands. As Clayton Christensen demonstrated in *The Innovator's Dilemma*, almost all industries can be disrupted by innovations that at first seem unlikely to be adopted—until demand shifts. Today, consumers are beginning to demand more meaningful experiences. Chart from *The Innovator's Dilemma* by Clayton Christensen (Boston, Mass.: Harvard Business School Press, 1997), xix. Reprinted by permission of Harvard Business School Press. Copyright 1997, Harvard Business School Publishing Corp.; all rights reserved.

Meanwhile, while the big company is casting about for new sustaining technologies, some idea that has been proven to be "untenable" in the market gets better and better—and then, all of sudden, the market shifts.

I'd like to use the idea of disruptive technologies to prove that the cultural shift I've described is real. I could probably describe the progression to meaningful experiences using other forms of evidence, but since Christensen is so readily accepted, he'll do.

The market prefers the start-up, which has the advantage of being the first mover—an advantage the big company can never really counter. Christensen provides numerous examples of this phenomenon in his book. I'd like to provide some examples of my own. Each one indicates that, indeed, we are moving toward meaningful brand experiences.

FROM FUNCTIONAL INNOVATION TO CULTURAL INNOVATION

In heading down this path, we shouldn't lose sight of what an experience actually is. According to Joseph Pine and James Gilmore, authors of *The Experience Economy*, an experience is a distinct economic offering—as distinct from a service as a service is from a product. Services deliver benefits. In contrast, experiences are staged to be memorable, personal, and sensorial. Each of the examples below fits these criteria. But in each case, the disruptive technology that has upset the industry has a cultural function associated with it. Each of these offerings allowed people to share, feel deeply, and accomplish something that matters to them or to others they care about. Likewise, each example also illustrates a design principle for companies considering designing experiences that matter. Let's get started.

In business category after category, smart brands have watched their market be overtaken by meaningful experiences that no one ever thought would work.

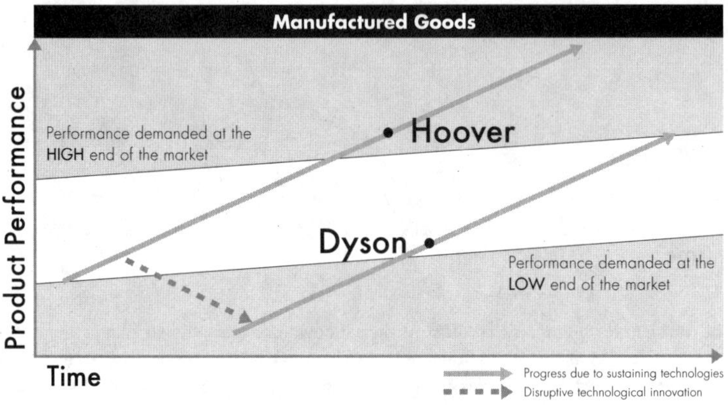

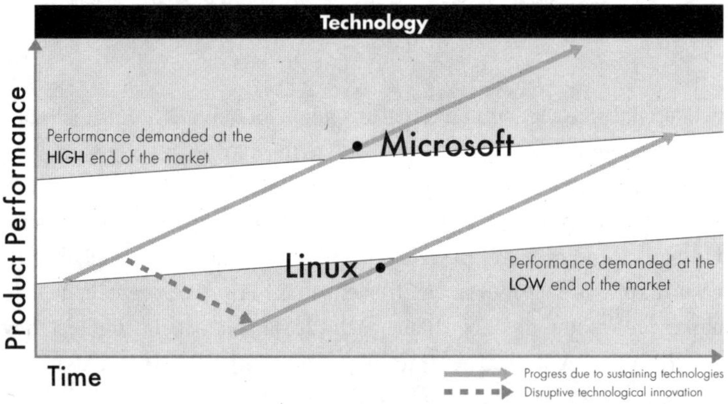

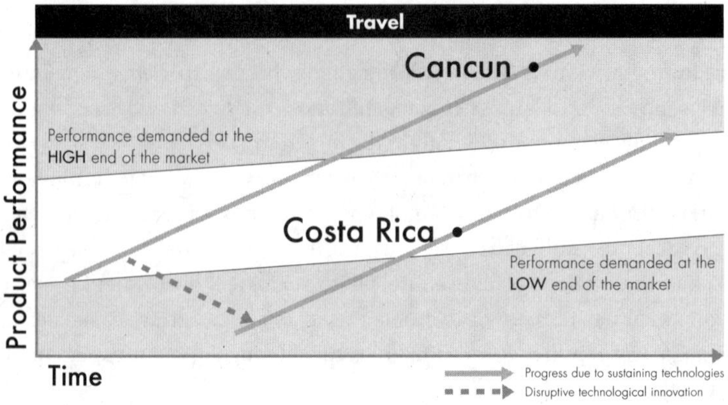

See figure 1 for an explanation of disruptive innovation.

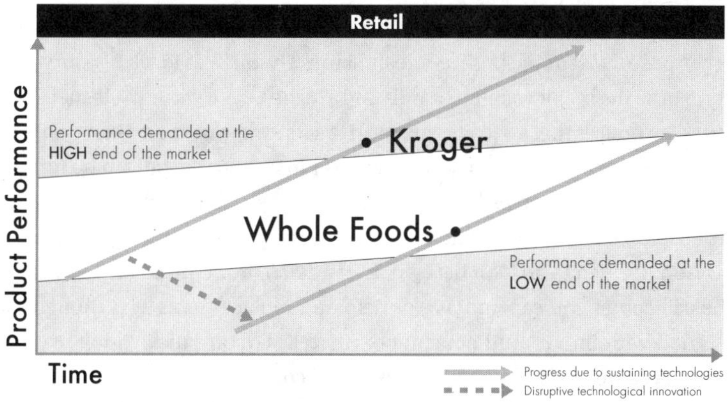

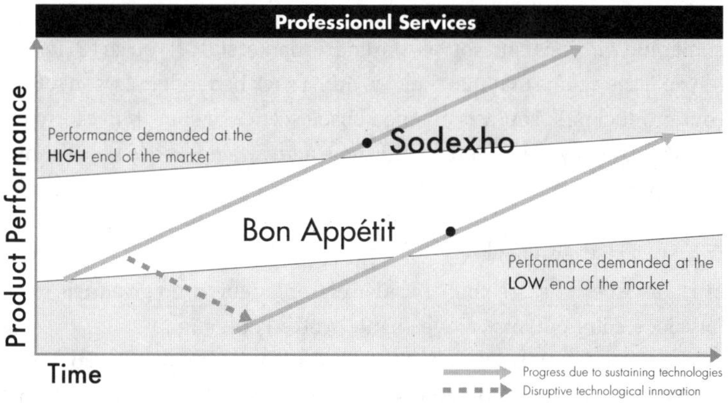

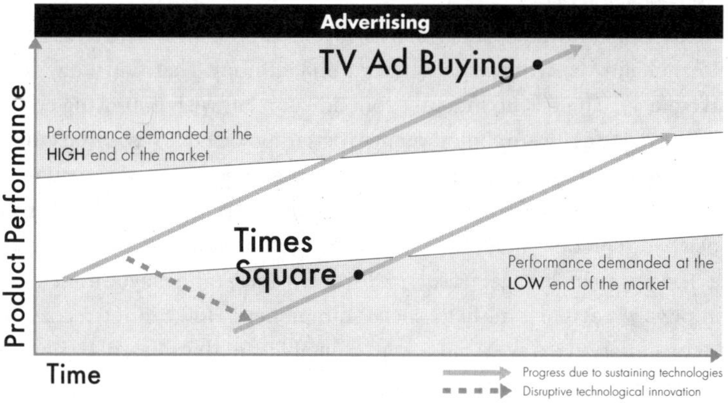

Dyson: Design with Intent

Less than two years since their entry into the U.S., Dyson vacuums now command 20 percent of the American market. Indeed, according to a number of reports, Dyson is now the number-one vacuum cleaner in the U.S.—and Hoover's stock has suffered greatly because of this U.K. upstart. Dyson is a phenomenal story about design with intent, or designing for a higher purpose than simple business goals. James Dyson likes to tell his story—much to the chagrin of all the major vacuum brands. In 1978, he buys a vacuum cleaner. After three or four uses, he notices that it's losing suction. He spends the next five years and 5,127 prototypes building the ideal vacuum, one that never loses suction, only to be turned down for years by the big companies because it didn't fit their paradigm. They sold low-cost, planned-obsolescence vacuums and made their money on vacuum bags.

So Dyson decided to go it on his own. Every detail, from the colors to the ergonomics to the call center you can contact for help and replacements, was thought through and designed with intent. And consumers can tell. Dyson quickly took over the U.K. market and became one of the richest men in the country.

The lesson for marketers and designers here was best captured by Google founders Larry Page and Sergey Brin, who said, "You can make money without doing evil."[3] Planned obsolescence was evil. Vacuum companies assumed no one really cared. Along comes someone who does, and you see the entire market shift. If you go to Hoover's Web site now, you'll see claims that that their vacuums suck better than Dyson's. But it's too late: if your product philosophy is planned obsolescence or some other form of buyer-beware thinking, then you lack intent and come across as deceptive to consumers. You can't be deceptive in today's market.

Linux: Be a Social Entrepreneur

If Dyson's story doesn't scare you, consider entrepreneurs who give their work away. Linus Torvald, creator of Linux, a free, highly evolved operating system, gives his intellectual capital away free. Read the headlines of almost any technology report today and you'll see "Oracle says Linux adoption faster than expected," or "Sun says Linux adoption stronger than expected." Now how is Microsoft to compete with free? Luckily, it is in a very strong position in the market.

The lesson for innovators is not simply to give your product away. The lesson is what Michael Porter and Mark Kramer call strategic philanthropy. That is, in today's competitive marketplace, "There is no inherent contradiction between improving competitive context and making a sincere commitment to bettering society."[4] If you think that all you have to do is get up in the morning and create shareholder value, then you're missing a major part of your competitive advantage. And you're putting your company at risk. Some social entrepreneur may come along and commoditize the market for a higher purpose. The way to hedge against such a disruptive force (and maybe even create your own disruptive force) is to think like a social entrepreneur. How can you realize the most value for consumers in a way that improves their ability to share, learn, be transformed, and care? How can you be the channel by which things that matter happen?

Costa Rica: People Enjoy Feeling That They've Helped

People seek after their own self-interest—that's a basic tenet of capitalism. It's what makes markets work. Nowhere is that more true than in the places people choose to vacation. Why do they go on vacation? To relax, to have a good time, and to see something new and exciting—to not do anything that looks like work. Cancun was built around just such a paradigm. So how do you explain the phenomenal success of Costa Rica?

In 2000, Costa Rica did over $1.1 billion in business; the country is pulling in well over one million tourists each year. Costa Rica's resorts are not nearly as big or extravagant as Cancun's. Both destinations have beaches and scuba diving—that's not a competitive advantage. Cancun's brand image is "fun in the sun," which fits nicely with the whole idea of self-interest. Cancun is also more convenient. But Costa Rica offers geotourism.

According to research conducted by the Travel Industry Association of America (TIA)—one of the hottest new trends in travel is geotourism, an evolved form of ecotourism. Ecotourism was about primitive settings and rich encounters with nature. You had to be pretty hardy to enjoy it. But it's what got Costa Rica started. TIA estimates that there are 55.1 million American geotourists. These are people who want a comfortable experience—amenities, showers, massages. But they also want their stay to have a positive effect on the local people and the places. They want to help while they enjoy themselves.

Costa Rica offers the perfect setting for geotourism: a preserved environment, a reputation for balance between local goals and tourism, and a brand that evokes empathy and intent. One example of how fast geotourism is catching on is Cross-Cultural Solutions, a nonprofit organization that offers volunteer vacations to Costa Rica and other places in the world. Started in 1997, this little organization offers two-week engagements that have attracted more than 10,000 people and helped to spark numerous other volunteer vacations. And people love it. It's the type of travel experience that matters.

Whole Foods: Market Through Your Experience

Kroger is a very big company. Price, convenience, product selection, and a comfortable shopping setting are the hallmarks of Kroger and other top grocery chains in the country. Grocery executives work tirelessly to get the balance just right: don't spend too much on the store environment or you'll have to raise your prices; get those Sunday mailers out so that people know where to get the best deal on staples. That's the paradigm within which major grocery chains work. But not Whole Foods.

For Whole Foods, grocery shopping is about contributing to a higher quality of life. The company is literally trying to transform the diet of Americans. That's very different from what Kroger is trying to do. What's interesting about the growth of Whole Foods is that you don't see any ads. Like Starbucks and Dyson, Whole Foods's disruptive marketing strategy was to create such a compelling shopping experience that it doesn't need to

More than 55 million people in the U.S. fit the description of geotourists. Consequently, Costa Rica is zipping past its undifferentiated fun-in-the-sun competitors.

advertise. The company puts its marketing dollars into its product design, and the result has been incredible word-of-mouth and reputation. A recent article in Whole Foods's hometown newspaper explains that Whole Foods's name shows up in all kinds of shows and movies, for which the company pays nothing. Because the design of the experience is so compelling, because the product is transformative, and because it stands for something, the Whole Foods brand gets placed for free.

Whole Foods does what Gilmore and Pine call "making marketing superfluous." But Whole Foods is not resting on its laurels. In October 2005, Whole Foods set up its first lifestyle store, dedicated to everything holistic about life—except food! You are able to buy apparel, handbags, paint, and much more. What the company is doing is not product extension. It's meaningful brand marketing through retail experiences.

Bon Appétit: Give Customers What They Really Want

Unless you are in the food industry, you might not be familiar with Sodexho, Aramark, or Compass. Each is a provider of professional food management services—which means that if you eat in a hospital, a university, a corporate cafeteria, or lots of other places, you are probably being fed by employees of one these companies.

It used to be that food service management companies determined the effectiveness of their operations by price per serving. Every potato, every piece of prime rib, was scrutinized to get the lowest price for their clients. Often the fastest way to reduce price was to reduce the skill set of the food preparers. Instead of a trained chef preparing the recipes and overseeing skilled laborers, you got people with minimal food preparation training. When you go down to your corporate cafeteria and remark that your food tastes like it came out of a box, that's probably because it did—to keep the price per serving down.

In October 2005, Whole Foods opened a store with no peppers, no soy milk, and no deli. But you are able to buy the lifestyle that is Whole Foods.

Then along come Bon Appétit, a food management company that charges extra but makes most of its entrées from scratch, doesn't follow menu cycles, buys pricey organic foods whenever possible, and ties every decision it makes to its higher objective—"to be the premier on-site restaurant company known for its culinary expertise and commitment to socially responsible practices." And Bon Appétit's clients can't get enough. What started as a catering company in 1987 is now one of the fastest-growing disruptive forces in food services. Compass, the largest food service company in the world, recently bought Bon Appétit, showing that this is a technology that will not be quitting soon.

Obviously, Bon Appétit does not focus its strategy on price per serving. Instead, it focuses on responding to the new menu demands of today's patrons. The company knows that people want fresh, wholesome, great tasting meals. It has shown that you can charge a premium when you create good things.

Times Square: Places Tell Stories Best

TV ad buyers used to be the potentates behind the advertising industry. They are still very powerful—much more powerful than yours truly. But the chips that began showing in the advertising windshield when cable came along have turned into full-blown, Web-like cracks, now that Tivo is a staple of household viewing. Consequently, most advertisers have turned their attention and resources to the Internet and to product placement. The problem for advertisers is that you can't tell a very compelling story in a Google ad, and when you product-place, it's not your story you're telling.

As Gilmore and Pine wrote in *The Experience Is the Marketing*: "People have become relatively immune to messages targeted at them. The way to reach your customer is to create an experience within them."[5] No wonder that companies like Ogilvy

One are turning their attention to Times Square, Chicago's Miracle Mile, and other experience venues.

Take American Girl Place—the most popular tourist destination in Chicago. It beats out the museums, the waterfront, and the Sears Tower. New York's SoHo district is so important to marketers that in 2002, when Levi's decided to stop the hemorrhaging of its 501 jeans, they went to Tony Arcabascio, Rob Cristofaro, and Arnaud Delecolle, co-founders of alife, a boutique design/retail firm in the SoHo district, for help. For three months, alife sold designer 501s exclusively at their store—nowhere else. But the stories and the word-of-mouth that the experience generated outstripped anything Levi's could have done with a traditional television commercial. No wonder that almost every major brand in the country has a place-based presence in New York, Chicago, or L.A. People love to hear stories about places almost as much as they love going to places to be told stories. And when you tell stories, you create cultural capital.

DESIGN MUST EVOLVE PAST CONVENIENCE

Sundance (vs. Hollywood), Newman's Own (vs. Kraft), Celebration Health (vs. your typical hospital)—the list goes on and on. In every category, there's a story about an organization or technology that is causing very smart people with big brands to say, "How did they do that?" In each of those cases, the market did not seem to exist for the good, service, or experience that was developed. Even though brand strategists, designers, marketers, researchers, and executives often thought about creating meaningful experiences for their customers, they often focused on the wrong issues and missed the opportunity.

Times Square is a place full of stories. No wonder Madison Avenue is looking closer to home for new ways of marketing products.

What's missing from all these stories is an experience strategy based on making things convenient: simple to use, easy to understand, or user-friendly. Unfortunately, in today's world convenience is often a code word for sustainable innovation—not disruptive innovation. The opportunity for design today is to go beyond making things convenient for people and start making experiences that people care about. Of course, products should be convenient—but everybody gets that. That was a competitive advantage ten years ago. You are not going to differentiate your product on convenience today. In most cases, what you will create is an incrementally better product or a marketing strategy for a market that needs fewer and fewer additional conveniences.

It makes sense that after the demand for convenience has been satisfied, the next big thing is demand for experiences that matter. It's telling that a recent *BusinessWeek* article on design was called "The Empathy Economy."[6] We have progressed from design being about making things simple and easy to design being about making people care. If you want to create tremendous value in today's marketplace, you should consider designing a meaningful brand experience.

Endnotes

1. David W. Norton, "Toward Meaningful Brand Experiences," *Design Management Journal* 14:1 (Winter 2003).

2. Clayton M. Christensen, *The Innovator's Dilemma: When New Technologies Cause Great Firms to Fail* (Boston, Mass.: Harvard Business School Press, 1997), xiv.

3. See *www.google.com/intl/en/corporate/tenthings.html.*

4. Michael Porter and Mark Kramer, "The Competitive Advantage of Corporate Philanthropy," *Harvard Business Review* (December 2002) 14.

5. James Gilmore and Joseph Pine, *The Experience Is the Marketing—A Special Report* (an e-document).

6. Bruce Nussbaum, "The Empathy Economy," *BusinessWeek* (March 8, 2005).

Chapter 21

The Road to Authentic Brand is Littered with Design

by David Lemley, President and Chief Brand Strategist, Lemley Design

Sophisticated products, the latest technology, persuasive marketing, and flashy graphics—it is all for naught without an abiding employee commitment to the brand. David Lemley stresses that this internal focus includes crusading leadership, staff engagement in making the brand real, and a culture that emphasizes values and ideology over compliance. It's an evangelical spirit that marks the intersection of brand building, business strategy, and design.

HANDS UP IF you are sick and tired of hearing about branding. Me, too. Brands, branding, and branded everything are everywhere. The pinnacle of oversaturation had to be when Tom Peters wrote *The Brand You*. Now we live amid a marching mass of billions of branded bipeds. And how about the brand books and brand gurus? It seems you can't swing a dead cat at a Chamber of Commerce luncheon without clubbing a branding expert in the back of the head. When did it all become so ubiquitous and meaningless? As Georgie Best was once asked, "Where did it all go so wrong?"

Way back in the beginning, branding used to refer to the searing of cattle with a permanent, prominent scar that claimed said cow for life and helped keep it out of the hands of thieves. Then, as a by-product of the Industrial Age, it became a cluster of fifty-cent words co-opted by the American Marketing Association to say in one hundred words what could be said in four: trademarks for corporate property.

Now the term branding sits in the Crock-pot with all the other buzzwords. Creative agencies are largely responsible for the confusion, as they quickly trademark everything under the sun to develop proprietary branding processes. We have branded branding. Clearly, this must be a sign of The Apocalypse™.

Somewhere on our journey from burning live leather on the range to prettying up the logo, color palette, and form factor, we forgot something: we forgot to deliver. You can make promises all day long—explicitly, through your product claims and advertised messaging, or implicitly, through tone and manner—but to be seen as real in an increasingly unreal world, you need to deliver on the experience you promise.

THE DEATH OF THE FOUR PS

In their book, *Building Great Customer Experiences,* Colin Shaw and John Ivens write that 85 percent of business leaders no longer feel that the traditional differentiators (product, price, placement, and promotion) make a sustainable business strategy. They go on to state that brand is the only sustainable business strategy in existence today.

RADICAL CHANGE

Our society has become extremely fragmented. We do less as families, groups, and neighbors and more as individuals. And yet, the fundamental condition of humanity is our need to connect and belong.

It's easy to see that anything in which we participate must be intentional.

The two places in which this intention has manifested itself in terms of radical change (which require our attention, as professionals standing at the intersection of

Consumers have created, in effect, tribes around brands they love.

business strategy and design) are the virtual world—where tribes are formed on the basis of affinity and like-mindedness rather than on geography—and the physical world, where we have Starbucks, the tribal gathering place, where the brand handles are easy enough for everyone to grab hold of and, thus, belong. But I promise not to bring up Starbucks again in this piece.

The Cluetrain Manifesto, by Rick Levine and colleagues, begins with one of my favorite lines ever written, "People of Earth . . ." and goes on to declare, "Markets are conversations." Since its publication in 2000, many of the authors' predictions have become commonplace. For the first time in history, consumers, not the companies that own the brands, control them. The consumers have created nomadic tribes centered around brands they love.

HOW I FIRST LEARNED THAT DESIGN ≠ BRAND

It was 1996. I was happy having achieved pretty much everything I ever wanted in the industry along my journey: to change the world, be recognized by my peers, and woo women. I had gotten as far as any thirty-year-old, self-obsessed hipster doofus imagines he can.

Then during one of those late-night, sleep-deprived bottle feedings, which only the parents of a colicky baby can fully appreciate, I was channel-surfing and found a news program that was lambasting one of our clients for alleged ethical violations and unfair labor practices in Asia. This woke me up from my "just do it, revolution" bliss as I was working on a new project with the man who had uttered those words into existence. And for the first time I began to see what is now front and center in our consumer-centric world: great design does not a brand make.

Great design can create interest. I agree with approximately 68,000 design firm Web sites in proclaiming that design creates emotional connectivity and that it may just be the thing that makes the difference. However, design style and clever imagery can be copied with ease—in fact, I challenge you to name one inspired motif that hasn't been ripped off at least a thousand times. (If you can think of one, send it to me so I can steal it.)

PRODUCTS DON'T MATTER

Here is a simple truth most product designers and innovation engineers don't like to hear: technology is irrelevant because it's a given.

For years, I struggled with a kind of blindness among businesspeople that defied my ability to address it: the belief that a good product was enough to make consumers loyal. A good product, even a great one, is not enough (Sony MP3 players and Zune, for example). Quality is a given in today's marketplace.

Why? Anyone can make a product that works and push it into the marketplace. Once there, if it is any good at all, it will be mimicked. And in the crowded, communication-saturated world we occupy, I expect my running shoes to help me correct the fact that I "pronate." I expect the moisture-transfer system in my polypropylene jogging suit to keep me dry when I sweat and my iTunes to sync up with my online workout journal. How or why all these things work is too much noise for me. In essence: Tell me the benefits, and I will choose on the basis of brand (the collection of opinions I have about you).

MEANING IS THE NEW BLACK

To quote my long-time client Robert Raible from our presentation this winter at the National Retail Federation: "People want more of the same, only with better features, but that isn't why we buy. We buy as a form of self-actualization." Raible continues, "In our consumer culture, people are no longer purchasing merely on the basis of need or utility. Consumption has become meaningful, and brands are often used as building blocks for the construction and maintenance of our personal identity."

It works something like this: If I chew this whitening gum wearing these Prada pumps while standing in line to buy RED at Bloomingdale's before I head to Patagonia, then what does this say about me? It's no longer enough to have your own world beliefs and to purchase products—people see the corporate responsibility aspect of brands as part of the cultural cachet they receive from alignment with those values by simply purchasing, wearing, and so forth.

BRAND STRATEGY IS A NEW BUSINESS MODEL

Compare the old model still used by many of today's organizations experiencing decline versus the new model that is the underpinning of all leading brands.

The Traditional Model: Compliance

- Decisions by committee
- Sink-or-swim culture
- Disgruntled employees
- Company distress and pressure for short-term gain
- Typically top-down ideas, handed out by management and imposed upon employees; also known as command and control and resulting in a brand product nobody will hate

The New Model: Commitment

- A fearless leader on a crusade
- Employee engagement
- Values-based culture

True vision can't be imposed on a company; it has to grow from the authentic, mutual purpose and passion of its people. True vision leads to commitment rather than compliance, confidence to create goods and services in a bigger picture—a brand people will love.

The traditional compliance business model features decisions by committee, ideas handed out by management and imposed upon employees, and results in a brand product nobody will hate, but nobody will love either.

Think about it, The Home Depot isn't about building materials but about empowerment: You can do it, we can help. REI isn't about hiking gear, it's about inclusion in a club that loves the outdoors, co-op values, and environmental stewardship. Starbucks isn't coffee; it's freedom to be you in the third place. . . . Dang, I did it again—but only because Howard Schultz stepped back into his leading role to "fix the brand so it keeps its promises."

DAVID MAISTER MAKES ME LOOK SMART (AND HANDSOME)

Harvard Business School professor, author, and recognized thought leader on the service business (and let's face it, except for all but the most commoditized of necessities, the Experience Economy has made everything a service business) David Maister recently completed a study he calls "The Profit Formula." Maister worked with 139 companies in fifteen countries trying to answer this question: What makes the most successful companies in the world? His conclusions show that we are in a new era. Here is what Maister found:

- The most money comes from consistently superior client satisfaction—which is entirely subordinate to internal culture.

The new model, commitment, draws from a values-based culture and engaged employees, as well as from a fearless leader. The result: a brand people can love.

- Businesses need employees who are engaged—not simply happy with their benefits package.
- It's about the wow factor. If your people are coming to work every morning saying, "Wow, this is exciting and fun—I get to be a barista again!" then they're feeling meaning and purpose.
- It comes down to the character, not the skills, of the individual manager.
- The person in charge must credibly be seen as having an ideology.

Or, as I like to say, ideology trumps systems.

INTERNAL BRANDING: AN ESSENTIAL COMPONENT

The brand must have buy-in from employees, and employee training must be implemented to instill a clear-cut understanding of new directives and goals if it is to be successfully implemented. Aligning the employees and getting them on board with the corporate brand is the first order of business. Didn't your mother teach you to clean up your mess before inviting company?

It's no coincidence that Nordstrom and REI made the top of the list in the National Retail Federation's survey of Top Retailers for Customer Service, as well as in *Fortune* magazine's Best Companies to Work For. Successful companies understand that a crucial element of connecting the customer to the brand is accomplished through motivated employees who themselves understand and buy into the brand. Every employee, front-line or not, should be viewed as a "brand evangelist."

Nordstrom encourages its employees to act "as if it's your name on the door." In turn, employees are empowered to make decisions that might improve customer service. REI calls its brand "a way of life." It encourages outdoor activity for its employees by providing big discounts on gear, free gear rental, and gear grants for personal outdoor challenges.

If employees fully experience an authentic brand, see it, and believe in it, they will effectively convey it to the customer. Clearly, retailers like Nordstrom and REI have given their employees and customers real reason to believe.

Collaboratively, businesses and their brand consultancies can define the unique brand attributes that have meaning for both employee and customer. These attributes, or pillars, of the brand, are the elements that describe its unique qualities. Communicated across every channel within the organization, they have the ability to connect with employees and customers on a personal, emotional level.

Once defined, these attributes need to be embodied and embedded throughout the company. From the CEO down through the retail ranks, from product design to advertising, in-store communications, signage, and POP displays, one overall identity and message must resonate. (Caveat: If the CEO of the company doesn't embrace the brand, live it, and make it a focus of the entire organization, all the revitalization efforts in the world will fall flat.) Employees who become brand evangelists are one of the most powerful tools in a company's arsenal. Furthermore, employees, in turn, can make evangelists of the customers by embodying the brand well and by making their customer service second to none.

THE FUTURE BEGINS NOW

The big challenge for brand strategists, design managers, and brand owners alike is to accept that organizations creating and running brands are made of people. Contradictory by nature, people and their modern consumer culture struggle to find meaning in our postmodern, democratized design world. The leaders of today already know what the rest of us need to learn: People will encourage transparent, authentic interactions with the brands they allow into their lives. Our job is to figure out how to create a framework that allows them to participate.

Companies need to find out and articulate why they exist (beyond profits), and that is where brand building, business strategy, and design intersect.

So, what about the brand manager or the design manager who is tasked with changing the sales figures without touching the business? It may be time to work on your résumé.

Chapter 22

Customer Loyalty and the Elements of User Experience

by Jesse James Garrett, Director, User Experience Strategy, Adaptive Path

In life, strong and fulfilling emotional bonds are fundamental to enduring relationships. Jesse James Garrett explores how this principle applies to products and customer loyalty. Conceptualizing design as integrating five layers of content—from strategic decisions to finely crafted details—he advocates developing a combination of function and information in each layer to create experiences users find compelling and satisfying.

CUSTOMER LOYALTY CAN seem elusive and magical to those trying to obtain it. However, there are a lot of good reasons for businesses to pursue customer loyalty as a strategic objective. Customers are expensive to acquire; keeping them loyal allows you to amortize those costs. Loyal customers are often willing to pay premium prices. Loyal customers can be your most effective marketing weapons, evangelizing for your product on your behalf.

Given all these benefits, it's only natural that businesses should turn to a diverse range of tools to develop customer loyalty. And everyone seems to have a different formula for making that loyalty happen. Develop a brand that resonates with your audience, and your customers will be more loyal. Improve your customer service, and your customers will be more loyal. Spend more money on marketing, and your customers will be more loyal. Strengthen your quality-control processes, and your customers will be more loyal. Invest in customer relationship management software, and your customers will be more loyal.

But initiatives like these don't build customer loyalty. Customers become loyal because of the experiences they have as a result of these types of initiatives. A resonant brand creates an emotional connection for the customer. Successful customer service delivers an experience that makes the customer feel important. Marketing initiatives reach out to customers even as they help the organization better identify its customers. Quality-control processes minimize the risk that the customer will experience product failure. Customer relationship management systems ensure a consistent experience across all the customer's interactions with the business.

The common thread here is the experience the customer ultimately has with the business because positive experiences create the emotional bond that leads to customer loyalty. But isn't something missing from the equation? What about the product itself? What role does it play in creating customer loyalty?

Of all the touchpoints customers have with your business, your product is the one touchpoint with which they are likely to spend the most time. The product is also the touchpoint likely to create the strongest emotional reaction because it is in the product experience that your brand promise is fulfilled. The product itself is your most valuable customer touchpoint, and creating a positive experience here is essential to building customer loyalty.

DESIGNING EXPERIENCES

It might seem as if experiences can't really be designed. Experiences are personal, emotional, and ephemeral—the subjective perception of a particular moment in time. But whether or not product designers think of their work in these terms, they are already in the user experience business. Every product creates an experience for its users. That experience can be the result of planning and conscious intent—or it can be the unplanned consequence of the product designer's choices. Which strategy would you prefer?

But creating an experience instead of an artifact requires a deliberate way of thinking about design. The decisions that result in a positive user experience are rooted in deeper, more abstract considerations. We can visualize these considerations as a series of planes, layered one on top of another, with more abstract considerations toward the bottom and more concrete considerations toward the top (figure 1).

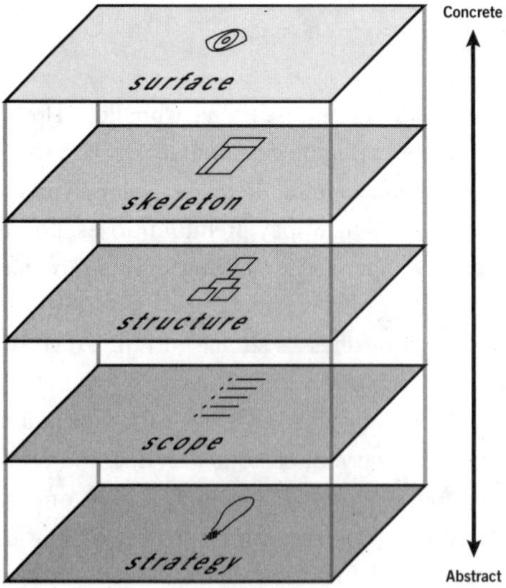

Figure 1. We can visualize the considerations that go into creating great user experiences as a set of five planes along a continuum from abstract to concrete.

At the most concrete level is the surface plane. Here, we address the sensory elements of user experience—the visual, auditory, and tactile stimuli the product will deliver to the user.

The choices we make about the surface are rooted in a more abstract set of considerations that I call the skeleton, or the arrangement and selection of design elements for maximum effectiveness.

The skeleton is the concrete expression of the underlying structure plane, where we articulate the flow of the experience as the user interacts with the product.

The structure plane deals with the relationships among the functional and informational elements of the product. The precise makeup and selection of these elements comprise the scope.

At the most abstract level is the strategy plane, in which we describe the overarching direction of the product, its place in the market, and the user needs and business objectives it must address.

Within each of these five planes, we have additional detailed considerations to take into account in designing the user experience. For many products—particularly complex technological ones—the problem of creating a successful user experience is compounded by a basic duality in the very nature of the products.

Some products are primarily functional, existing to enable a user to perform a task or accomplish a goal. Other products are primarily informational, existing to communicate to a user. But a diverse and ever-larger group of products has both functional and informational aspects. Consider the design of a public space, such as an airport or a library. The design will include functional considerations, such as helping users move through security or check out a book. But the design will have informational considerations as well, communicating to users the status of flights or a schedule of events.

To talk meaningfully about the elements of user experience, we must incorporate this duality into the five planes. Dividing the planes down the center allows us to fill in specific terms for the various elements, and it enables us to see how the elements work together to create positive emotional experiences that lead to customer loyalty (figure 2).

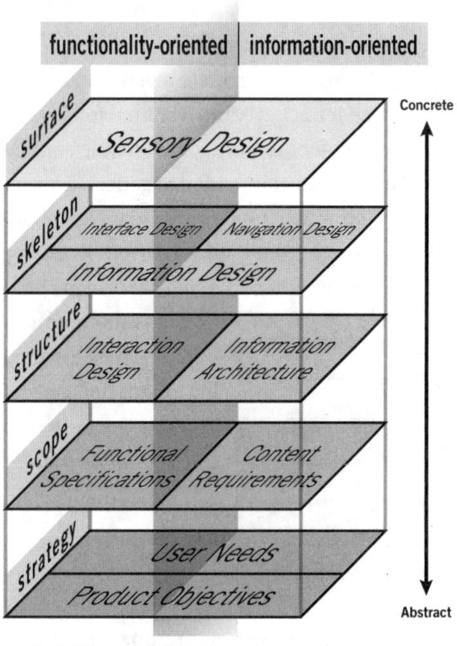

Figure 2. The elements of user experience are organized according to a basic duality in the nature of products that incorporate both task-oriented and information-oriented experiences.

I developed these ideas (as a model called The Elements of User Experience, in my book of the same name) in the course of my work designing Web sites because it is on the Web that the collision between the task-oriented and information-oriented nature of products is most apparent. But these same principles apply to any product with both functional and informational aspects—that is, any product that must both help users accomplish tasks and communicate with them.

PLANE BY PLANE

Strategy is the foundation of every user experience. But to result in a successful experience, the strategy must balance the business's objectives for the product against the needs and expectations of the product's users.

User needs include the concrete goals and objectives users have for their interactions with the product, as well as the less tangible emotional characteristics of the experience they desire. These needs are typically uncovered through research and analysis of the behavior and expectations of users as they relate to our product (or the product of our competition). Attention to user needs is the essential foundation to building customer loyalty.

But every product exists as much for the business that produces it as it does for the people who use it. We articulate our understanding of the strategic role of the product for the business through product objectives. These objectives determine how we measure the success of the product.

Some products generate revenue only once, when they are sold. Other products continue to generate revenue over time for as long as they are actively used, as in the case of any product that requires consumable supplies, such as a razor or a photocopier. Some products are never intended to generate revenue. For instance, Microsoft takes a $71 loss on each Xbox 360 it sells because the company plans to make its money on software for the unit, not on the hardware itself. Knowing how we will measure the success of our product helps us to make smarter design choices to support those product objectives.

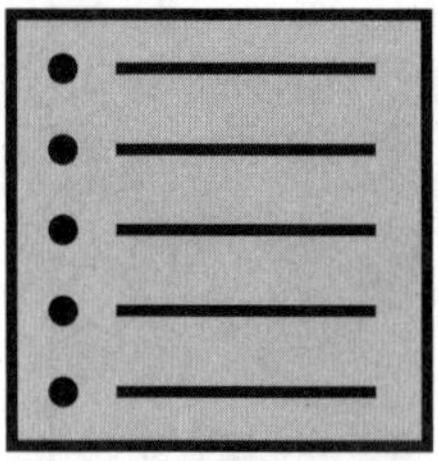

Scope is the entire set of features the product will include. In defining scope, we must consider both the functional and the informational aspects of the product. As a result, we have two separate scope exercises—functional specifications and content requirements.

Functional specifications sound technical, but they're not. They simply represent the set of operations the product will enable the user to perform. Functional specifications for a mobile phone, for example, may include details of user tasks, such as placing calls, answering calls, or changing the ringtone. These specifications do not describe the technical underpinnings of these features; instead, they describe the features as they are presented to the user.

Content requirements describe the information the product will need to communicate to the user. For a mobile phone, content requirements might include detailed descriptions of the various status indicators or other messages the phone must be able to convey. Content is frequently textual, but it need not be—wallpaper images or games included on a mobile phone would be considered part of that phone's content.

Smart choices about scope can have a significant impact on customer loyalty. No matter how effectively the features of your product are designed, if they aren't the right features—that is, if they don't align with user needs and expectations—users will come out of the experience feeling confused or let down. Having the right features in place is essential to creating the positive user experience that creates customer loyalty.

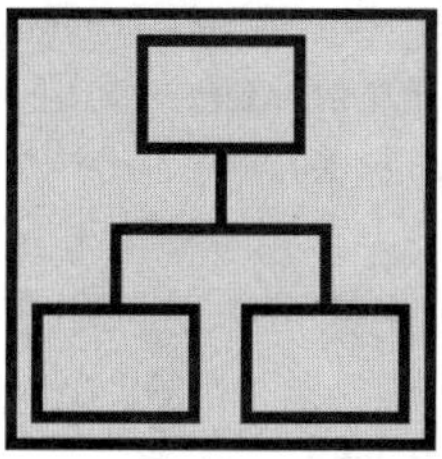

Structure is where the user experience starts to take shape. Structuring functionality requires attention to issues of interaction design, mapping out the flow of the user's movement through a task or from one task to the next. Looking at the informational aspect of the product, we must solve problems of information architecture, organizing and arranging the information so that people can understand it and use it.

Interaction design and information architecture intertwine most prominently on the Web. Pages on a Web site can freely intermingle functional elements and informational ones. The high-level structures of a site—its sections and subsections—are likely to be developed through information architecture, but they may contain application components (such as forms) that require interaction design.

Information architecture and interaction design can be vital contributors to customer loyalty because both these disciplines require an intimate understanding of the psychology of the user. By understanding the flow of a task—the natural way a user goes about achieving a goal—we can develop the interaction design to mirror user expectations, as well as sometimes predict what users will need before they request it.

Successful information architecture reflects the way users think about the subject matter of the content, as well as the language they use to talk about it. Not only does this help users find content they're looking for, but it has an important emotional impact, as well. Good information architecture makes the product feel familiar and comfortable, like having a conversation with someone who shares your background and point of view. This creates the positive emotional resonance that makes users want to spend more time with the product.

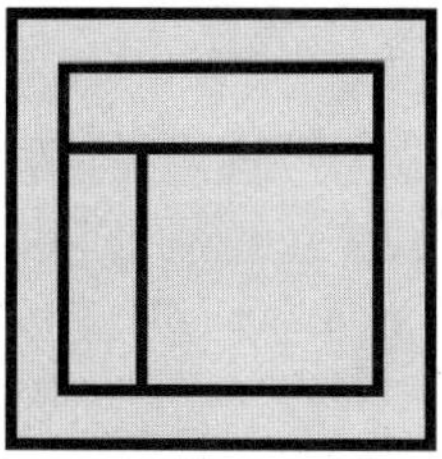

Skeleton issues come into play when we move beyond understanding how the experience will flow for the user and start defining what form that experience will take. We give form to interaction design through interface design, or the selection and arrangement of controls the user will interact with. Anyone who has driven a variety of rental cars, for example, can tell you that the same interaction flow—such as adjusting the mirrors, turning on the windshield wipers, and engaging the parking brake—can be accomplished through a wide range of configurations of switches, buttons, levers, and knobs.

We give form to information architecture through navigation design, the selection of elements to facilitate the user's movement through the available content. Successful navigation designs must accomplish two goals: they must communicate to the user the choices available to them, and they must help the user access the content of his or her choice. The table of contents in a book serves as navigation because it includes page numbers that allow users to jump directly to a chapter. A simple list of chapters without page numbers would not serve the same navigational function.

Both the functional and the informational aspects of a product benefit from good information design, crafting the presentation of informational and functional elements so that they can be easily understood. In a space like a retail store, information design is essential to help users operate within that environment. Clear signage or other visual cues are important way-finding devices that help customers to locate the features and products available in the store. In an information-rich environment like a museum, these information design choices can make the difference between a confusing experience and a rewarding one that drives repeat visits and customer loyalty.

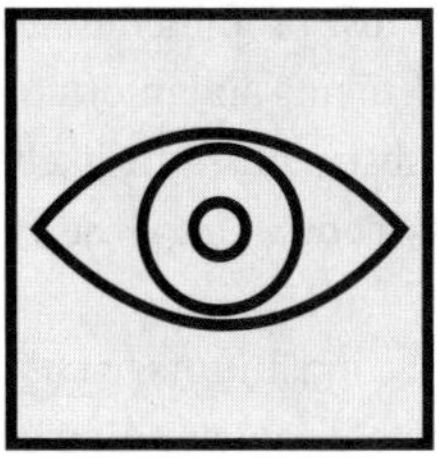

Surface considerations are often the first to come to mind when we think of the design process. This realm of sensory design includes visual choices, such as color palettes and typography; sound elements, such as the background music in a shopping mall or the beep of a microwave oven; and tactile qualities, such as the textured handle of a power drill or the click of a button on a remote control.

Choices about sensory design should not be made on purely aesthetic grounds, however. The decisions we make here must reinforce and support all the choices we've made about the other elements of the user experience. You can make all the right choices about the flow of a user task, the controls to facilitate that task, and the necessary labeling of those controls, but if the visual design makes it difficult for users to read those labels because the controls are cluttered with unnecessary decorative elements or poor typographical choices, the experience falls short.

Sensory design in and of itself can have a powerful effect on customer loyalty. The power of sensory stimuli to evoke human emotion is well known; indeed, it is the basis of all forms of art. This emotional dimension to experience can, in many cases, persuade the user of the value of a product. Great sensory experiences are ones we want to return to over and over again.

MAKING IT HAPPEN

Customer loyalty is all about making customers feel good about their relationship with your business. It's a lot like the personal relationships we have with friends or colleagues. People want to spend time with people who make them feel good and well-appreciated. We evaluate the relationships we have with businesses in the same way.

In a very real sense, your product is the embodiment of your business for the customer. For customers to feel they have a good relationship with your business, they must first feel they have a good relationship with the product—and that begins with the user experience. The savviest marketing strategies and the most efficient customer service processes won't deliver loyal customers if those customers don't have a positive experience with your product.

Your customers are on your side; they want to be loyal. They want to have positive experiences, and they want you to succeed in delivering them. The unhappy customers who send you disgruntled email or call your help desk with expletives don't really want to see you fail. They turned against you because their experience with your product wasn't what they had hoped for.

Loyal customers are high-value customers. And every customer wants to be a loyal customer. But first, you have to enchant them.

User experience is a complicated business, but if you understand all the elements involved, it isn't an unsolvable problem. With attention to the right details, the designer can seem like a real magician.

Chapter 23

Experiential Design Drives an Established Brand to a Youthful Market

by Judi Jacobs, Writer and Producer, State Farm Creative Services
and Jeff Hackett, Manager, State Farm Creative Services

State Farm's involvement with teen driver safety is a natural extension of its history with auto safety in general, dating back to the introduction of guard rails and seat belts. Here, Judi Jacobs and Jeff Hackett explore how the company's in-house creative team designed a youth-inspired, interactive experience with a twofold purpose: to deliver a compelling commentary on safety and, more subtly, to introduce the corporate brand to a new audience.

AT THE HEART of any company—at the heart of any brand—is the promise it makes to its customers. State Farm has been delivering promises in the form of insurance policies since 1922.[1]

Coupled with its business objectives is a social responsibility to promote personal safety through research and education. In particular, State Farm has made significant efforts to reduce car accidents for teenage drivers—the leading cause of death among teenagers in the United States. State Farm's involvement with teen driver safety is a natural extension of its long history with auto safety initiatives, dating back to the introduction of highway guard rails and seat belts.

One project with a unique peer-to-peer approach is making a big difference in many schools and communities. It is called Project Ignition. Coordinated by the National Youth Leadership Council (NYLC), this program encourages driver safety awareness projects in high schools throughout the country. Using the Web, video, print, and performance art, students creatively express their passion for changing risky driving behaviors. The top ten student projects are then showcased at a national conference, with the students competing for a $10,000 grant to continue their work in promoting teen driver safety.

CREATIVE SERVICES GETS INVOLVED: MAKING A BRAND CONNECTION

Creative Services is State Farm's in-house creative department, located at the company's headquarters in Bloomington, Illinois. The team consists of 181 design, media, and technology experts who provide creative thinking and media expertise to corporate departments and business partners throughout the United States and Canada.

Creative Services' involvement with Project Ignition started with a request from the company's marketing department to enhance State Farm's presence at the NYLC national conference. With an understanding that research fuels creative thinking, a small creative team visited the conference to get a sense of the overall experience. Once onsite, team members quickly recognized a branding opportunity with the teen audience that went well beyond the initial request to design booth space for a corporate presence. Project Ignition seemed to provide a unique fit from the perspective of social responsibility. Dedication to education and safety were apparent in both State Farm's efforts and those of the NYLC program.

The Project Ignition program encourages driver safety awareness projects in high schools throughout the country. State Farm Creative Services created IgnitionLand to better showcase student projects and to encourage the students to interact, share ideas, and learn from each other.

At the conference, the individual student teams were clearly passionate about their respective projects, but there was no discernible emotional connection to the conference experience. It became apparent that the creative team needed to leverage the strong emotional connection the students had with their projects and then amplify that buzz at the next year's conference. As the team interviewed the students, they learned that some were so devoted to their work that they had missed their high school proms to attend the event. Another group of students had paid the extra expense to rent vans so that they could bring their entire team to the conference, traveling more than 13 hours to get there. Students' passion for their work permeated the hall. As the winners were announced on the final day, many students cried openly when their schools failed to take home the top prize.

Using the power of design, the creative team hoped to develop a consistent look and feel in a highly interactive environment, which would transform the experience and raise brand awareness with the students, who for the moment, had little knowledge or experience with State Farm. As work began, the team found it both exciting and daunting to connect an eighty-five-year-old company that helps customers recover from the unexpected with an audience that typically defines the future as the next weekend.

Because successful branding seeks to create long-term relationships with customers, keeping the conversation going is vital. The State Farm team, wanting to start an effective conversation with these potential customers, recognized that they first needed to speak a common language.

DESIGN THINKING: CREATING A PERSONAL EXPERIENCE

To kindle a relationship with the high school students, Creative Services needed to understand their point of view and develop relevant communications that spoke in a voice to which teens could relate. Ultimately, the creative team had to design an experience—transforming the existing conditions of the NYLC conference into one that would resonate with the students.

In their daily work at State Farm, members of the creative team would typically start from a common awareness and knowledge of a particular product or service and then expand their thinking. But designing the Project Ignition experience reversed the process. The team began by first deconstructing what they inherently knew about the teen audience. Their anecdotal approach, based on their own experiences as parents, aunts, and uncles, was then distilled into a handful of common truths. Once the team members felt they were properly grounded, and that the youthful market platform was firm, the building process began. All the members of the creative team, from the writer to the art director to the creative manager, immersed themselves in teen culture, careful to stay away from anything too trendy. It was agreed that getting the tone right was perhaps even more critical than developing the messages. The students would instantly and ruthlessly judge as disingenuous anything perceived as preachy or condescending.

In addition to their life experiences, team members examined volumes of existing research on the teen market segment and added an in-house performance technologist to research key insights related to the audience. Not surprisingly, much of the research revealed what was already common knowledge—the teen world is much louder and far less concerned with the conventions of a polite society than most other audiences.

Without the benefit of design school or film class, the student projects were often crude and clumsy from a technical aspect, but they scored a direct hit with the essential elements of design thinking. The teens knew their audience, which meant that their loosely designed projects powerfully communicated in a unique and memorable voice. In effect, their pitch was perfect.

At one school, several students staged a particularly grisly accident scene, which they videotaped and broadcast via a closed-circuit network throughout the school. It was evident from the copious amounts of fake blood that the students had no interest in a soft-sell approach. Simply put, they had lost friends due to reckless driving and wanted the over-blown images to serve as a cautionary tale.

Despite an obvious lack of production resources, the video project was effective because it was a genuine, passionate expression of the message. It was also clear to the creative team that any attempt to mimic the student work would be dismissed as a transparent attempt at ingratiation. The team recognized that providing a meaningful experience for the students would require authentic touchpoints—moments of engagement among the students, NYLC, Project Ignition, and the State Farm brand.

The atom—the visual chosen by the creative team to best capture the concepts of energy and positive change, was central to the Project Ignition experience.

HITTING THE TEEN MARKET

Starting with a visual aimed at capturing the passion and enthusiasm of the students, the team came up with the formula e = pi: Energy equals Project Ignition. The central visual element was a frenetic, modern-looking version of an atom. Each student project represented a spark of creation, and when combined with other sparks from other students, parents, and community leaders, it held a powerful, almost atomic potential for change.

The team agreed that there was a visual freshness to the atom icon, which had replaced some of the initial, more obvious ideas—broken windshields and smashed fenders—images that were clearly too literal. As one team member put it, "This was not about the car, but the driver. Not about the problem, but the solution."

In addition to building a relationship with the students, the creative team also wanted to connect the students to one another, to encourage them to share ideas. While on-site, the team noted that the physical space created a barrier to interaction. Student exhibits were tucked in a corner, away from the main traffic flow. Compounding the lackluster interpersonal experience, the students had been charged with the design and construction of their own booths. The result was chaotic, lacking visual consistency or connection to the Project Ignition theme.

To better provide the students with an appropriate platform to showcase their work and provide recognition for their projects, the creative team went back to the atom concept. The team believed the students should be the nucleus of Project Ignition. To get there, designers reworked the floor plan, prominently placing the student booths in a new area named IgnitionLand. Colorful banners representing past winners flanked the entrance and defined the space.

By establishing formal boundaries, IgnitionLand provided the students with an effective forum to promote their work. It encouraged interaction among student teams and those attending the conference—providing a comfortable area for conversations, project demos, and the exchange of ideas.

To further promote interactivity around the safe driving theme, the design team created two video driving games for this event. "React to That!" tested the student's ability to maneuver through difficult road conditions, such as bad weather, sleep deprivation, and various levels of DUI. "Total Distraction" exposed student drivers to cell phone usage, a hot coffee spill, and an unruly passenger, the most common in-car situations and distractions for teen drivers, based on State Farm research. After successfully completing the road tests, the students took home T-shirts and buttons emblazoned with the atom logo.

Another important element in developing the experience was to encourage a sense of community. Working together, the creative team and students built a large mosaic at the conference. Each student chose a plastic tile and wrote a message on it, then placed it on an ever-expanding mosaic wall. Messages often focused on camaraderie born of project work or school pride; some spoke to the loss of a friend or family member from a car accident. When the mosaic was complete, the students found they had created more than a piece of art. The mosaic became a testimonial for all of those who were involved in saving lives.

If IgnitionLand was the centerpiece for the experience, the awards program, held on the final night of the conference, was the climax. The creative team recognized the potential of this event to provide lasting memories. The year before, the awards portion of the event consisted of a simple production with little audio or visual support—essentially, a congratulatory handshake at the conclusion of the conference. Now, renamed the Awards Festival, the program included a dramatic video introduction edited from portions of the student projects and framed in high-end graphics, featuring lights, music, and big-screen projection of the nominees.

The show's video opener illustrated the collective energy of students. Emceed by a professional actor, the staging and production resembled the MTV Video Music Awards. With TelePrompTers, professional sound mixing, and teen assistants to help distribute the awards, the revised awards festival better celebrated the student's work and captured the passion of the event.

OUTCOMES

During the course of the Project Ignition campaign, almost every area of the Creative Services department played a part in delivering target-specific communications. The initial concepts were developed by a core creative team comprised of an account manager, a creative manager, an art director, and a writer/producer, all supported by techni-

At the Project Ignition Awards Festival, students were treated to an MTV-like awards show experience.

cal coordinators. Performance support specialists provided research on the teen market and additional content research throughout the project. Writers developed key messages and translated them into youth-oriented copy for event materials, speeches, signage, Web sites, and media releases. The authoring team programmed video driving games. Print and electronic designers created the look and feel for IgnitionLand, the multimedia Web site, and designed the hardware for Project Ignition's top award. Video directors, producers, editors, and audio post-production specialists were responsible for the video and music featured in the awards show, the Project Ignition Web site, and IgnitionLand.

From the first visual impression of the atom logo to the creation of IgnitionLand through the design of the awards presentation, the creative team defined success primarily as a celebration of the student projects, and secondarily as a stronger connection to the brand.

When surveyed on their reactions to the new event experience, students said they appreciated the changes. They remarked on State Farm's effort to make the conference experience professional, yet appropriately targeted to the youthful audience. It was apparent that the students felt comfortable in the IgnitionLand environment, and they were delighted with the new activities—particularly the video games, which subtly encouraged networking among the teens from various towns and states.

The MTV Awards-style presentation of the project competition was extremely popular. Some of the students described it as a "sitting-on-the-edge-of-your-seat" kind of experience. The multimedia approach created a powerful energy throughout the hall. One teen lamented that he had not participated in Projection Ignition prior to his senior year, so he could not attend more than one conference. Now, as an even stronger advocate of the program, he encouraged underclassmen at his school to get involved early to take advantage of this unique opportunity to help change risky behaviors, as well as to have some fun with the experience.

The relationships forged among the students and the Creative Services team left a lasting impression on both groups. Some teens said they were surprised that State Farm representatives could be so laid back—high praise from teenagers. On the other side, the State Farm team continued to be amazed and inspired by the students' energy and dedication—atypical behavior for many in this age group.

But beyond the positive comments and shared feelings, the most important metric is the steady increase in student participation. Since its launch in January 2004, student applications for Projection Ignition have nearly doubled.

Beyond the peer-to-peer recognition of the issues, news media coverage of the student campaigns helped to boost community awareness and involvement in teen driver safety. In one community where the local school earned top honors for its project, seat belt usage increased appreciably, while the number of accidents declined. In addition, the driver's education teacher for that school has repeatedly been asked to help other schools in the area establish Project Ignition programs.

Like the promises State Farm makes to its policyholders, the Creative Services team attempted to live the company's brand by creating a memorable experience that mirrored the level of passion the students brought to their own projects.

Endnotes

1. State Farm is the registered trademark of the State Farm Mutual Automobile Insurance Company.

About DMI

DMI, the Design Management Institute, connects design to business, to culture, to customers, and to the changing world. We bring together business people, designers, educators, researchers, and leaders from every design discipline, every industry, and every corner of the world with strategic conversations. The results are transformational. Over the decades, DMI has been the place where the world's most experienced, creative, and ambitious design leaders gather to share, distill, and amplify their knowledge.

DMI is a nonprofit (501c3) educational organization with more than 1,500 members in forty-four countries. The Institute connects design leaders to the inspiration, knowledge, and community they need to succeed. Our vision is to improve organizations worldwide through the effective integration and management of design and design principles for economic, social, and environmental benefit. Our mission is to be the international authority, resource, and advocate on design management, and our objectives are to:

- Assist design managers in becoming leaders in their profession
- Sponsor, conduct, and promote research
- Collect, organize, and make accessible a body of knowledge
- Educate and foster interaction among design managers, organizational managers, public policy makers, and academics
- Be a public advocate for the economic and cultural importance of design

Over the years, DMI has created the largest body of knowledge about design management in the world by producing thirty-four case studies with Harvard Business School, publishing eighty issues of the *Design Management Review* and *Design Management Journal* (adding up to over 850 articles), and producing over one hundred conferences and two hundred workshops and seminars around the world. This book is an anthology of some of our best articles in the area of design thinking.

www.dmi.org

Editor Biography

Thomas Lockwood is the president and a member of the Board of Directors of the Design Management Institute (DMI) and publisher of the *Design Management Review*. He is considered an international expert in the area of innovation and design leadership and the integration of design and business. Prior to working in the public sector, he managed brand and design at Sun Microsystems and StorageTek and ran his own design firm for a number of years. Lockwood is a visiting professor at Pratt Institute in New York City. He holds a PhD and MBA in design management from the University of Westminster in London, and a BA in marketing and visual design from Eastern Michigan University. He is a design consultant to corporations and countries and has lectured and led design and brand workshops in twenty countries and serves on numerous boards and academic councils throughout the world.

Authors' Biographies

Chris Bedford, president of Karo Group, has helped a roster of blue-chip clients focus and streamline their brand stories over his twenty-five-year career. He's been a member of the DMI International Advisory Council for nearly a decade. Karo Group is a brand agency that has been helping create inspiring brand stories for over thirty-seven years for clients in Canada, the United States, Mexico, South America and China. Using interdisciplinary processes and thinking, Karo creates meaningful emotional connections between branded goods and services and the consumers they are intended for.

Phil Best, vice president of product design and innovation at LPK, is a true veteran of brand design. Best spent the majority of his career at Procter & Gamble. He is credited with building the global design organization at P&G and establishing design as one of P&G's core competencies. With Best's counsel, LPK's product design and innovation group has grown significantly with visionary focus on consumer insights and structured ideation. Best is also responsible for managing the LPK's trends and verbal identity groups, and is the senior executive managing the home creative unit.

Brigitte Borja de Mozota is professor of management science at the Université Paris X in Nanterre, France. She teaches marketing, innovation management, and strategy, with a specialty in design management at the ESSEC Business School in Paris, Université Nancy 2, the European Institute of Design (Toulon), and the Audencia Nantes Ecole de Management. Borja de Mozota is especially interested in research pertaining to design management; she is author of the reference book *Design Management*; and she gives numerous speeches and seminars on design management. Editor of the *Design Management Review*'s special *Academic Journal,* she also set up DMI's International Scientific Committee. Borja de Mozota was also a founder and board member of the European Academy of Design (EAD) and of the association Cercle du Design et de la Marque. She was nominated in 2002 as France's design expert at OAMI (the European Commission office for trademarks and designs) in Alicante, Spain.

Kevin Clark is a brand and business strategist, author, experience designer, and a sought-after creative facilitator and keynote speaker. He is a thirty-year veteran of IBM and serves as program director, brand and values experience, corporate marketing and communications. Clark is the author of *Brandscendence: Three Essential Elements of Enduring Brands* (published by Kaplan/Dearborn).

Rachel Cooper is codirector and professor of design management at Lancaster University's creative research lab, ImaginationLancaster (U.K.). She is also the director of the Lancaster Institute of Contemporary Arts, and has written several books in the field of design, including two with coauthor Mike Press (*The Design Agenda* and *The Design Experience*), and more than two hundred research papers. Cooper is currently the commissioning editor for a Gower series on design for social responsibility. In May 2007, she was commissioned by the U.K. government's Foresight program to write a scientific review on mental wellbeing and the built environment. She is also editor of *Design Journal* magazine and is president of the European Academy of Design and on the Arts and Humanities Research Council.

Chris Downs, Ben Reason, and Lavrans Løvlie cofounded live|work in 2001 with the vision of establishing service innovation and design as a credible alternative to mainstream improvement methodologies. Together, they challenged clients to think differently about service and demonstrated the benefits of applying design tools and techniques to service issues. In doing so, they inspired a new generation of service designers. Seven years later, live|work has a global reputation for thought leadership in service thinking and for delivering value to blue-chip private and public sector organizations in the U.K. and the Nordic region.

Heather Fraser is the director of Rotman Designworks, a design-based education and innovation center at the Rotman School of Management, University of Toronto. She is an adjunct professor of business design. Fraser joined Rotman in 2005 with more than twenty-five years of experience in business design and in brand design and communications gleaned from her roles as researcher and brand business leader at Procter & Gamble, brand steward and managing director at Ogilvy & Mather, and managing partner and builder of TAXI Advertising & Design. At the Rotman School, she leads the development and application of business design methodologies, local and international partnerships, and student programming.

Jesse James Garrett is cofounder and president of Adaptive Path and a widely recognized technology product designer. His book, *The Elements of User Experience*, has been called "brilliant," and "essential," and is considered one of the seminal works on user-centered design. Garrett is a frequent keynote speaker addressing audiences around the world on product design, user experience, and innovation. In 2005, he gained worldwide attention for coining the term "Ajax" and defining the concepts behind this emerging trend in Web technology. Jesse is the recipient of *WIRED* magazine's 2006 Rave Award for Technology.

Christa van Gessel, MSc, is Zilver's first employee. She obtained her master's in strategic product design through a user insights project at Philips Research (Delft University of Technology, 2006, cum laude). Van Gessel combines great passion for people with strong design research skills. She started at Zilver after several traineeships (PARK, Tri-co) and activities in the design management domain.

Brian Gillespie is director of strategic design at Molecular, an experience design and technology consultancy with offices in Boston, New York, and San Francisco, and a member of the Isobar network. He leads multidisciplinary design teams in strategizing, designing, and developing digital customer experiences for a wide range of clients, including JPMorganChase, Rentokil-Initial, miCoach, and Adidas's innovative new brand-driven customer experience. As part of the global Isobar network, he values the opportunities for design collaboration with sister companies on multichannel digital experiences. Brian is a graduate of the University of Westminster's design management MBA program and has a degree in law from University College Dublin.

Marc Gobé is an author, designer, futurist, and filmmaker, and president of Emotional Branding, LLC, an experimental and futuristic think tank. Translated in fourteen languages his bestselling book *Emotional Branding* initiated one of the most powerful movements in modern marketing by bringing the focus on consumers as the ultimate power in branding strategies. As cofounder and former copresident of Desgrippes Gobé (now brand-image), Gobé was a pioneer in combining the disciplines of brand strategy, human factor research, product design, graphic design, and architecture to engage consumers emotionally along different points of the brand experience.

Alexis P. Goncalves is an independent consultant in the area of business innovation, working with clients in the U.S. and Brazil. He has worked for Citigroup, American Express, and Accenture both in the U.S. and internationally. At Citigroup he led the global customer experience management practice.

Jeff Hackett manages the creative leadership group in design and development within State Farm Creative Services. Prior to joining State Farm, he managed a corporate visual communications team and cofounded Simms & Hackett Advertising. His media experience includes producing and reporting at CBS affiliates KOLD-TV, WCIA-TV, and WLBH AM/FM. He holds a degree in speech communications from Eastern Illinois University.

Judi Jacobs is a writer and producer for State Farm Creative Services. She earned a journalism degree from Loyola University in New Orleans and served as a staff writer for the *Times-Picayune* in New Orleans. She worked in the public relations field for trade organizations and at her own consulting firm before joining State Farm.

Julian Jenkins is a senior consultant with 2nd Road, a consulting firm dedicated to incorporating design thinking into the world of business. He specializes in both information design and human systems design, and has worked with major public and private sector clients on design projects, especially in the context of management reporting. As a firm, 2nd Road is increasingly working on installing design thinking and capabilities across entire organizations as a path to strategic innovation and organizational transformation.

Mark Jones is the service design and innovation lead at IDEO's Chicago office. He helps clients uncover unmet consumer needs and then design and develop innovative service experiences that meet, and exceed, those needs. Jones frequently lectures about service innovation strategies and teaches service design at the Institute of Design at IIT.

Sabine Junginger is a lecturer in design at ImaginationLancaster and at the Lancaster Institute for the Contemporary Arts, both part of Lancaster University in the U.K. Junginger studies the roles of design, designers, and designing in the organization. Her work is informed by organization and management theories, interaction design, and product development. Junginger received an MA in design in communication planning and information design and a PhD in design from Carnegie Mellon University. She regularly contributes to international conferences in both design and management, having delivered keynotes and lectures at international business and design conferences.

Jerry Kathman is president and CEO of LPK, the largest independent brand design agency internationally, with offices in North America, Europe, and Asia. Kathman is recognized within the industry as a leading authority on the role of design in brand building, providing Fortune 500 companies with insights into both the opportunities and pitfalls of taking a brand beyond national boundaries. LPK leverages relevant consumer, shopper, and market insights to create value, sustain leadership, and transform businesses, and has developed brand design franchises for some of the world's most successful companies, including IBM, Pampers, Olay, Hershey, Gillette, AT&T, Hallmark, U.S. Bank, Samsung, Novartis, and Kellogg.

Tony Kim is professor of design management at IDAS, the graduate school of design at Korea's Hongik University. His teaching and research interests include strategic design systems in digital business, in emerging technology environments, and recently in ubiquitous computing environments. His recent research includes trend- and scenario-based future design. His interest in international design has led him to develop and manage cooperative programs between IDAS and the University of Art and Design in Helsinki for design research and education. Prior to joining the faculty at IDAS, Kim was director of Samsung's Advanced Technology Center, where he led emerging technology research and training for corporate technologists. Kim holds an MBA in international design business management from the Helsinki School of Economics and Business Administration and a PhD in mechanical engineering from the University of Michigan.

Anson Lee is the director of customer experience strategy for the Karo Group, and is passionate about using customer driven insights to guide creative strategy and push creating boundaries. Karo Group is a brand agency that has been helping create inspiring brand stories for over thirty-seven years, for clients in Canada, the United States, Mexico, South America, and China.

David Lemley is a lip-syncing eighth-grade talent show loser who went on to found his own brand design firm. For over twenty years as president of Lemley Design, he has focused on holistic branding programs and design strategies for some of the most respected companies in the world, including Pepsi, Nike, Starbucks, REI, and Wal-Mart. Lemley is an alumnus of the Art institute of Seattle and University of Washington. He has been a visiting professor at several colleges and continues to speak and write about brand strategy, design, and brand revitalization.

Marty Neumeier is president of Neutron, a design think tank in San Francisco. He's the author of a series of "whiteboard overview" books, including *The Brand Gap, Zag,* and *The Designful Company,* as well as the pocket-sized *Dictionary of Brand.* Neumeier divides his professional life among three activities—consulting with corporate leaders; writing and speaking about brand, innovation, and design; and developing brand programs for marketing professionals and Fortune 500 companies across all industries.

Dave Norton, PhD, is the founder and principal of Stone Mantel, and is internationally recognized as the cutting-edge thinker on what makes brand experiences meaningful. He has lectured at Harvard and Columbia Business School, and at *Fortune* magazine's annual summits. His seminar series, Strategies for Creating Meaningful Brand Experiences, has been praised by attendees from companies such as Microsoft, Royal Caribbean International, Kraft, and Disney. Norton's research capabilities have been embraced by entities as diverse as Fortune 500 Internet businesses, small countries, and multibillion-dollar consumer goods companies. Stone Mantel is an insights agency focused on finding the marketing experiences that matter most to customers.

Chris Rockwell is the founder of Lextant, a user experience consultancy dedicated to informing and inspiring great design through a deep understanding of people, their experiences, and their desires. By combining design with behavioral sciences, Rockwell and his team have provided innovation clarity and organizational alignment for product, retail, brand, and interactive design programs. A frequent speaker and thought leader, Chris was recently named adjunct faculty in design at The Ohio State University. He also sits on the advisory board for Virginia Tech's Department of Industrial and Systems Engineering.

Erik Roscam Abbing, MSc MDM, is founder of Zilver brand driven innovation™, a design management consultancy in the Netherlands. Abbing holds a master's in industrial design engineering (Delft University of Technology, 1995, cum laude) and in Design Management (Inholland/Nijenrode, 2005, cum laude). He worked for ten years as a product designer (Flex, Zilver design), and now teaches at the Delft University of Technology and at Eurib in Rotterdam.

Roberto M. Saco is owner and principal at Aporia Advisors, a management consultancy based in Florida. Working with clients in the Americas, Aporia specializes in service design and sustainability, process management, and organizational change. Saco worked for two decades at American Express, mostly in strategic planning and service operations for both domestic and international units.

Fran Samalionis is a partner and a practice lead at IDEO. Samalionis leads the service design and innovation group responsible for helping clients create sustainable service strategies and innovate commercially viable services that consumers love. She has pioneered the use of prototyping in the design of services, making otherwise intangible experiences real.

Ron Smith is an award-winning product designer and customer experience strategist. Using over twenty years of experience designing products for IBM, he works with clients inside and outside IBM around the world to create experience strategies, and captivating experience designs. He is currently a brand experience design strategist with IBM corporate marketing and communications.

Craig Vogel is the director of the Center for Design Research and Innovation in the college of Design Architecture, Art and Planning (DAAP) in the University of Cincinnati (UC). He is also a professor in the School of Design with an appointment in industrial design and coauthor of the book *Creating Breakthrough Products* with Professor Jonathan Cagan, and one of three authors of the book on innovation and organic growth, *Design of Things to Come*. During the last twenty-five years, Vogel has been a consultant to over twenty companies, and advised and managed dozens of research projects and design studios collaborating with industry. He recently cofounded the Live Well Collaborative (LWC) a joint venture between UC and P&G. His education experience includes over twenty years of teaching at all levels of undergraduate and graduate design education at the Institute of Design, IIT, The School of the Art Institute of Chicago, Carnegie Mellon University, and University of Cincinnati.

Index